A DISSIDENT LIBERAL

THE POLITICAL WRITINGS
OF PETER BAUME

PETER BAUME
Edited by John Wanna
and Marija Taflaga

A DISSIDENT LIBERAL

THE POLITICAL WRITINGS OF PETER BAUME

Published by ANU Press
The Australian National University
Acton ACT 2601, Australia
Email: anupress@anu.edu.au
This title is also available online at press.anu.edu.au

National Library of Australia Cataloguing-in-Publication entry

Creator: Baume, Peter, 1935– author.

Title: A dissident liberal : the political writings of Peter Baume / Peter Baume ; edited by Marija Taflaga, John Wanna.

ISBN: 9781925022544 (paperback) 9781925022551 (ebook)

Subjects: Liberal Party of Australia.
Politicians--Australia--Biography.
Australia--Politics and government--1972–1975.
Australia--Politics and government--1976–1990.

Other Creators/Contributors:
Taflaga, Marija, editor.
Wanna, John, editor.

Dewey Number: 324.294

All rights reserved. No part of this publication may be reproduced, stored in a retrieval system or transmitted in any form or by any means, electronic, mechanical, photocopying or otherwise, without the prior permission of the publisher.

Cover design and layout by ANU Press

This edition © 2015 ANU Press

CONTENTS

Foreword vii
Introduction: A Dissident Liberal—A Principled Political Career xiii
1. My Dilemma: From Medicine to the Senate. 1
2. Autumn 1975 17
3. Moving Towards Crisis: The Bleak Winter of 1975 25
4. Budget 1975 37
5. Prelude to Crisis 43
6. The Crisis Deepens: October 1975. 49
7. Early November 1975. 63
8. Remembrance Day. 71
9. The Election Campaign 79
10. Looking Back at the Dismissal 91

SPEECHES & OTHER PRESENTATIONS

Part 1: Personal Philosophies
Liberal Beliefs and Civil Liberties (1986) 109
The Mud of Prejudice (1989). 117
Purpose in Politics (1990) 121
Valedictory Speech: The Senate (1990) 127
Farewell to Politics (1991). 133
Philosophical Liberalism: Patron's Address to the Young
Liberal Movement (1994) 137
Liberalism and Robert Nestdale: A Memorial Oration (1994) 139
Liberalism Discarded (2004) 145
Caring for People (year unknown). 147
Four Careers (2012) 155

Part 2: The Liberal Forum Contributions

The Birth and Emergence of the Liberal Forum, 1985–1987 (1987). 165
Parliamentary Eulogy on the Death of Senator Alan Missen (1986) 177
Australian Liberalism: The Continuing Vision — Press Release from the
Liberal Forum (1986). 181
Quitting Shadow Cabinet (1987) 183
Easter at Point Lonsdale (1987) 197
Reflections on a Trip to Queensland (1987). 203
Executive Government and the Funding of Parliament: Threats, Crises
and Constitutional Confrontation (1989) 207

Part 3: Policy Concerns

Equal Employment Opportunity (1987) 213
Social Policy and Disadvantage (1995) 223
Welfare and Taxation (1987) 229
A Separate Policy for Aboriginal Australians: A Paper to the
Liberal Forum (1987). 235
Immigration Motion in Defence of Non-Racial Selection (1988) 239
War Crimes Amendment Bill (1988) 245
Legalisation of Drugs (1994) 251
Taking on Tobacco (1997). 255
Madness and Hypocrisy: Drug Policy in Australia (2000). 263
The Australian Drug Review of 1991 (1992) 269
NSW Parliament: Voluntary Euthanasia (1996) 273
AIDS and Discrimination (1999) 277
An Apology to Aboriginal Australia for the 'Stolen Generation' (1997) 283
Australian Racism Today and Aboriginal Disadvantage (1997). 287
Aboriginal Health (2000) 291
Rationing in Health (1998). 295
Health: An 'Awful' Debate (2011) 301
Bibliography 313

FOREWORD

It is now a long time since the Dismissal on 11 November 1975. In brief, there had been a unique stand-off between the Senate and the House of Representatives over the Budget and Supply and the matter was resolved at the eleventh hour by the Governor-General Sir John Kerr, who dismissed Gough Whitlam summarily as prime minister and appointed Malcolm Fraser in his place. Before 1975, no prime minister had been dismissed against his will by a governor-general, although Sir Philip Game, the then Governor of New South Wales, had dismissed the state Premier Jack Lang in 1932.[1]

Elsewhere the events of 11 November might have led to revolution or been resolved by military intervention. In Fiji, a military takeover followed an election result unacceptable to a powerful minority;[2] in India, the Constitution was suspended by a president who determined that emergency powers were required.[3] In Australia, there was no such extra-constitutional intervention, disorder being confined to demonstrations in Australian capital cities on 11 November and a crowd of 1,000 angry people who demonstrated outside the Parliament that evening.[4] Letter bombs were sent to the Governor-General and to the Queensland Premier, injuring two public servants. Nevertheless, the deadlock between the Senate and the House of Representatives was resolved,

---

1 Sir Philip Game was Governor of New South Wales when he withdrew the commission of John Thomas Lang as Premier of New South Wales on 13 May 1932.
2 A government led by Timoci Bavadra won the Fijian general election held in April 1987, defeating the predominantly indigenous Fijian administration of Ratu Sir Kamisese Mara. The Bavadra Government was supported, especially by Fijians of Indian background. It was overthrown in a military coup led by Lieutenant-Colonel Sitiveni Rabuka on 14 May 1987, in which non-Indian Fijians regained control of that country.
3 Indian president Fakhruddin Ali Ahmed declared a state of emergency on 26 June 1975 based on an alleged threat to internal security. Opposition MPs and 676 opponents of Indira Gandhi were arrested and press censorship was imposed. The Parliament, without the Opposition, later ratified the declaration. These events followed the finding by the Allahabad High Court that Prime Minister Indira Gandhi's election in 1971 was invalid, and its disqualification of her from membership of any parliament for six years.
4 *The Australian*, 12 November 1975: 1.

in the first instance by extraordinary vice-regal action, and validated later by Australians voting at an election. There was no sustained violence and the transfer of power was peaceful.

I was present throughout that Parliament as a freshman senator, having won the tenth Senate seat in New South Wales, in 1974. The Coalition then had an equality of Senate votes—enough to block any proposal and deny Labor a Senate majority. Labor thought it would get a Senate majority on election night in 1974, but quickly realised, as did my people, that I would win and Labor's Peter Westerway would lose narrowly.

I was new to politics and to public life—having come from the relative security, order and comfort of the practice of medicine—very green and very much needing to learn my new craft. But the Twenty-Ninth Parliament I entered was the focus of crisis from the start and later the eye of the constitutional storm. There was little time to learn, especially in 1975. For all this turbulent and difficult Parliament, I was there in Canberra—inexperienced, undoubtedly ignorant, certainly shaken, and yet exhilarated and involved, and determined to observe and record some of what was going on about me.

There have already been a number of books about the events of 1975. Most have been written by journalists who observed the events,[5] by academics,[6] by interest groups,[7] and by principal actors in justification of the roles they played.[8]

No longer do I have any such agenda. No longer do I have any need to justify publicly what we did, or to assert a Panglossian view of events past.

I was unknown in 1975, the most junior member of an activist Senate. Apart from casting my vote in Senate divisions, I played no significant role in determining events or their outcomes, had no advisory function to the decision-makers, no frontbench position or parliamentary office, no pivotal role or leverage. All that I did (and it has been recorded in several places in print)[9] was to question, for a month, the course of events that led to the deferral of Supply in late 1975, although I had changed that view after 14 October when Rex Connor was the fifth Labor minister to resign or be dismissed.[10] The demotions and dismissals of ministers in the Whitlam Government were as follows: Gordon Bryant was demoted from Aboriginal Affairs to Capital Territory on 9 October 1973; Frank Crean was demoted from Treasurer to Minister for Overseas Trade

---

5   See, for example: Kelly (1976, 1984); Hall and Iremonger (1976); Solomon (1976); Tennison (1976); Reid (1976); Oakes (1976).
6   See, for example: Horne (1976); Penniman (1977); Encel et al. (1977); Sexton (1979); Ayres (1987).
7   See, for example: (IPA 1976).
8   See, for example: Freudenberg (2009); Kerr (1978); Whitlam (1979); Barwick (1983).
9   See *National Times*, 20 October 1975: 6; Kelly (1976: 255); Oakes (1976: 155); Whitlam (1979: 72).
10 Senate Hansard, vol. S66, 1975: 1,065.

on 21 November 1974; Lionel Murphy resigned on 9 February 1975 to go to the High Court; Speaker Jim Cope was forced to resign on 27 February 1975; Jim Cairns was demoted from Treasury to Environment on 5 June 1975, and then dismissed from the ministry on 2 July 1975; Moss Cass was demoted from Environment to Media on 5 June 1975; Clyde Cameron was dismissed from Labour and Immigration on 5 June 1975 and appointed to Science and Consumer Affairs on 6 June 1975; Lance Barnard resigned to become Australian Ambassador to Sweden in June 1975; and Rex Connor was dismissed from Minerals and Energy on 14 October 1975.

Throughout the period of deferral of Supply—the actual constitutional confrontation—I was there in the Senate every sitting day and voted in every division with my colleagues.

Now we are almost 40 years on. Passions have cooled and it is possible at last to record, examine and discuss calmly, with the benefit of inside knowledge, some of those events and those times.

In 1990, when I first edited these reflections into a manuscript, almost all the main protagonists of those events had retired from public life or had died. Sir John Kerr retired as Governor-General on 8 December 1977. He lived for some time outside Australia and has generally been treated rather poorly, especially by some of those most affected by what he did. Gough Whitlam led the Labor Party to the election in 1977 but retired from Parliament on 31 July 1978. Bill Hayden, who later became Governor-General, had been a minister in the Whitlam Government of 1975, was subsequently Leader of the Opposition and then foreign minister under Bob Hawke. Malcolm Fraser retired from Parliament after he lost the election of 1983. Phillip Lynch, Rex Connor, Bill Snedden, Lionel Murphy, Ivor Greenwood, Jim Keeffe, Ron McAuliffe, Reg Wright, Frank Stewart, Eric Robinson, Bob Katter Snr, Kevin Cairns, Eric Bessell and Alan Missen were all dead. Retired from the Parliament were Speaker Cope, Presidents Cormack and O'Byrne, all surviving ministers of the Crown from 1975 except for Paul Keating, 20 members of the then shadow ministry, and 53 of the 60 senators of that Parliament. The celebrated retirements of Lance Barnard and Lionel Murphy and the death of Bert Milliner all preceded the Dismissal. Many of the main players who had gone were destroyed, completely or in part, immediately or later, by the Dismissal and by their roles in it.

The only then Labor minister still in Canberra in 1990 was Paul Keating and the surviving Liberal shadow ministers from 1975 (in the order of their seniority at that time) were Andrew Peacock, Harry Edwards, Michael MacKellar, Peter Durack, John Howard, Ian Wilson, Ian Sinclair and Bruce Lloyd, not all of whom became ministers in the Fraser ministries between 1975 and 1983. Steele Hall sat in the Senate in 1975 as the only representative of the Liberal

Movement, but in 1990 was a Liberal member of the House of Representatives, as were former senators Fred Chaney and Kathy (Martin) Sullivan. The only Labor senators from that time remaining in the Senate in 1990 were John Button and Peter Walsh; the only remaining Liberal senators were Peter Durack and me.

During all the period of the Budget sittings in 1975, I maintained a diary daily, writing a few lines each night or early in the morning. For the time before that I maintained a collection of notes and personal papers. Another diarist of those times was my colleague Chris Puplick. His diaries cover a longer period and include his comments when he worked, during the relevant period, as a member of my staff. He made his diaries available to me for use in the present enterprise.

Because there is no other manuscript by a parliamentarian with a diary of that time (and certainly no book by a bit player with no continuing personal axe to grind), I believe it is proper for me, from notes written at the time, to record what it was like from the inside—what it was like to be there to face the events as they occurred, with the picture as it unfolded; what it was like to have faced the pressure of being part of a decision to defer Supply, and then to have maintained that position and, finally, to have been part of the landslide election victory at the end.

From this distance of time, my perceptions have altered and softened. They are also clearer. I am less passionate in my judgement of our opponents, less vehement in my opinion of their actions, less passionate in my defence of our strategy, less absolute and arbitrary in my assessments, and in particular I am less certain of the wisdom of the course we took.

All this I will discuss in the succeeding chapters, drawing where necessary on contemporary notes and material, on the Hansards, on the Journals (the official records) of the Senate, on the newspapers and, above all, on my own contemporary notes.

In this manuscript, I emphasise my minor part and my own insignificance in the events. This is at once a strength and a weakness: while my access to 'inside' information was less than for frontbench colleagues, my capacity to avoid some of their tunnel vision and particular judgments was rather greater. But I was a member of the parliamentary Liberal Party. I did sit in every meeting of the joint parties. I did talk daily with major figures. I did report to public meetings about the situation and about our options. I did reassure them about our determination. I did discuss daily with colleagues where we were and where we thought we might be going. I did talk daily to members of the Canberra Press Gallery. I was subject to great pressure. I did breathe in daily the atmosphere and the sense of the drama as it unfolded.

In addition, I was a senator and not a member of the House of Representatives. Although the confrontation was between the two chambers, it was in the Senate that the main action occurred, and it was in the Senate that events were determined and in which I voted on every vital division. Those with a continuing sense of hurt and injustice will blame me for those votes, while those without deeply entrenched attitudes or bitter memories may feel curiosity about the whole affair. This series of insights will complement some other published material and because of that this manuscript should be of value to those who, while never having served in a parliament, wish to understand the events of that time as seen by a parliamentarian.

Peter Baume
Sydney, May 2014

INTRODUCTION: A DISSIDENT LIBERAL—A PRINCIPLED POLITICAL CAREER

John Wanna and Marija Taflaga

Introducing Peter Baume's Political Writings and Selected Speeches (including his unpublished diaries)

Peter Erne Baume MD, AC, served in the Australian Senate from August 1974 until January 1991, representing the people of New South Wales as one of their initially 10 and then 12 senators. As a member of the Liberal Party, Baume was a dissident liberal, very much his own man, who often baulked at toeing the party line, and was not afraid of crossing the floor against his party colleagues. He was a highbrow classical intellectual of Jewish faith with professional training in medicine. He tended not to suffer fools gladly but equally was not elitist or aloof in his interactions with others and could be tolerant and empathetic in his demeanour. Like Max Weber, he regarded politics as a vocation, a special calling for those committed to serving the public interest throughout their lives;[1] and yet when he came to serve in the legislature and experienced the rough and tumble of political life he often despaired at the lack of principles, vision or even basic understanding of many of his party colleagues. He resented other politicians who ostensibly posed as leaders of the community yet who adopted positions on public policy based on next to no information and were simply prejudicial in making their minds up on issues of national importance (at one time referring

---

[1] See Baume (2000); and his speech later in this volume entitled 'Four Careers'.

to them as the 'fat arses' of the political system). Baume was in many ways ahead of his time but drew his inspiration from an earlier heyday of social liberalism.[2] As a humanist, he was prepared publicly to champion unpopular causes or fight for issues that were seen as marginal but would become mainstream a generation later. But he was never solely the token bleeding heart; he could just as easily advocate tough issues that were unpalatable to the body politic, such as the need to ration increasingly expensive health services and begin a dialogue with the community about how rationing would be implemented.[3] He subsequently recalled, looking back on his career, that many of his views were 'heterodox' and that people 'have not understood' that he had 'been a bit of a "Cassandra"'—a denigrated seer with the power of prophecy in politics. But some of his closest colleagues, like Steele Hall, went further and argued that people like Peter Baume found it hard to be in politics, and to live within its rigours and strictures.

Baume's political career began when he was suddenly catapulted into the constitutional crisis of 1975; it was a daunting initiation and a baptism of fire for the professional idealist. He entered Parliament as a new senator after the double-dissolution general election of May 1974 forced on the Whitlam Labor Government by an obstructionist, hostile Senate. With increasing personal misgivings, he witnessed the traumatic events of the blocking of Supply in 1975, which led to the sacking of the Whitlam Government and the installation of a caretaker government led by Malcolm Fraser. As a new Opposition backbencher, he was not a major player in the unfolding crisis but neither was he an innocent bystander; he was an active participant who did not broadcast his reservations. Like the other 'small-l' Liberal senators in parliament at the time, he disagreed with the tactics but went along with the strategy of displacing a recently re-elected government. He then spent seven years in government with the Coalition, from 1975 to 1983, becoming sequentially a short-term minister in the portfolios of Aboriginal affairs, health, and education, serving a combined total of just two-and-a-half years in the ministry. For a man of many talents, his ministerial appointments were all too brief to make any lasting impact or legacy. After that, he spent a further seven years in opposition during the Labor era, under Prime Minister Bob Hawke, watching the Government's economic reforms but mainly witnessing with increasing discontent the growing neoliberal radicalisation of his own side of politics. He became increasingly disillusioned with politics in general and especially the right-turn in the Federal Liberal Party, and in September 1990 he announced to the Senate that he would resign his seat in January 1991. He spent his post-political career as a professor of community medicine in New South Wales and was active in a number of health-related

---

2 Sawer (2003: 171–3).
3 See Khadra (2010: 192).

lobby groups, civil rights bodies and government reform commissions, before turning his skills to university administration by becoming Chancellor of The Australian National University and advocating social policy issues.

Peter Baume was born in January 1935 and enjoyed a relatively privileged upbringing in Sydney's Northern Beaches. Of German–Jewish descent, his family has a long involvement and interest in politics.[4] His grandfather, Frederick Baume, a lawyer by profession, was born in Dunedin, New Zealand. He served in the New Zealand Parliament, representing the progressive Liberal Party in the seat of Auckland from 1902 until his death in 1910. The New Zealand Liberal Party was a reformist 'social liberal' party interested in equality, public education and ameliorative social policies. Peter's grandmother Rosetta was also a community activist and social campaigner. She established the Auckland Civic League in 1913, and was an early suffragette who stood for Parliament—the first to do so in New Zealand. A distant uncle named John Jacob Cohen was Speaker of the Legislative Assembly in New South Wales. Peter's uncle Eric Baume (also named Frederick) was a prominent Sydney journalist, editor, broadcaster and author, who had a fascination with the proto-fascist New Guard movement in the 1930s. After Peter's entry into politics, he was followed by his cousin, Michael Baume, who was Member for Macarthur in New South Wales and then became a federal senator from 1975 to 1983 as the Member for Macarthur and as a NSW senator from 1985 to 1996.

Peter Baume's education and early career were devoted principally to medicine, attaining his initial qualifications from the University of Sydney, before further study in Sydney, the United Kingdom and the United States. In 1969 he received a Doctor of Medicine (MD) from the University of Sydney. He turned his attention to health policy issues and began a more active involvement in public life in the early 1970s, especially crystallised around the public health policies of the Whitlam Government and the introduction of Medibank. Having joined the Liberal Party in 1971, he initially stood for preselection in 1972 in the federal seat of Berowra (a northern suburb of Sydney, later supposedly one of Sydney's most 'bogan' regions). Baume ultimately lost the contest (for which he was later thankful), along with other future luminaries of his generation, John Howard and Ian Macphee. Yet, the contest had whetted Baume's appetite for politics and gained him the attention of John Carrick, the General Secretary of the NSW Branch of the Liberal Party. Carrick encouraged Baume to consider a political career in the Senate instead of in the lower house. Accordingly, Baume stood for preselection for the Liberal Party in New South Wales and was elected as a senator for that state at the double-dissolution election of 1974, winning the last spot on the list of elected senators, but only after waiting for weeks for counting

---

4   See Sawer (2003: 167–71).

and preference allocation to confirm the final place. His maiden speech was more forgettable than a memorable pièce de résistance or work of artistic merit; it was laced with pure political partisanship, lambasting the performance of the Whitlam Government, which he charged with failing to look after the little man. He championed the power of the Senate to supervise lower house governments, complained about increasing unemployment, housing affordability and defence capabilities, and argued that the Coalition had a strong record on social welfare while indicating he opposed Medibank as a universal health insurance system. This was in striking contrast with his valedictory speech at the end of 1990, where his emphasis was on the endurance of the Senate as an institution in contrast with the fleeting presence of individual senators.

His first year in federal politics in 1974–75 was truly tumultuous. He watched as the Whitlam Government imploded and was finally dismissed, unable to secure passage of its Budget through the Senate. As a new senator, Baume seemed slow to realise the consequences of what was going on and that long-standing conventions were being broken for short-term opportunism. As his essay on the 1975 crisis reveals (which is part narrative diary and part contemporaneous reflection), he remained a bemused onlooker to the dramatic events of 1974–75, but along with his Coalition colleagues in the Senate he possessed a crucial vote. It was often reported that Baume was one of the 'wavering senators' who were looking to break ranks and allow the Supply Bills to pass, but while he had sincere misgivings, his resolve hardened during the crisis, especially after it was revealed that the mineral and energy minister Rex Connor had misled Parliament. Others who were reputedly wavering during late 1975 included Don Jessop, Kathryn Martin and Alan Missen.

Baume noted that during those terrible months of the second half of 1975, he kept a daily diary, recording his observations and views, and these notes then became the basis of his essay on the Dismissal contained in this monograph. He insists that these diary accounts were contemporaneous: there was no rewriting of history, no revisionism, no hagiography, no tempering of the record with the wisdom of hindsight. His primary document gives, among other things, an account of a newly elected if relatively unimportant backbench senator caught up in affairs of great moment.

His initial prominence in Federal Parliament came as a result of his deep interest in social policy issues and the importance of effective parliamentary scrutiny. He chaired the Senate Standing Committee on Social Welfare and produced a major report on the growing consumption of illicit drugs, called *Drug Problems in Australia: An intoxicated society?* (1977). He followed this with a pioneering study into the paucity of policy evaluation in government programs and the failure to report outputs or achievements to the Parliament. His two-volume report entitled *Through a Glass Darkly: Evaluation in Australian health and welfare services* (1979) became an important milestone in the encouragement of better reporting of program performance by government agencies. At the time, Baume was aghast that Commonwealth agencies could secure budgetary resources for their intended programs but not report on progress and achievements, or evaluate the efficiency and effectiveness of their activities. Many senior public servants interested in better public policy outcomes welcomed his report as a wake-up call to the political executive to focus on results (not on how much inputs they expended) and take program evaluation seriously. He won many plaudits for his insistence on what now would be called evidence-based policy—again acting as a harbinger of future predispositions.

With the Fraser Government already enjoying the services of two ministers in the Senate from New South Wales (Senator Bob Cotton and Senator John Carrick, later Sir John), Baume's progression into the ministry was slowed. Serving an apprenticeship as deputy senate whip from October 1977 and then government whip from February 1978 until the 1980 election, Baume was promoted to the front bench as an outer minister responsible for Aboriginal affairs. Life as a minister was hectic but not quite Hobbesian ('solitary, poor, nasty, brutish and short')—not least because he spent relatively little time in situ in three different portfolios. He served for just 19 months as Aboriginal affairs minister, three weeks as health minister in 1982 (but then a further three months more as acting minister after the dismissal of Michael Mackellar), and finally 11 months as education minister. When given the choice by Fraser between the portfolios of health and education in 1982, Baume quickly chose the latter, but his tenure was abruptly ended when the Fraser Government was defeated at the snap election of March 1983. Only in the last two portfolios was he a member of Fraser's Cabinet, for approximately 12 months.

It was no accident that Fraser selected Peter Baume as his Minister for the Interests of Indigenous Australians. Baume was part of a key group within the Fraser Government advocating for the Government's human rights agenda. As Fraser's Minister for Aboriginal Affairs, Baume took up what was at the time a fringe issue in his party, arguing that a separate policy for Aboriginal people would benefit them in terms of social policy and human welfare. Baume was also tasked with formulating a long-overdue response to the House of Representatives Standing Committee on Aboriginal Affairs' report *Aboriginal Health* (1979) on the poor state of Aboriginal health in Australia. The task was a challenge for Baume, having to balance the states' rights mantra of the Liberal Party with the low-priority status given to Indigenous affairs. Baume's solution to maintain much of the existing status quo of cooperative federalism, with the states retaining responsibility for running Indigenous health services, was contentious as it disappointed advocates who had wanted a greater federal role. Yet there were victories: Baume secured the increased participation of Aboriginal people in the design, delivery and evaluation of Indigenous health programs and a 15.3 per cent increase in funding for the Aboriginal affairs portfolio. During Baume's time as minister, all Federal Government agencies adopted an administrative definition of Aboriginality based on descent, self-identification and community recognition.

Scandals claimed the ministerial careers of Michael Mackellar (Minister for Health) in the 'colour television' scandal and later John Moore, as the responsible Minister for Customs, who did not follow procedure to investigate his fellow minister and seemingly covered it up. As a result of these departures, Baume was sworn in first as health minister and then as education minister—both positions representing rapid promotions from his initial appointment. Baume's promotions to health and education also saw his elevation into the Cabinet. As education minister, he also courted controversy. Baume took on the vexed question of education funding for non-government schools—known then as 'state aid'. Baume promised to increase funding by 7 per cent for private schools in 1982 and a further 2.5 per cent in 1983. Poor private schools, mostly Catholic, were the beneficiary of these increases, which brought their funding base up to 40 per cent of a government school's standard costs. Although he did not remain long in any of his ministerial positions, he was nevertheless passionate about the issues in his three portfolios.

On losing office, Baume continued as the Shadow Minister for Education and Youth. He held this position until December 1984 when he was sidelined by Andrew Peacock, and given carriage of the status of women portfolio. After the surprise leadership change in 1985, the new opposition leader John Howard added community services to Baume's existing responsibility for the status of women. Baume subsequently came to believe that Howard knew that he had not voted for him in the leadership ballot, but that the new leader wanted an articulate liberal voice in the Shadow Cabinet; Howard also later called on the Liberal Party to re-endorse Baume at his subsequent preselection. Against the wishes of many of his colleagues, Baume supported widening the coverage of equal employment opportunity (EEO) legislation. After fighting with his conservative colleagues on the issue, he resigned from the Shadow Cabinet on a point of principle (collective solidarity) on 26 March 1987, a month before the crucial vote on the legislation. He then duly crossed the floor of the Senate in April 1987 to vote with the Labor Government on a bill to extend EEO to Commonwealth statutory authorities—extending its reach into the wider public sector, a stance that won him many plaudits from women and social reformers.[5]

---

5   See Sawer (2003: 173–6).

INTRODUCTION

Once he resigned from the Shadow Cabinet, Baume was never to return and would spend the next four years again on the Opposition backbench (although he was offered a lower-level appointment by the next leader, John Hewson, in 1990, but by that time he had had enough and refused). By then he was becoming seriously disaffected with the 'increasingly dominant radical conservatism of others' in his party—especially the Howard backers and neoliberal 'Dries'. Two of his close parliamentary colleagues, Ian Macphee and Chris Puplick, had by then been ousted from Parliament—Macphee in a bitter preselection fight against the New Right's David Kemp, and Puplick lost his Senate seat for a second time at the 1990 election. Baume spent the final years in Parliament as an increasingly marginalised dissident within his own party. With little committee work to occupy him, he chose to join two parliamentary groups—one a liaison group for the prevention and treatment of AIDS, and a second championing the international work of Amnesty International. His work on AIDS with Neal Blewett and the then shadow minister Peter Shack fought against the rise of a scare campaign around AIDS both publicly and within his own party. The result was a bipartisan consensus that resulted in timely proactive interventions and mobilised a massive public awareness campaign, especially in the gay community. As a result of Baume's and others' work across the political divide, Australia was one of the few countries where AIDS did not become a partisan issue, which significantly improved patient outcomes and the overall public health of Australia. In recognition of his work, Baume was made a life governor of the Kirby Institute of the University of New South Wales in 2014, together with Neal Blewett.

Nevertheless, by 1990 Baume had made the decision to move on; and in a brief personal statement, he notified the Senate on 19 September 1990 that he would resign in the near future as he had been appointed as professor and head of the Department of Community Medicine at the University of New South Wales. His resignation took effect from 28 January 1991. While a professor at the University of New South Wales, he became the tenth Chancellor of The Australian National University in 1994, a position he held until 2005, when impaired hearing forced him to resign.

Becoming a Conviction Politician: Assembling social liberal principles and ideas

Peter Baume began his formal career in politics to do some good for his fellow citizens, not as an ideological protagonist or a conviction politician. He was a moderate Liberal with a rationalist bent and a policy interest in health and medical matters. Gradually, his parliamentary career and the party machinations he experienced forged a more crusading politician to emerge and sharpened his principled positions. He was also influenced by other progressive voices in Parliament and among his close circles—for instance, his fellow moderate Liberal Forum members with whom he shared an abiding commitment, and from Labor's side mentioning that Neal Blewett was particularly influential in Baume's own stance on the decriminalisation of marijuana. By the early 1980s, his thinking was changing and becoming more nuanced, if at times unpredictable. He developed a social conscience and believed in collective responsibilities, and committed himself to helping those in less fortunate circumstances than others. Baume emerged as a 'small-l' liberal or liberal humanist, extolling the virtues of social liberalism—à la J.S. Mill, L.T. Hobhouse, T.H. Green and J.A. Hobson.[6] In taking this position, he readily distanced himself from the Classical Liberals—the earlier liberal tradition associated with John Locke and Tom Paine that placed personal freedoms and private property over other considerations—and from the newly emerging neoliberalism drawing on Ayn Rand, Frederick von Hayek and Milton Friedman, and epitomised in the governments of Margaret Thatcher and Ronald Reagan. He felt there was an important role for government in modern societies, not simply enforcing codes of law and order but also in building a civilising culture in the social order and developing human capital with investments in education for the benefit of future generations.

Social liberalism for Baume was nuanced and flexible. It would often seem a grab bag of divergent contentious ideas, but was a platform that somehow made sense and informed his stances on divisive contemporary issues. Along with a handful of like-minded colleagues in the Parliament, he looked to his normative values and ethics to shape his opinions and provide some coherency to his positions on contentious social issues; and he was not afraid to speak out against the powerful, whether in society or in his own party. With the benefit of hindsight, it is clear that he was often more convinced of what he was *against* than what he was for, and many of his heterodox speeches begin from this premise. He made principled defences of refugees and asylum-seekers, Aborigines, gay people and AIDS sufferers, drug-users, the seriously ill or infirm, disaffected youth and the aged. Many of these marginal groups he thought of as victims of prejudice, discrimination, disadvantage, neglect, or all of the above. Accordingly, he saw his role was to speak up for the 'little man' who was ground down by the system. He also began to publicly champion some celebrated issues such as voluntary euthanasia, Aboriginal health, racism, drug liberalisation and, later, a non-discriminatory immigration policy. Conversely, he was not afraid to argue for collective rights against individuals who have transgressed, as in the case of his championing of war crimes legislation and exposing the infiltration of former Nazis into Australian society.

---

6   Sawer (2003).

In policy development, he preferred a Burkean orderly progression rather than radical shifts driven by ideology. Occasionally, he expressed some essentially libertarian sentiments about the sanctity of the freedom to make personal decisions and choices, and not be ruled by an overly regulatory 'big brother state'. His support for drug law reform was another libertarian stance—unusual for a member of the medical profession. He was no economic rationalist but could contemplate controversial economic issues, as with his advocacy for rationing health services, prioritising care and his critique of overservicing by the health industry.

Baume's most important contributions to public policy debates were his unconventional and at times maverick opinions given in a series of important speeches—self-composed and thoughtfully crafted and delivered mostly in the early to mid-1980s. He was a major dissident voice prepared to defend unpopular or controversial causes largely to sympathetic audiences, knowing but not actually caring that the national media and his conservative opponents would note his contrary opinions. In this collection, we have selected and included his most important speeches under three headings: his political philosophies and conviction-based adherence to 'small-l' social liberalism; his responses to the increasingly factionalised and dysfunctional Liberal Party and its hijacking by the neoliberal forces of the Right; and his contributions to contemporary policy debates hoping to introduce some greater reasonableness into the often ideological arguments. Here we read about the formation of his beliefs and those inspirational influences that helped form his political ideas, especially his view that politics was a noble cause dedicated to serving the greater good. We also read about the formation of a loose factional grouping of social liberals under the label the Liberal Forum, which had pretensions to being the intellectual vanguard of the Liberal Party. Finally, the collection includes his major policy speeches, in which he defends social policies, redistributive taxation, Aboriginal health policies and social provision, the plea for an official apology to Aboriginal Australia for the 'Stolen Generations' (more than a decade before it was actually delivered by Kevin Rudd in 2008), education about illicit drugs and euthanasia, and the removal of racial selection in immigration policy.

Factional Power Plays

As a backbencher, Baume had the time to record his observations of the factional power plays affecting his party in a daily diary. Political diaries from non-Labor parliamentarians in Australia are relatively rare. Baume's diaries from various years in the 1980s are deposited in the library of The Australian National University, in Canberra. These political diaries offer a rare and important insider's view of the political machinations at a key transition point in the

Liberal Party's history. They recount the pressures politicians endure and the power plays that affect them and in which they act as combatants, but they also describe the human feelings of those who commit their lives to politics, the difficult journeys, the 'what-ifs', the betrayals and boredoms, the dog-eat-dog world of career politicians, and the disappointments at what can realistically be achieved in parliamentary terms. Baume's diary entries are unvarnished, often brutal or unkind in their honesty, and full of minutiae indicating the pressures on and peripatetic lifestyle of serving politicians. They are part political observations of events and circumstance, part reflections and opinions about close colleagues, and part personal concerns with the dilemmas of family life as a busy politician. These diaries should be recommended reading for any budding politician intending to run for office, as they provide a valuable insight into the life that awaits them if they succeed. They have been tidied by these two authors but not edited or changed in any way or amended with the benefit of the wisdom of hindsight.

Given the numbers of people who go into politics, political diaries all too infrequently see the light of day. When they do appear, they are often invaluable to political scientists and historians wanting a first-hand account of the times, conflicts, impressions and so on. Peter Baume's diary entries reflect an era in which the Federal and NSW branches of the Liberal Party had hit on hard times. Riven by ideological divisions at the federal level, and increasingly open factional warfare in the NSW branch, the 1980s represented an era of transformation for the Liberal Party at both levels of the party. Baume was one of the leading lights of the 'Wets', along with Robert Hill, Alan Missen, Ian Macphee, Chris Puplick, Steele Hall and a much younger George Brandis, as the historical tide of 'small-l' liberalism was fast receding. His dissident views often put him at loggerheads with his more mainstream party colleagues. Indeed, some Australian Labor Party (ALP) politicians felt that Baume was a decent parliamentarian who would sit more comfortably in their party with his views on social justice (although he would baulk at the party discipline and union dominance).

The Liberal Party has always sought to deny the existence of factions within the party because it is a key point of differentiation from the ALP and goes to the core of the Liberals' philosophical self-identity as a party of independent-minded representatives. However, by the mid-1980s, groupings within the Liberal Party, both nationally and within some state branches, started to form that went beyond personality cliques. Most of these groupings would never take on the discipline and rigidity of factions in the ALP, but they provided important organising and strategising opportunities for Liberal members during this time. Baume's political career, and membership of two of these groups, illustrates the difference between the organisation and operation of moderate factions at the federal and NSW division levels.

INTRODUCTION

At the NSW level, Baume was a member of the inner circle of the powerful faction known prosaically at the time as the Liberal Forum Group ('the Group', or at times the 'Black Ankle'), which coalesced into a political force in New South Wales in 1984.[7] Baume was also a founding member of the Liberal Forum at the federal level, which was an informal association of moderate Liberal members in Canberra. The Federal Liberal Forum, originally a clandestine group within the broad church of the larger Liberal Party, was officially formed in February 1985 and was irreverently named by its members the 'Black Hand' (from which Baume's self-mocking nickname for the NSW branch—the 'Black Ankle'—originated). Baume's account of the formation and aims of the Liberal Forum reveals the growing alienation and dislocation that he and other moderate Liberals felt in the party room: Baume wrote that with the formation of the Liberal Forum it was for many social liberals 'the first opportunity to be part of a sympathetic, collegial group pursuing compatible ideological goals'.

The formation of the Liberal Forum Group in New South Wales was a response to the rise of a grab bag collection of radicals on the right, including the Australian League of Rights, the Citizens' Electoral Council and the Captive Nations Lobby and Conservative Christians, which were seeking to establish new branches of the Liberal Party in the electoral wastelands of western Sydney. These right-wing infiltrators were known as 'The Uglies' by the traditional North Shore Liberal establishment.[8] Led by Lyenko Urbanchich and a young David Clarke, 'The Uglies' exploited the Liberal Party's undemocratic voting rules, which gave all branches equal status despite membership numbers in an attempt to gain more power within the State Council during the late 1970s.[9] The tactics of Urbanchich's group, and later the rise of the 'New Right' with its emphasis on neoliberal economics and (often, but not always) nationalistic social agenda, represented a major incursion into the urbane social liberal agenda that had dominated the NSW division of the Liberal Party from its earliest days as a more free-market and free-trade oriented political party. The effect of these aggressive new tactics spurred moderate voices in New South Wales, such as Baume, to increasingly engage in factional behaviour and the formation of the Group.

The Group's success as a faction lay in its deliberate decision to eschew discussion of policy and NSW party leadership in order to lessen the chances of the formation of sub-factions and dilution of its overall political efficacy. Indeed, Baume's reflections on the activities of the group were businesslike in tone. Thus, in New South Wales, the Group became a powerful bloc through the skilful deployment of raw numbers and the unceasing management of branches. When Baume was a member of the Group, its power as a faction was only

---

7   Hancock (2007: 238).
8   Hancock (2007: 164).
9   Hancock (2007: 160).

starting to assert itself, but it had a number of significant wins, which included maintaining Baume's position in a winnable seat in the Senate in 1987 (with the additional help of John Howard). The faction was also successful for a while in blocking the ambitions of the hardline right-winger Bronwyn Bishop (whom Baume in his diaries seemed to loathe with a passion bordering on paranoia). By the mid-1990s, nothing could be achieved without negotiation with the Group. Yet the conflict between the Group and 'The Uglies' (later to become known by the moniker 'the Taliban') would lead to the escalation of infighting and increasing factionalisation of the NSW branch, which would set the tone of political relations at the state and federal levels until this day.

Although the Group as a formalised faction was specifically intended to manage preselections and internal party appointments within the NSW Branch of the Liberal Party, the Liberal Forum, in contrast, especially from Baume's point of view, was both an ideas group and a forum to discuss the faction's tactical position. A key reason why the Liberal Forum manifested itself differently to the Group at the federal level was a result of widespread disapproval of factions within the Liberal Party and the lack of infrastructure to enable factions to flourish. NSW politicians who might be heavily engaged in factional or factional-like contests at the state level had no natural home when they arrived in Canberra. This was in stark contrast with the ALP, whose factions at the state and federal levels virtually fed into each other. Moreover, as the Liberal Party was the dominant national political party during the long years of the postwar boom, the need for factions was not readily apparent. Differences in policy preferences could be managed effectively by the existing structures within the Liberal Party. However, as the postwar Bretton-Woods settlement broke down from the mid-1970s onwards, and the business-as-usual approach was no longer an option for Australia, the Liberal Party was forced to consider which new policy framework would guide the relationship between citizens, markets and the state into the future. So, at stake at the federal level were not preselections or positions within the Cabinet (as they were in the ALP); the main battleground was now focused on ideas and the future direction of the Liberal Party.

For Baume, the Liberal Forum's role was to 'counter the arguments and intellectual dominance achieved by the conservative and libertarian elements within the party' and in Australia's intellectual debate more generally. Baume and his fellow factional members were defenders of Fraser's legacy, particularly in public administration and social affairs, although many would have concurred with the view that by 1983 the rudderless Fraser Government probably deserved to lose at the March election. The Wets had been slow to recognise the gradual 'drying out' of the Liberal Party since Billy Snedden—a leading 'trendy' within the Liberal Party—had lost the leadership in 1975.[10] Baume's diary records a meeting at his home where the NSW group decided to back Fraser—and thereby ensured his victory. Given the dominance of Fraser as prime minister and the heavy impact that the 1983 defeat had on Dry members, much of the process had happened quietly. It was only after the 1984 election, when a slew of retirements from the party saw the return of many more Dry members into the opposition parties, that the shift in the party's outlook was readily apparent to social liberals like Baume.

Contemporaneous news reporting tended to suggest a level of political organisation on the part of the Wets, which as Baume's diary reveals, was simply not there. The Liberal Forum was less well organised than its forerunner, the Dries, had been during the later years of the Fraser Government.[11] Baume and his fellow travellers were largely an ad hoc political grouping that met fairly infrequently every six to eight weeks. Baume's diary also reveals the growing importance of today's Senator George Brandis to the formation and workings of the Liberal Forum and its tactical organisation, alongside Tom Harley (Alfred Deakin's great-grandson) and Yvonne Thompson. Before he became a party stalwart and factional warhorse, the young Brandis, then an idealistic promoter of social liberalism and an important factional tactician, would cut his political teeth fighting a rearguard action against the incoming tide of neoliberal economics and a muscular social conservatism that increasingly came to characterise the party in the late 1980s and early 1990s.

As the 1980s dragged on, Baume increasingly came to recognise that his neoliberal colleagues regarded the Liberal Forum as the 'cockroaches in the corner', out of step with a party that was increasingly less interested and intolerant of the social-liberal views he represented. While the Wets were successful in providing a public critique of the rightward direction of the Liberal Party, the political goal of the Wets was not well defined beyond the promotion of a modern version of liberalism. Baume and his dwindling brigade of 'Black Hand/Black Ankle' supporters were drawn into factional disputes. As Liberal Forum members, they regularly discussed the tactical position of their faction, particularly during the 1987 election as the federal party was facing its third consecutive defeat at the polls. Brandis, Harley and Thompson edited *Liberals Face the Future* (1984). The Liberal Forum produced *Australian Liberalism: The continuing vision* (1986), regularly released occasional papers and undertook important speeches. Despite these efforts at public persuasion, the Group was not free of internal tensions and such conflicts required a fine balancing of personalities and the internal political machinations. One issue that dogged the Forum membership

---

10 Head (1989: 490).
11 See Hyde (2003).

was the constant attention given to and media discussion of prominent Wet Ian Macphee's leadership ambitions. The media at the time had come to the assumption that Macphee was the official leader of the faction (incorrectly as it transpired), whereas no such internal discussion about leadership had ever taken place.

Baume's recounting of Wet factional activity reflects the faction's precarious position. Much time is dedicated to crisis management and offering consolation and support to other faction members. As Baume became more politically isolated and struggled to find the resources to engage courteously with party members he held in low regard, it is clear that Baume gained solace from his involvement with the Liberal Forum, where he would linger over the details of philosophical and tactical discussions that he had found pleasurable and intellectually stimulating.

Perhaps the greatest illustration of the limitations of the Liberal Forum as a politically oriented faction (such as the Group clearly was) occurred in 1989. As a factional member, Baume remained in the dark over the lightning leadership coup that replaced John Howard with Andrew Peacock as federal leader in that year. Baume remained in complete ignorance of the plotters, even though some key actors, such as Puplick, were close colleagues and Liberal Forum members. It illustrates the limits of the forum's utility as a political grouping and the overall limitations of factions within the Liberals more generally, as discussed above. At the federal level, the Black Hand simply could not compete with the more coordinated (but by no means well-organised) work of the Dries. Indeed, as Baume's diary records, the careers of several leading moderates were destroyed during this period, including Macphee, Puplick and, eventually, Baume himself.

Drawing towards the end of his political career in late 1990, Baume's diary increasingly reflected a man weary of politics and struggling to conceal the contempt he felt for some of his colleagues. His interactions with his colleagues became more limited and he disengaged from their politics. The factional interactions that once gave Baume much intellectual stimulation and enjoyment became facile and sterile. He despaired about the future of liberalism and the hijacking of his cherished Liberal Party, and grew weary of attending Parliament. By 1990, he was isolated in politics and opted to change career for the better. By contrast, in this fading political light, we see a re-blossoming of his family and his own inner life, and a growing sense that politics is not the only thing of importance to him. Baume's speeches from this period are generally uplifting and optimistic, yet his diary accounts are far more pessimistic and despondent while conveying remorse over the banalities and brutalities of political life.

Baume's contribution to public life in Australia was as a progressive medical practitioner and educator, a dissident politician who managed to have influence on the body politic beyond his predominant position as a humble backbencher, and finally as an advocate of principled causes. Some would venture his career was partly that of a prophetic Cassandra, partly a St Jude as the patron saint of lost causes, and partly a platonic guardian less comfortable in the Machiavellian machinations of modern party politics.

References

Baume, Peter. 2000. Service in three careers. *Medical Journal of Australia* 173: 643–6.

Brandis, George, Harley, Tom and Maxwell, Don. 1984, *Liberals Face the Future*. Melbourne: Oxford University Press.

Hancock, Ian. 2007. *The Liberals: The NSW division 1945–2000*. Sydney: The Federation Press.

Head, Brian. 1989. 'Parties and the Policy agenda 1978–1988.' In Brian Head and Allan Patience (eds), *From Fraser to Hawke: Australian public policy in the 1980s*. Melbourne: Longman Cheshire.

Hyde, John. 2002. *Dry: In defence of economic freedom*. Melbourne: Institute of Public Affairs.

Khadra, Mohamed. 2010. *Terminal Decline*. Sydney: Heinemann.

Sawer, Marian. 2003. *The Ethical State?* Melbourne: Melbourne University Press.

Thompson, Yvonne, Brandis, George and Harley, Tom. 1986. *Australian Liberalism: The continuing vision*. Melbourne: Liberal Forum.

1
MY DILEMMA: FROM MEDICINE TO THE SENATE

Gough Whitlam became prime minister of the first Labor government to take office in Australia for 23 years after Robert Menzies led the Liberal Party to victory in 1949. Whitlam's Labor Party triumphed at the general election of 2 December 1972 by winning eight seats and sweeping out the Administration of William 'Billy' McMahon.[1] At that election, the Labor Party won 67 seats, the Liberal Party won 38 seats, and the Country Party won 20 seats.

I have always felt somewhat sorry for Bill McMahon. He was never a likeable person, and I did not ever like him. His voice was as unpleasant as Gough Whitlam's voice was impressive, his looks were against him, and he was a self-centred and untrustworthy colleague. Yet I felt sorry for him. He had been blackballed as Liberal leader by the leader of the Country Party John 'Black Jack' McEwen, following the death of Harold Holt, after which John Gorton had come from the Senate to snatch the premiership. Then he had taken over the prime ministership in a nasty palace coup against the liberal Gorton just in time to face the irresistible tide of Whitlam and the Labor revival. McMahon has been described by Laurie Oakes as being 'indecisive as a leader, confused in debate, unappealing on television, and unconvincing on the hustings'.[2]

---

1 Mayer (1973).
2 Oakes (1976: 228).

But even had he been more attractive, more likeable and more in tune with the aspirations and sentiments of the community and the times, it is doubtful that he could have withstood that tide.

In any event, once the Labor Party took office, McMahon was replaced quickly by the liberals. Bill Snedden became leader in 1972 and remained leader until the Fraser coup of 1974. A man of liberal views, Snedden never really stamped his authority on the Liberal Party or the Parliament. His leadership was always insecure—and was seen to be insecure by the press and by his enemies. It is one measure of the limitations of Gough Whitlam's political judgment that he chose to destroy Snedden in Parliament so completely, thus making more certain the advent of Malcolm Fraser and the eventual destruction of Whitlam's own government.

In the early 1970s, soon after joining the Liberal Party, I had been approached by Don Dobie, Member for Cook in southern Sydney and an assistant minister, to consider running for Parliament. An initial try for the seat of Berowra had been unsuccessful (as it had been for John Howard, Bob Ellicott, Jim Cameron, David Arblaster and Vi Lloyd—all of whom, like me, later ended up in Parliament), but I had been noticed by Nigel Bowen and John Carrick, and was able on 29 June 1973 to win preselection for a place on the next NSW Liberal Senate ticket. That preselection took place at the Boulevarde Hotel on William Street in Sydney. Bob Cotton won the first position and there were 20 of us seeking the other Liberal position in the team. We were all shut together in one large room, and there we stayed together for the whole day.

What an extraordinary scene it was in that room. There were party faithfuls who sat together and chatted, party eccentrics who carried on their own eccentricities, and newcomers (many of them to shine later in party affairs) nervously sitting around. The experienced had novels to read or packs of cards with them; the rest of us just endured the time. And, most extraordinary of all, there was Julia Freebury, the abortion law reform campaigner who had joined the Liberal Party so that she could nominate and address a college of 75 leading Liberals for only the cost of her nomination. She moved professionally during the day to speak with each of the candidates about abortion law reform. During her speech to the preselection college, she spoke on the same subject.

As the only 'outsider' in the whole preselection, she was rather more dispassionate than the rest. She later told friends that she had come expecting the preselection to have been determined in advance. It was only when she felt the tension rising and saw the nervousness of candidates that she realised that there was no designated candidate and that she was witnessing a true trial of strength. Perhaps she was only partly correct. Chris Puplick, who later became a close friend and associate of mine, was a preselector that day. He tells me that he was 'under instructions' to vote for me. Incidentally, it was Puplick's aphorism that most people in political parties are 'lonely, mad or ambitious' to a greater or lesser extent that was well illustrated that day.

Towards the end, John Jobling, an unsuccessful candidate that day but later whip in the Legislative Council, returned from the lavatory to tell us that only Milovoj (Misha) Lajovic and I remained in the ballot. Ten hours after it had all begun, the 20 candidates were called back to the electoral college. All eyes were on me and I knew then that I had succeeded. The announcements followed, some speeches were made, whisky was drunk, I phoned home with the news, and we were off and running.

After the preselection, I was summoned to meet the most senior NSW Liberal Party senator, the Honourable Sir Kenneth Anderson. He greeted me with something like the following: 'Your job is to sit on stages, introduce people if asked to, give votes of thanks if asked to, and otherwise to keep very quiet. Do you understand? Would you join me now for a cup of tea? Milk? Sugar?' This was rather an abrupt and disquieting introduction to the glory of being a preselected candidate and Ken Anderson was fierce in delivering the message. But he was in fact a gentle, friendly, wise man and became a supportive friend. He had been a prisoner of the Japanese at Changi and on the Burma railway, as had John Carrick and Tom Uren. These doughty politicians from two opposing parties showed consistent support and courtesy to each other and there was something in this Changi association that transcended the daily conflicts of federal politics.

The election of 18 May 1974 was precipitated when, on 10 April, Senate Opposition leader Reg Withers moved an amendment to the first of three Appropriation Bills, which, when carried, was treated by the Government as a denial of Supply.[3] The amendment was to demand that there be a general election held in association with the expected half-Senate election.

My contemporary notes give some flavour of the campaigning. I have written:

> One night a parking station took 20 minutes to find my car and I missed a flight to Armidale as a result. I was due to join Ian Sinclair for his campaign opening but had to watch helplessly as the aeroplane taxied out without me. A charter plane got me to Armidale by 10 pm to reach the meeting just as it closed. My arrival caused great excitement and no little comment in the local paper that the Liberals had been so keen to keep their commitment that a charter aircraft had been used. After the meeting I went to the home of David Leitch, the local state member and a medical colleague.

---

3 Fraser (1983: 355); Reid (1976: 205).

Next day I drove 400 km to Newcastle and joined Bill Snedden. During the afternoon Snedden's press secretary came to me and said: 'Bill is losing his voice. What are you going to do about it?'

What could I do about it? I knew nothing about ENT [ear, nose and throat] work and I had no hand in setting up Snedden's speaking arrangements. A friendly ENT surgeon in Sydney listened to my plea for help for an unnamed political friend and then replied: 'Well, the first thing I can tell you is that your political friend is not a trained public speaker.' Much hilarity and mirth ensued from the Snedden team when this was relayed on. My Sydney medical friend did however give us some good advice which included almost total rest to Bill's voice except when he was actually speaking on a platform.

With great gallantry Snedden proceeded on to Maitland to address a noisy street meeting from a truck. Later that night he spoke at the Newcastle Town Hall where no Liberal leader had spoken for 20 years. It was an unforgettable evening. Liberal and Labor supporters came to blows, blood was spilt, more than 50 police were needed, and one agitator actually tried to climb down drapes from the dress circle to attack speakers on the stage below.

We received enormous and beneficial press coverage and earned some well deserved credit for his courage and determination.

Later in the campaign I drove to Wollongong, then flew immediately to Albury, arriving too late to eat. I was taken straight off to a campaign meeting with David and Ruth Fairbairn who then put me, together with some soup and a pizza, on to the train. That train deposited me at Goulburn at about 5 am and I was met by our regional president Pat Osborne. Pat took me to his magnificent Lake George property *Currandooley* for a quick breakfast. Then we drove 200 km to Cooma for street meetings, then to Nimmatabel [sic] for a camp draft, then back to Cooma airport for a flight back to Sydney where I drove out to Luddenham for another function until midnight.

The 1974 election was unusual in that it became only the third double dissolution of the Parliament since Federation. A double dissolution is an election in which all senators and all members have to face the electorate on the same day, instead of having half the senators continue on, as happens with most Australian elections. It was probably only because it was a double dissolution that I was elected. Since the introduction of proportional voting for the Senate at the 1949 election, Labor had more often than not won three of the five seats contested in New South Wales. So although originally selected for the generally unwinnable third position (out of five to be elected) on the Liberal/Country Coalition Senate team in New South Wales, I suddenly found myself number five on our ticket for the larger election with a likely chance of our winning five places. As it turned out, it was still a close-run thing: we won the fifth position in New South Wales only after 35 days of counting votes and then only by 31,736 votes out of the 2,702,903 votes cast. I defeated Labor's Peter Westerway, who then went to the Commonwealth Public Service and rose to a senior level in the Department of Communications. Except for some university positions, it was my first time in any elected public position. I was then 39 years old.

My wife, Jenny, and I were actually at a dinner party at the home of Senator Bob Cotton's daughter Annie and her husband, David Ferguson, on 22 June when my mother-in-law phoned to let me know she had heard on the radio that I had been elected. The Liberal Party either did not know or had not bothered to let me in on the secret. On my return to the table, I was asked the usual question of a doctor: 'Do you have to go?' I was able to answer with 'no'. Conversation at that dinner party was vigorous, interesting, civilised and non-political, so I did not burden the group at table with my news.

Because the voting systems are different for the House of Representatives and the Senate, and because the quotas for senators vary between states, it is possible to achieve different electoral outcomes in the two parliamentary chambers even at the simultaneous election for both chambers as a result of a double dissolution. This is what happened in 1974. After some uncertainty early in the counting, the Whitlam Government secured a second term in office by winning 66 of the 127 seats in the House of Representatives. But at the same election it won only 29 of the Senate places in a chamber of (then) 60 senators.[4] The Liberal and Country parties won five places in Victoria and Western Australia, six places in Queensland, four places in South Australia and Tasmania (Michael Townley was at that stage an independent senator),[5] and five places in New South Wales. My victory—the last place to be determined—ensured that the Government would not enjoy a Senate majority and that Steele Hall would exercise great influence. The election also saw the total disappearance of the Democratic Labor Party (DLP) from the Senate after 19 years. In fact, it was to the former office of defeated DLP senator Jack Kane that I was directed when I sought my office accommodation in Sydney.

I had only three or four weeks to prepare for my transfer to a new life. This involved phasing down a busy consulting medical practice, reorganising my links with the Royal North Shore Hospital (RNSH), paying off some of my dedicated personal medical staff (my personal secretary, Naomi Kirkpatrick, came with me and stayed, with one break, until 1989), finding the new office and mastering some of the logistics associated with its functioning, learning

---

4   The Senate was increased from 64 to 76 people in 1983 by an amendment to the *Commonwealth Electoral Act 1918*.
5   Senator Michael Townley sat as an independent from 1971 to February 1975, and again from 5 June 1987. He was a Liberal Party senator from February 1975 to 5 June 1987.

a little of my duties, responding to the many letters and invitations, getting an office in the provisional Parliament House, finding some accommodation in Canberra, and preparing my family for new challenges.

Renegotiating my relationship with the RNSH proved to be somewhat prolonged, difficult and disappointing. Unsure of my future in politics, I requested a long leave of absence from the hospital, as had been granted to some other medical colleagues from time to time. My appointment at RNSH involved both patient care and teaching. A request was made in a letter of 18 March 1974 to the general medical superintendent in the following terms:

> Dear Doctor Vanderfield,
>
> I write concerning the possible outcome of the forthcoming Senate Election. If I am unsuccessful in that Election then no adjustment of my present practice with relation to the Hospital will be required. If I am elected a Senator for New South Wales then an adjustment will be necessary and I write to enquire about possible ways in which this might be achieved.
>
> If elected it would be necessary for me to cease my regular duties at the Hospital and my regular practice of internal medicine. I believe that the Hospital requires 3 months notice of any such move and I hereby foreshadow such notice should it be required.
>
> It is not my desire to sever my relationships with the Royal North Shore Hospital. I would remind you that I came to the Hospital as a medical student at the beginning of 1956 and have been continuously associated with the Hospital in my professional career since that time. If elected I would have a six year tenure in the Senate provided there was not a Double Dissolution of Parliament. At the end of that time I might be defeated and wish to return to medical life.
>
> I write to ask the Board of Directors through you to give consideration to offering me some continuing form of association with the Hospital in the event that I am successful at the Senate Elections. Such an association might allow me to continue to make a contribution to the life of the Hospital on a less regular basis and could be to our mutual advantage.
>
> I remain
> Yours sincerely,
> Peter Baume

Not only was my request for special leave refused but also my hospital appointment was determined within six months. This occurred because, coincidentally, the normal quadrennial reappointments fell due at this time. I did apply for reappointment and for long leave of absence but was refused both. The leave of absence was refused first in the following letter sent to me on 15 July 1974:

Dear Doctor Baume,

I refer to earlier correspondence and our discussions of 3rd July regarding your future position at the Hospital. Your letter and your request for leave were considered by the Board at its meeting this week. I informed the Board of your future plans, as you outlined them to me, now that the outcome of the Senate elections was known.

The Board recognises the unique situation which has occurred and offers its congratulations on your election to the Senate. However the Board feels that it cannot depart from the policies it has always followed with regard to extended leave and feels unable to meet your request in this regard.

The Board asked that I convey its appreciation for your services to the Hospital, both as Resident Medical Officer in earlier years and as an Honorary Assistant Physician during the last eight years.

Yours sincerely
I.R. Vanderfield
General Medical Superintendent

The medical board of the hospital, the body representing the medical staff, was unhappy about this decision and made separate representations to the hospital board on the matter. At a meeting of the section of physicians on 23 July 1974, a move was initiated by Professor Douglas Piper to have the matter appealed through the medical board to the hospital board of directors. That motion from the section of physicians was moved at the meeting of the medical board on Tuesday, 13 August 1974 by Dr Murray Lloyd and seconded by Dr Ian Thomas. The minutes of that meeting of the medical board record that 'successive speakers stressed the high quality of Dr Baume's services to the Hospital and the community … The motions were carried without dissent and with acclamation'.

Accordingly, a letter was written by Dr Ian Hales, honorary secretary of the medical board, to Dr Vanderfield on 4 September as follows:

Dear Dr Vanderfield,

At the meeting of the Medical Board on Tuesday 13th August, the Medical Board follow [sic] due notice of motion from the Section of Physicians unanimously passed the following motions:

1. That the Medical Board notes with pride the election of one of its members, Dr Peter Baume, to the Senate and commend [sic] the spirit of public service which it believes motivated him.

2. That the Medical Board accepts that he will be unable to fulfil his various hospital commitments during his tenure of office.

3. That, being conscious of Dr Baume's contribution to the hospital in undergraduate and post graduate teaching, research, and patient care, the Medical Board believes that it is in the interests of the hospital to retain him in some appointment.

4. That the Medical Board recommends to the Hospital Board that Dr Baume be appointed to a position that will permit him to retain his clinical seniority for a period of three years, after which time there should be a review. This position should not require him to give clinical service to the hospital. It is suggested that this could be done by appointing him as an Honorary Physician with special leave of absence for three years.

It would be appreciated if you could bring these resolutions to the Board of Directors of the Hospital.

Yours sincerely,
Ian Hales
Honorary Secretary, Medical Board

But the board was unmoved. On 8 October 1974, Dr Vanderfield advised me of the termination of my hospital appointment in the following terms:

Dear Dr Baume,

The Board at its last meeting dealt with the statutory four yearly appointments to the Honorary Medical Staff, which included your application of the 20th June. I wish to advise that the Board decided it was unable to approve your reappointment in view of your present circumstances as indicated in your previously submitted letter of 18th March.

The Board also gave further consideration to your position generally, in the light of representations made by the Medical Board. However, the Board felt it was unable to alter its previous decision, conveyed to you in my letter of 15th July. The chairman, Sir Lincoln Hynes, would like to talk to you about this when a suitable occasion presents.

Yours sincerely,
I.R. Vanderfield
General Medical Superintendent

I responded on 29 October 1974 as follows:

Dear Dr Vanderfield,

Thank you for your letter of the 8th October 1974 informing me that the Board had found itself unable to approve my re-appointment or to make any concessions towards me in terms of leave or special appointment.

I am grateful for the consideration that the Board has given to my application and I am grateful for the opportunity I have had to work at Royal North Shore

Hospital. I would be pleased if you would thank those of your colleagues who have helped over the years and pass my thanks on to those of your Senior Department Heads who have given me so much assistance and support.

I am grateful for support which you personally have given me over a period of fifteen years in a variety of situations. I hope that my long term association with the Royal North Shore Hospital is not completely broken.

I remain
Yours sincerely,
Peter Baume

It was disappointing to read in a subsequent annual report of the hospital that it had been necessary for me to resign my appointment. I had not resigned; I had been sacked and it was wrong of the hospital to say otherwise.

As a Jew, I decided to wear a yarmulke for my swearing in and to ask for a Hebrew Bible, which was provided immediately. For all my time in Parliament, I have always worn a yarmulke for daily prayers and have absented myself for the High Holydays and for the Passover whenever these clashed with sittings of the Parliament. In 1990, it happened that I was the only Jew in the Australian Parliament. Although other Jews have served during my time, none has been, like me, in the Liberal Party. Some of the other identifying Jews were Joe Berinson, Moss Cass and Barry Cohen. Dick Klugman was a cheerful agnostic. Lewis Kent and John Coulter, both born of Jewish mothers, identified themselves otherwise. Cohen tells the story of a day when he had forgotten to bring a yarmulke for his swearing in and explained his problem to Whitlam. Gough, the veteran of many Jewish communal functions, took Cohen to his desk, opened a drawer and asked him, 'Which colour would you like?'

A surprising telegram of congratulations had arrived from Senator the Honourable Sir Magnus Cormack, President of the Senate, whom I had never met. Although I was a little surprised, I came to learn in time of the unfailing courtesy and generosity of this colleague. By all accounts, he had been a good president during the first Whitlam Parliament.

Jenny accompanied me to Canberra for the first meeting of the Twenty-Ninth Parliament on 9 July 1974. More or less at random, I had booked us in to a motel in Manuka for those first few days. When the great day of the opening of the Parliament arrived, there was a heavy, pervasive Canberra fog and the Commonwealth car seemed to appear from out of nowhere and to take us back into a white blanket of nothingness. It was all unreal, exciting and symbolic of the great adventure we were undertaking into the unknown.

After we new senators had been sworn in, it was time to elect a new president. We had 29 Coalition senators with a Liberal independent, Michael Townley; Labor had 29; and then there was Steele Hall. So the possibility existed for a 30–30 tie and a draw from the hat, for which Senate Standing Orders provide that the name of the unsuccessful candidate shall be the one drawn.[6] Sitting there, new and polished, proud and inquisitive, with my wife sitting with Lady Cormack and others in the President's Gallery, I waited to take part in my first election for the President of the Senate. The Clerk Jim Odgers called for nominations; there were two. Labor nominated Senator Justin O'Byrne from Tasmania; the Opposition proposed the retiring president, Magnus Cormack. Each then 'addressed' the Senate with the identical formulaic words: 'I submit myself to the will of the Senate.' Each of us was given a ballot paper on which to write one name, and then the leaders, Lionel Murphy and Reg Withers, were invited to act as scrutineers while the votes were counted at the table by the clerks.

The result was 31–29 to O'Byrne, which was a great surprise to everyone—including Justin O'Byrne. But there it was: Steele Hall had almost certainly voted for the Government, as expected, but so had one of our senators! Who it was has never been revealed and the late Reg Wright actually collected damages after one commentator suggested it might have been him. My wife, Jenny, reported later that Lady Cormack nearly fainted when the result was announced, although she assured everyone present that her disappointment was for Magnus, not for herself.

Justin O'Byrne was the Father of the Senate—that is, he was the longest-serving senator, and he was an adequate president. I well remember that he became ill about a year later and I was asked to see him by a Labor senator and former student, Don Grimes. Grimes could have attended to the medical problem himself but was concerned that his colleague might mistrust his opinion because of local Tasmanian political considerations. For this reason, he sought a 'neutral' (that is, non-Tasmanian) doctor. Our teaching relationship dated from the time, many years earlier, when as a medical registrar, I gave tutorials to the student group of which he was a member. But at the time I saw Mr President, the Senate was in a frenzy of activity passing Bills—an event that occurred twice yearly at the end of each sitting period when accumulated legislation was cleared in double quick time to allow senators to get out of Canberra. So the president was in and out of the chair briefly as the various stages of different pieces of legislation followed each other with great rapidity. I was trying to consult medically in the passage behind the chair and it took some time to catch him long enough to determine that he needed to go to hospital—which he did.

---

6   Standing Order 7(4), formerly Standing Order 22.

From the moment that Parliament assembled in July 1974, even with a Labor president, the possibilities of disagreement between the houses, of deadlock and of constitutional crisis, were real. The temptation was there for the Liberal and Country Opposition to obstruct the Government in the Senate and so make it unworkable. As the Government reeled from crisis to crisis without any help from us, losing electoral support and the confidence of the people, the temptation to use Senate power became irresistible, as has been described in detail by many writers.[7]

After we got to work, I made an unmemorable maiden speech on the second day as my side wanted me, as the only Liberal doctor, to be ready for some health legislation soon to be debated. The convention was that one could not participate in debate vigorously, or accept interjections, until one's first speech was out of the way. I remember that second day when so many of us participated in what our seniors called 'the Maiden Stakes'. No one had warned me in advance to be ready. On the contrary, I had been advised to take it quietly and settle in before even thinking of speaking. As it was I had only one day or so to prepare what should have been (and was not) a significant and thoughtful first contribution.

Senator Bob Cotton used to tell the story of a maiden speech (perhaps his own) in which the chamber was full of colleagues sitting solemnly and listening in silence with eyes ahead and arms folded. When the speech finished, he alleges that a note was passed up with the words, 'I have a vacancy for a rabbit trapper—do you want a job?'

Soon after this, we had some health legislation and I spoke from a position of some knowledge. At the end of the speech, Steele Hall passed down a note complimenting me on 'a real parliamentary speech'. It meant a lot coming from a former premier of South Australia. Senator Don Grimes from Tasmania, who followed me, stated:

> It is rather strange for me to be speaking after Senator Baume in these circumstances. Many years ago Senator Baume taught me medicine.[8] Honourable Senators may be surprised to know that he did not teach me philosophy, politics, economics or anything else.
>
> Senator Jessop: It is a pity he did not.

---

7   See, for example: Reid (1976); Whitlam (1979); Schneider (1980). In each of these, large sections are devoted to the processes leading up to the deferral of Supply on 16 October 1975.
8   At the time Don Grimes was a final-year medical student at the Royal North Shore Hospital, I was a medical registrar who took his group for some tutorials. Incidentally, of the parliamentarians or significant political figures with an association with that hospital, only Bob Woods and I served the Liberal Party. Grimes, Moss Cass, Dick Klugman, Peter Wilenski and Doug Everingham all joined and supported Labor.

> Senator Grimes: It may be a pity but, unfortunately for Senator Jessop, I went on reading after I read Adam Smith's book which was written 200 years ago.[9]

I always did like Grimes!

Early in the Parliament we had the only Joint Sitting of the Houses to be called pursuant to the constitutional provisions relating to double dissolutions. On 6 and 7 August 1974, we all crowded into the House of Representatives chamber (and so I have sat officially in both chambers) for set-piece debates and votes along party lines to allow the Labor Government to obtain passage of six double-dissolution Bills. We new parliamentarians had the very back rows as befitted our lowly status. After dinner, Bill Snedden took several of us down to sit with him on the front bench for half an hour. It was a thoughtful gesture. It was during this sitting that I first saw the crossing of the floor by a parliamentarian: Country Party MP for the Northern Territory Sam Calder, who crossed the floor to vote with Labor on a Bill to provide Senate representation for the territories. He had told us in a party meeting of his intention and need to do so—and had received the 'blessing' of his colleagues, not that he required that to take the course he did.

During that same joint sitting, Steele Hall made a blistering attack on the resistance of the Coalition parties to electoral reform. Hall had, as premier of South Australia, pushed through an electoral reform Bill to remove a long-standing rural gerrymander. As a result of this courageous and correct action, his party had lost government. About a year after my election, I visited South Australia and was driven from Narracorte to Adelaide by a conservative group of South Australian legislative councillors who spent the entire four-hour trip telling me why I should not continue to feel respect and sympathy for Hall. They did not convince me then and have not convinced me since. He is a fine Australian, a fine liberal and a good friend.

As a senator, I became entitled to employ two staff. One was Naomi Kirkpatrick, who became my personal secretary. She had been with me in medical practice and understood my ways of working. She was married to an Irishman, Rea Kirkpatrick, who was badly afflicted with rheumatoid arthritis. In 1989, she finally had to call it a day as her husband's disability had by then become so severe as to require her to become his full-time carer.

My other staff member was Christopher Puplick. He accepted a job offer made by me on Friday, 14 March 1975 and remained with me until he entered the Senate himself. This outstanding Australian was even then a major figure within the Liberal Party. He is co-author of one of the few coherent books on Liberal

---

9   Senate Hansard, vol. S60, 1974: 296.

Party philosophy,[10] has been national president of the Young Liberal Movement of Australia, was on the Federal Executive of the Liberal Party during 1974 and 1975, has been a long-time diarist of events around him, and was a senator for New South Wales from 1978 to 1981 and 1985 to 1990. His defeat in 1990 was a victory for conservative elements who have never been able to accept his more liberal views. Puplick was a founder of the Liberal Forum and a powerful and feared contributor to Senate debate. He has been my friend for many years.

Soon after Chris joined my staff, I received a furious letter from the late Lady Violet Braddon, then a force in the Liberal Party, demanding that I sack Puplick. I have kept that rather unpleasant letter, which, if it did nothing else, put me on notice as to some of the more unreconstructed and vicious attitudes in the party that I had been elected to represent.

Our numbers in the Senate provided us with a powerful weapon. The question was then (and remains in retrospect) how we should use that power. Since all government measures passed in the House of Representatives while the Government held its numbers, the Senate votes were the only indication of the real tactics of the opposition parties or of the willingness of the Government to compromise if pressed hard enough. Assuming that Townley would vote with us, we always had sufficient numbers to block any proposal and, when Steele Hall was with us, we had numbers sufficient for the passage of an affirmative resolution. This was because tied votes in the Senate are determined in the negative, the president having a deliberative but not a casting vote. It is the failure to appreciate the full implications of this that led many people to assert that the constitutional crisis of 1975 could not have arisen had Labor had its proper complement of senators.[11] Such a proposition is incorrect. It would have been more correct for people to assert that the events could not have occurred in the manner they did. The events could still have occurred, using different procedural means to take advantage of tied votes (and therefore, of negative outcomes to any vote). The matter is discussed in more detail later in this manuscript.

The summary for the Budget sittings of the Senate for 1974 shows that six Bills were affirmed at the joint sitting, 141 Bills passed both Houses, two Bills with Senate amendments awaited further consideration by the House, two Bills had been returned from the House with Senate amendments disagreed to, two Bills originating in the Senate were awaiting consideration by the House, two Bills had

---

10 Puplick and Southey (1980).
11 See, for example, Whitlam (1979: 60).

been deferred, 25 had been negatived at the second reading, and 10 remained on the notice paper. There had been 12 successful amendments to the second reading of Bills and 184 amendments to the clauses of Bills.[12]

By the end of that period, I had made some speeches and felt comfortable in the chamber. I had already decided to limit my interventions to those matters on which I knew something (rather than responding automatically to requests from my seniors to speak whenever they needed another speaker) and had decided also, following some fatherly comments by South Australian Senator Condor Laucke, to 'play the ball and not the man'. That is a decision that each parliamentarian has to take individually. Some elect to 'play the man' and these become the 'bucket droppers' of Parliament. They play it tough and are treated accordingly within Parliament. They can expect to receive no mercy if ever they seek the indulgence of their chamber in a moment of need. Those who decide to play the ball (that is, concentrate on the issues and not the personalities) are likely to find, later in their careers, that people remember and appreciate this and are willing to help in difficult moments. Such an occasion occurred for me in 1979 when I breached the privilege of Parliament. I had briefed a journalist about the contents of a forthcoming senate committee report and that journalist then wrote a story before the report was tabled. I went straight into the Senate, explained what I had done and left it to the chamber. Although I had laid myself open to severe disciplinary action, the senators, including tough Labor senators, all just looked the other way.

During that first period, the leadership of Bill Snedden was challenged—an event that has been described extensively in books dealing with that Parliament. I had noticed that Malcolm Fraser wandered into my office a couple of times and had seemed unusually interested in the views of a new and inexperienced backbench senator. Still, flattery has always been a potent weapon in politics and I was flattered. The actual question at that 1974 challenge was the 'spill' motion—'that the leadership be declared vacant'. That motion was defeated. At that party room meeting, the NSW contingent voted generally for stability by supporting Snedden, although we were, as described later, to change our vote in March 1975.

After that first unsuccessful challenge, the party room emptied quickly and John Carrick and I noticed that Fraser was standing alone looking a bit forlorn. We asked whether he would join us for a cup of tea and he agreed readily. Our motive was simple: we wished to start the healing and binding of wounds and this was a good way to begin. We wandered from the party room to the tea room to find a large table almost full with people from the parliamentary Liberal

---

12 *Business of the Senate July–December 1974*, The Senate, Canberra.

Party. We would have sat down but Malcolm asked first of a very senior person at the table whether he or the others would mind our joining them. 'Yes', came the answer, 'we would mind'. So much for the quick healing and binding of wounds! Fraser, Carrick and I sat at another table, drank our tea and, in time, were joined by others.

By the end of my first Budget sitting, it was clear that the year ahead would be one of crisis and difficulty. The Government was determined to effect change quickly and, partly as a result of the speed with which it moved, many of its actions were untidy or unconventional and laid ministers open to criticism. It was clear, too, that our people were considering all the options available to them in the year ahead, and the press was already canvassing another deferral of Supply as one of these.

I returned to Sydney at the end of that year for Christmas and New Year with my wife and two children. We decided to have a decent break and took ourselves to Lord Howe Island for a marvellous holiday. Although I returned from that holiday refreshed and ready for the year ahead, I did not know it would involve me in some of the most dramatic events in Australian political history. The story of those events is contained in the following chapters of this 1975 manuscript.

2

AUTUMN 1975

This was my second sitting period[1] in Parliament. This time I would not come to everything new. I had some feeling for the job, for the chamber, for the people, for the institution. I had established an office, had somewhere to stay in Canberra, had competent staff, and knew how to organise transport, how to find food and how to use the library. I had friends within ministerial offices and within the apparatus of the Opposition. I had made friends with senators and members, and with their staff. In the electorate, I had made progress, too. Constituents, party organisation people and community groups had established networks with me and there was plenty to do. Yet rather than being a time of steady work and consolidation, of building on that base, the period was to prove one of drama and high tension in which the groundwork was laid for the dismissal of the Government on 11 November.

During the first six months of 1975, I was to travel abroad for Amnesty International, was to vote at a second and successful leadership challenge, and was to see an acceleration of the stumbling incompetence and uncertainty that marked this last year of the Whitlam Government. The details surrounding the search for loans from overseas sources, irregularities in executive council

---

1   A session is defined in Odgers (1976: 619), as follows: it 'begins with an official opening by the Governor-General and ends either by prorogation or by dissolution of the House of Representatives'. What we casually refer to as the Budget Session or the Autumn Session are more properly called autumn or Budget sittings, although there is no official citation to which to refer.

proceedings, the resignations and demotions of ministers, the forced resignation of Speaker Jim Cope on 27 February 1975—all have been dealt with at length in other books and do not need repetition here.[2]

I now had a superficial knowledge about politics and Parliament. This was still more than most outsiders had then or have now. As I have seen in many other areas, this little knowledge gives rise to overconfidence, misinterpretation and complacency. It takes some years to understand that the world of politics is like an onion—one can see the vegetable but then one can peel off the skin and see another and different layer of the same vegetable—or perhaps a different vegetable. It is sad that so many of my newer colleagues still have to learn slowly by trial and error the subtleties and nuances of political life—just as I had to do in that first dramatic Parliament.

It was a period, too, during which I learned something of the operation of senate committees. I served on a committee chaired by Labor Senator Jim Keeffe that examined the dreadful environmental conditions of Aboriginal and Torres Strait Islanders. We travelled as a committee to places I had never seen nor thought about, from Laura on Cape York to Oodnadatta, and to Cape Barren Island. It was very productive serving with experienced and skilful senators like Keeffe, Gordon Davidson and Neville Bonner.

Neville Bonner was my friend as well as being a colleague. Senators sit in pairs and Bonner and I shared one of the red leather couches in the chamber of the provisional Parliament House. On my first day there, he indicated that we should each put some cash in the dry inkwell and thereafter we drew on that 'bank' to pay for tea in the restaurant. On one occasion, too, I remember that during a speech I was enraged by Labor and so was provoking Labor senators to interject. I did not see the president rise to his feet to restore order and did not stop shouting out what passed for a speech. Bonner did not hesitate to take hold of my coat-tails and pull me back down with a surprised thud. He told me severely, 'Whenever that man stands up, you sit down, my boy.'

In the Parliament that followed (when we were in government) we had Baume (the only Jew), Bonner (the only Aborigine), Lajovic (the only recent migrant) and Missen (the true liberal) all seated near each other; we used to laugh and call it 'Cockroach Corner'—the place where all the unconventional and difficult people were put together.

---

2   See Fraser (1983: 357).

The story associated with a trip to Oodnadatta with my senate committee is worth telling.[3] We had come into Oodnadatta, unwelcome to some in the small South Australian town and welcomed warmly by others. In fact, we found a community polarised about our visit. We had Lois O'Donoghue[4] with us, who was at that time acting South Australian state director of the Department of Aboriginal Affairs. She brought some supplies on the aeroplane for her mother, who still lived in the Aboriginal encampment just outside the town. She found that her mother had suffered an injury within the previous 24 hours and so was away from us for much of the day arranging medical attention for her.

We stayed at the Transcontinental Hotel in Oodnadatta, a remote town in arid country and at that time on the main train line between Adelaide and Alice Springs. Because of a mouse plague, all exterior doors on the hotel (including those leading from the bedrooms to the wide verandahs) were kept shut and we could open doors only from our bedrooms to the interior passageway. We were allocated two to a room, my companion being Gordon Davidson.

The first difficult moments came at our public meeting in the evening. Some locals attempted to have us answer their questions, their general thesis being that too much was being done for blacks. Jean Melzer, a member but not chair of the committee, set the matter right by leaning across and saying in a voice she had probably used in some tough political meetings in Victoria: 'Let us get it straight. This is our meeting and we will ask the questions.' It was a most effective intervention and stopped the interlocutors dead.

After the meeting, we returned to the hotel, had some drinks and then retired to bed. Jean Melzer and Lois O'Donoghue were in one room, Davidson and I were in a second room, Jim Keeffe and the pilot were in a third room. We had not long gone to bed when there was a great commotion and the publican, apparently drunk, came up the passage roaring words to the effect of 'Where is he? I'll kill him! Let me at him! I'll kill him!' There were great noise and movement outside, with the publican's wife vainly hanging on to his arm and begging him to settle down. Not sure who was about to be killed, I searched my own conscience and, finding it clear of any immediate offence, then whispered, 'Gordon, are you asleep?' Gordon Davidson answered in a whisper, 'What do you think? Of course I'm not!' We got up and peeped out, to see the faces of Jean Melzer and Lois O'Donoghue just up the hall, peeping out from their room. We saw no sign of Jim Keeffe.

---

3   Senate Hansard, vol. S127, 17 May 1988: 2,293.
4   Later Lowitja O'Donoghue.

The noise continued somewhere close by at a high level and we retired to the relative safety of our beds. Then a local policeman appeared and took control. He subdued the publican but then a new problem presented itself. The publican's wife, in desperation, had locked herself and her baby in a bedroom opposite ours and the publican would not or could not provide a key to allow the door to be opened. Eventually the local policeman put his shoulder to the door and splintered it, so allowing the rescue of the wailing infant and its mother. The publican was taken off by the police and the wife and baby were taken off by neighbours. Somewhat shaken, we went back to sleep—eventually.

In the morning, we did not know what to expect. We need not have worried; someone had cooked some breakfast and no mention was made by staff of the horrendous events of the previous night, of the shattered door still swinging on its hinges, or of the absence of the publican and his family. We never did confirm who it was the publican had intended to kill, or why.

When we went to Laura in north Queensland, I had some education of a different kind. We were there to see the Quinkan caves and Aboriginal cave paintings and were in the care of Percy Trezise, but discovered on our arrival in this tiny Cape York hamlet that the local graziers had erected a small stockyard in the middle of town and stocked it with cattle to make a point to us about the unmet need for beef roads to serve the cape.

It was on this trip that I discovered the cane toad. The shower for the little pub was a communal affair separate from the main building and with corrugated iron roof and walls. The walls did not extend from top to bottom so that anyone having a shower was visible—as to his or her head, and lower legs—from outside. This also meant that cane toads, abundant in the area, could come freely into the ablutions block, which they did regularly. So, to have a shower one had to shoo out the cane toads and then continue to discourage them while one washed. My daughter remembers me coming home and telling her about these toads, which are poisonous if eaten. She remembered the story incorrectly, believing that the toads were aggressive and that their bite was poisonous. She wondered then, aged nine years, what dangerous and crazy occupation her father had got himself into.

It was on that same trip that the local Aboriginal community took us out for a bush barbecue. It was only after it finished that I learned that I had eaten barbecued bush tucker—that is, barbecued indigenous wildlife. As a Jew, I wondered vaguely later whether all the bush tucker had been kosher; I neither knew nor worried terribly much.

During the autumn sittings there was also my work as secretary of the Policy Committee of the Parliamentary Party, chaired by Don Chipp, who was then the relevant shadow minister. For the record, he was good to work with and he taught me a lot I needed to learn, and I feel nothing but gratitude towards him for his tutelage during this time. He in turn has described me as 'an able and sincere senator from NSW' and also included me in his list of 45 parliamentarians from the Thirty-Fourth Parliament (1984–87) whom he 'rated as capable of making a significant contribution to this country in a government'.[5]

At this stage, I still spent two hours weekly (7–9 am on Mondays) consulting in my medical rooms at the North Shore Medical Centre. These were patients with whom I had a long-term relationship and some old patients whose difficult problems the local doctors did not wish to treat. In any event, I was at that stage anything but secure in my new political role and kept a small practice running as a hedge against an uncertain future. This was something I continued until late in the decade when I gained promotion and became unable to provide proper ongoing availability to my patients.

On Sunday, 12 January 1975, I flew to Jakarta as part of an Amnesty International mission to Indonesia. That country had arrested tens of thousands of its citizens at the time of an internal uprising in 1965 and had held many of these people, without trial, in custody for a decade. Amnesty selected a team led by Dick McGarvie (then president of the Victorian Bar Council) and including Neil Gilmour (then president of the Australian Council of Churches), Dr Dick Klugman (then Labor MP for Prospect in New South Wales), Lenore Ryan of Amnesty International (Australia), and me. We had with us an Amnesty International officer (W. Huang) who was to service our delegation and to whom we gave cover and protection.

Arriving in Indonesia late in the afternoon, I found myself held up at immigration. I had, with some difficulty, obtained a visa for Indonesia before leaving Australia. No doubt I was photographed and observed by security while my (valid) visa was questioned, examined endlessly and checked again and again. Our delegation was not welcome in the country just as I had not been welcome at the airport, and for the next 10 days we were studiously not received by the officials we approached. It did not matter that we were not 'received officially'. During all this time, our Amnesty officer made a lot of contacts and gathered a large amount of information—doubtless followed by security all the time.

---

5   Chipp and Larkin (1987: 171, 113).

I doubt we achieved the release of any political prisoners, but it was one means of concentrating attention on Indonesia. Also, we were able to gather material that was disseminated worldwide by Amnesty to inform a wider public of the vast number of breaches of due legal process by the Indonesian authorities.

Sometime soon after my election I had established good contact with radio station 2WL in Wollongong through Brian Surtees. During most of 1975, I did radio segments for 2WL—commentary on politics rather than straight news—to 'balance' that by local ALP members. This meant that I commented before, during and after the constitutional crisis. I also recorded radio segments irregularly in Newcastle. At the same time, I maintained active constituency work, particularly in the western suburbs of Sydney.

My children were both attending primary school on the comfortable and privileged upper North Shore of Sydney. They attended private schools, which expected regular parent attendance and participation—which they got from us. Demanding as political life was, it was still an improvement on the medical life I had left, so we found it possible to improve our family life even with the full schedule demanded of us by politics. This seems to be an indictment on the life demanded of successful consultant physicians, then and now.

Also at this stage I was regularly writing a column for the *AMA Gazette*, a fortnightly newspaper produced by the Australian Medical Association (AMA) that went to a majority of Australian doctors. It had the advantage of making me more widely known and the disadvantage that some of what I wrote enraged the readers. It was at least a rich source of letters from doctors.

In retrospect, the forcing of that 1974 election was an error by our leadership, though, of course, it helped me. Had Snedden and his colleagues been more patient, 1975 would have seen a normal election at which Labor would have been defeated handsomely and without the disruption and crisis that are now part of history. The events of 1975 were also a mistake—they were unnecessary—as I have said elsewhere.[6]

Matters began to heat up when Malcolm Fraser became Leader of the Opposition on 21 March 1975, and took the fight to Gough Whitlam in Parliament and to Labor generally in the country. Until then the Opposition had not matched Whitlam in Parliament and did not enjoy the support of the community.

---

6   Nolan and Hocking (2005).

A story about that change of leadership: Malcolm Fraser had challenged Bill Snedden for leadership of the parliamentary Liberal Party in November 1974 and lost on that occasion (actually Tony Staley's motion to have the leadership declared vacant was defeated).

My relationship with Snedden had always been ambivalent. On the one hand, I admired his relative liberalism and his innate decency; on the other, I had always resented his refusal to allow me to attend the first meeting of the parliamentary party after my election (my result was not then known with certainty), possibly because he could not be certain of how I would have voted in any showdown. It was reported to me that Bob Cotton objected strongly on my behalf and actually opposed Phillip Lynch for deputy leader as a protest. But Snedden's failure to handle Whitlam was his final undoing; above all, we wanted someone to win for us and it seemed that only Fraser could do it.

When Fraser challenged again in March, the fortunes of the Opposition were even worse than they had been four months earlier. On the Sunday before the decisive leadership ballot, almost all NSW Liberal senators and members gathered quietly at my home in Gordon to discuss what our attitude might be in the forthcoming vote. This meeting has never until now become public knowledge; it was our desire to keep it secret that led to no invitation going to the late Bill McMahon. It was at that meeting that we agreed that a change of leadership was necessary. There has been a lot of speculation about the change of vote by the NSW bloc, but it has not been known generally that the change was formalised at a meeting in my home on that Sunday, 16 March 1975. The change in leadership duly occurred at a meeting of the parliamentary Liberal Party on Friday, 21 March 1975.

The party meeting of 21 March was tense and difficult. It has been described accurately in some books, to which interested readers are directed.[7] That it could be described so accurately by outsiders is a measure of just how readily the proceedings of the party meetings—supposedly private—were (and are still) conveyed to journalists in return for favourable treatment. The role of a freshman senator in that titanic struggle was to say little, let the warriors battle it out and make some rational judgment for himself. I remembered the unpleasantness of the earlier challenge to Bill Snedden's leadership when the 'spill' motion was unsuccessful. It is a matter of record that the spill motion succeeded in March 1975 and Fraser became leader. I seem to remember that John Gorton got up and walked out when this happened. He later sat as an independent and retired from the Parliament at the next election when he was

---

7   See, for example, Kelly (1976: 116, 128), where the change of NSW view is discussed without any reference to the meeting on that Sunday.

unsuccessful in attempting to win a Senate place for the Australian Capital Territory. It was a sad event as I admired him greatly as a person and as prime minister.

By the time the autumn sitting finished, the Government looked pretty awful. The loans affair was already running, the ministry had been destabilised, the speaker had resigned after being repudiated by his party in a vote in the House, public confidence in the Government was evaporating, and there was speculation even then that the Liberal and Country parties might try to force an election before year's end, using tactics similar to those used in April 1974.

We were certainly giving the Government a hard time in the Senate. Many years later, at a social function, Lionel Bowen, at the time acting prime minister, referred to the Senate as the graveyard of legislation. That was a typical House of Representatives and typical executive view. The Senate is, and will be for many years, a chamber where one must negotiate and compromise to get legislation through; such a course does not appeal to members of the House of Representatives or to ministers of the Crown, all of whom expect the views of the Government to prevail unchallenged in the Parliament at all times.

During the first half of 1975 we considered 132 Bills. Of these, 90 were passed by both Houses, 22 were negatived (in the Senate), one was laid aside in the House of Representatives, three were discharged in the Senate and one was referred to a senate committee. So the Government continued to have a tough time and we continued to reject about one-quarter of all its legislation. Looking at it the other way round, the Government, even without a working Senate majority, still managed to get about three-quarters of its legislation through Parliament.

The strain on Senate ministers was intense and several collapsed physically. First, there were fewer ministers in the Senate than in the House and therefore each Senate minister had a heavy load representing colleagues in the House. This meant that Senate ministers had the problem of trying to pilot difficult measures proposed by House of Representatives colleagues through the hostile Senate. Second, the Government did not have control of the business or procedures of the Senate and so had a miserable time trying to organise and implement a program to meet government priorities and needs. Third, because the Opposition could dictate some of the procedures, it was possible for Opposition proposals to be introduced and debated, and for debates to continue for as long as the Opposition decreed. I did not envy Labor Senate ministers their situation.

3

MOVING TOWARDS CRISIS: THE BLEAK WINTER OF 1975

Winter in Canberra is bitter and cold. This is not surprising; Canberra is located in the Australian Capital Territory within the Southern Tablelands of New South Wales some 600 metres above sea level. One of the attractions of this capital city is that it does have definite seasons. So it is that we look with pleasure at the autumn colours and enjoy the blossoms in spring. But equally, the summers are hot and the bush flies troublesome, while the winters are cold, dreary, bleak and bitter.

Politicians cope with this in good years by scheduling the two long breaks—the recesses—in the winter and the summer, so as to avoid the times of greatest heat and cold in Canberra and confine our sitting periods to the more pleasant months and seasons. More than that, the time of these recesses is when many politicians travel overseas, getting away not only from Canberra but also from Australia.

Cabinet ministers are not so lucky. The Budget cycle began in December each year and came to a climax with the Budget cabinet meetings in the depths of winter (when the Budget was presented in August). This then allowed the Budget to be made ready for presentation to the Parliament in mid-August when senators and members returned. So cabinet ministers had to be in Canberra during the very worst part of the year. Many years later, I was a minister in the Cabinet and underwent this experience. One of the things that made it more bearable was the care I received from an exceptional car driver named Patrick Torpy.

Pat used to get me to Parliament House, then get my gear home and turn on the heaters in my unit. It meant that things were a little less bleak when, eventually, I returned home from endless Cabinet and committee meetings.

The year 1975 was atypical in many ways, including an atypical pattern of parliamentary sittings. For a start, the scheduled sittings of the Senate continued somewhat late, to 12 June, just 10 days short of the winter solstice. Second, the Senate returned in July, in the depths of winter, for unprecedented sittings related to the emerging loans affair. In this chapter, some of these events will be described as they affected this backbench senator and as they contributed to his understanding of the loans affair.

When the Senate rose for the winter on 12 June, the standard motion was passed giving leave to all senators until 19 August, the planned date of the Budget, but it was passed with an Opposition amendment to permit the recall of the Senate if needed before that date.[1] Our forcing of that amendment (with our 'legitimate' numbers before the death of Bert Milliner) signalled our belief that we might want to recall Parliament during the recess—a recess to which the Government was looking forward and which it needed to allow it to rest, recuperate and regroup.

We could be certain in 1975 that Labor ministers got no real relief over the winter. Their fatigue would not have gone, the tension remained on them as they battled over the form and content of the forthcoming Budget, and Senate ministers in particular would not have obtained much needed rest and recuperation.

I returned to Sydney when the Senate rose and got straight back into a hundred activities that had been put aside while Parliament had demanded my presence and commitment. There were meetings, outings, dinners at home and at other people's homes, political meetings, commemoration concerts, senate committee trips and public hearings, flag presentations, Australian Assistance Plan meetings, naturalisation ceremonies, dental appointments, school holidays, and so on.

Late in June 1975, I travelled to Launceston to take a tiny role as one of an army of workers for the Bass by-election caused by the resignation of Lance Barnard from the Parliament. Our candidate was Kevin Newman and I found a well-organised and determined operation when I arrived in Tasmania. Like a large number of colleagues, I did all I was asked to—and we achieved an enormous swing (of 14.3 per cent) to win the seat from Labor. So great was our victory that the result is generally reckoned as the start of a roll that carried us right

---

1   *Journals of the Senate—56th Session*, 1975: 817.

through to December and to victory in the general election. Certainly, it was a devastating blow for the Labor Party and for the confidence of Labor leaders and strategists.

One of the stupider things that the prime minister did during this campaign was to argue publicly with a man who questioned some injudicious statements about the Baltic states, which had been incorporated against their will into the USSR during World War II. The prime minister managed to alienate all Baltic voters to the disadvantage of Labor. These events are recorded well in other books.

The senate committee on which I served was very busy with visits to Aboriginal communities in Walgett, Bourke, Cobar, Adelaide, Point McLeay, Mildura, Redfern and Fitzroy. What we learned (and what had not been known to me before) is that Aborigines in different locations live quite differently to one another and face different problems. Traditional Aboriginal people faced problems with basic services—with the availability of clean water in sufficient quantities to allow them to care for themselves and their children, for adequate supplies of fresh food, for adequate hygiene, and so on. Completely urbanised Aborigines faced different problems—many of them the problems of poverty, isolation and alienation from mainstream structures and services seen in many depressed minorities of any kind in our large conurbations. The third group—then called 'fringe dwellers' and later called 'town campers'—had almost the worst of all worlds: no place, no roots, no purpose, no acceptance, no resources, and no hope. Later, when I became Minister for Aboriginal Affairs, I found that my greatest heartbreaks were in relation to those attempting to make lives for themselves and their families on reservations close to the towns of non-metropolitan Australia. I might add too that the greatest expressed sympathy for Aborigines seemed to come from those living in all-white neighbourhoods.

Nationally, however, the loans affair continued to develop. Documents continued to appear—a trickle at first and a flood later. Ministers made more and more statements, but more and more of these proved to be inconsistent one with another. So it was that our leader, Reg Withers, activated the contingent notice and petitioned the president to recall the Senate. This occurred on Wednesday, 9 July at 4 pm. The Opposition wanted certain senior officers of the Public Service to answer some critical questions to which the Government was determined no answers would be given. The Senate was recalled to settle the matter.

On our reassembling, one of the first things done by Mr President was to table the ruling of Sir Garfield Barwick, the Chief Justice of the High Court (sitting as a Court of Disputed Returns), on the qualifications of Jim Webster to sit as a senator,[2] a matter that had been activated by motion of the Senate three

---

2   Senate Hansard, vol. S64, 1975: 2,687; *Journals of the Senate—56th Session*, 1975: 597, 605, 618, 628.

months earlier.³ Jim Webster had a family business that was alleged to have had some dealings with the Government and the question was whether this disqualified Webster from sitting in Parliament under the provisions of Section 44 of the Constitution. The court ruling was in Webster's favour.

Mr President also announced to us the death of Senator Bert Milliner on 30 June.⁴ Milliner had been ill for some time and had, in fact, been granted leave of absence by the Senate on account of ill health on 13 May 1975.⁵ The failure of the Queensland Government to replace him with a proper Labor senator was one of the worst actions of that or any year and contributed greatly to the bitterness associated with the crisis that followed and to the means used by the Coalition to prosecute that crisis.

The Government opened proceedings by tabling a mass of documents related to loan raisings by it and by previous (non-Labor) governments, to correspondence on the loans affair, to certain legal opinions, to correspondence with Mr Khemlani, and to telex and other communications by ministers⁶ (and it tabled more two days later).⁷ The Leader of the Opposition Reg Withers then gave notice that he would move that certain senior officers be called before the Bar of the Senate to give evidence on matters related to the loans affair on Tuesday, 15 July 1975.⁸ These were the most senior officers in the Departments of Treasury, Minerals and Energy and of the Attorney-General, together with a statutory officer, the Solicitor-General. Although people had been called before the Bar of the Senate previously, the procedure was used very rarely. Here I was, almost within my first year in the Senate, about to see it happen again—and to a swag of the most senior public servants in the country.

The Government had intended its action in tabling papers to be pre-emptive in that it hoped sufficient information would be revealed to satisfy the press and public. But Withers immediately branded the action as inadequate and arrangements were then completed for witnesses to appear a week later. Summonses were served on the officers, all of whom indicated dutifully that they would attend as required. Meanwhile, the prime minister and some ministers challenged the right of the Senate to call and examine senior officers even on matters of fact. As a result of those challenges, on 15 July, Senator Withers moved another motion, reaffirming the right of the Senate to call and examine witnesses at the Bar of the Senate, which was agreed to on 16 July.⁹

---

3   Senate Hansard, vol. S64, 1975: 2,687; *Journals of the Senate—56th Session*, 1975: 645.
4   Senate Hansard, vol. S64, 1975: 2,697.
5   Senate Hansard, vol. S64, 1975: 2,703.
6   Senate Hansard, vol. S64, 1975: 2,710.
7   *Journals of the Senate—56th Session*, 1975: 831.
8   House of Representatives Hansard, vol. 168, 1941: 719.
9   House of Representatives Hansard, vol. H of R6, new series, 4 Eliz II, 1955: 1,625.

What was already occurring was that the prime minister and his ministers were challenging rights of the Senate conferred on that House of Parliament by the Constitution and by established practice. There are quite valid and powerful arguments that go to the continuing relevance of some of those powers but, while the powers exist as they do, it is the duty of those who serve the Senate to resist all attempts to limit or 'write out' those powers. This was a part, and not the least part, of the battle then before us. What was occurring was one more skirmish in that never-ending battle between authority (represented by the Crown or by the Executive) on one hand and the people (represented by the Senate) on the other.

I represent the Senate as 'the people' quite deliberately. While the House of Representatives is democratically elected—and undoubtedly so—it is by its make-up the electoral college for the Executive and is always a tool on which that Executive can depend for support. Indeed, it was on 3 October 1941 that a government was last defeated on the floor of the House of Representatives[10] on a vital matter, and I do not expect it to happen again without some extraordinary concatenation of circumstances. The Senate, on the other hand, partly as a result of its election by a system of proportional representation, is finely balanced in its composition, often without a government majority. (My problems related more to the effects of good dinners and wine on senators than they did to their formal allegiances.) Since then the Senate has been a real legislative chamber in which governments must fight and negotiate for support if their legislation is to pass, a chamber in which argument is listened to and amendments accepted to legislation, albeit reluctantly.

In 1975 one of the sub-agendas was the determination of the prime minister of the day to assert and establish a dominance of the House of Representatives not contemplated by the framers of the Constitution; conversely one of our sub-agendas was to resist and repel such an attack. It is now a matter of history that the prime minister failed in his objective *qua* the Senate.

I understood then too little of the import of what was going on. It was hard to keep up with the action and with the twists and turns that occurred each time we met. I realised that this was 'big league' stuff and that we were moving to virtually uncharted territory; in spite of this comprehension, I was struggling to follow the tactics being used by some very smart and experienced leaders on both sides of the debate. Every point that I understood, they understood better. For each procedure I devised in my mind, they had devised and then executed more subtle and more powerful and more imaginative procedures.

---

10   Senate Hansard, vol. S64, 1975: 2,729, 2,763.

When the witnesses eventually appeared, I was even more perplexed. The subtlety of the situation was considerable. On one hand, the Senate was exercising one of its undoubted powers. It was taking positive steps to elicit information otherwise being withheld. On the other hand, the press and public were watching closely and were, we suspected, very ready to publicise and criticise any evidence of bullying of those appearing—as had happened in the infamous Browne–Fitzpatrick appearance before the Bar of the House of Representatives[11] 20 years earlier. So we were determined not to bully and not to give any suggestion that witnesses would be treated other than with the utmost courtesy.

The Government, however, had no intention of conceding the possibility that the activities of the Executive could be scrutinised by the Senate. Such reluctance seems laughable now; we now examine officers of the Public Service in depth about programs and expenditures not once but twice each year, in estimates committees, and each such examination lasts for as many hours as is necessary to obtain all desired information. But in 1975 the Government instructed each of its senior officers, by letters from ministers, to claim Crown privilege for all substantive questions, and the Solicitor-General wrote himself claiming the same privilege. We responded with a motion asserting the rights and privileges of the Senate, pointing out that the Labor Party had itself demanded the appearance of an officer of the Public Service before the Bar of the Senate in similar circumstances in 1967, relying on exactly the powers we were now seeking to use. Our motion was carried.

I had imagined that our inquisitors might pursue the witnesses—we had formidable advocates in Withers, Greenwood and Wright, for example—but in the event Withers carried most of the questions and he did not challenge the claim of any witness to privilege. Reg Wright had a prolonged and fascinating exchange with Sir Maurice Byers about the nature of the privilege he was claiming; it makes good reading still[12] and indeed is required reading for anyone making a serious study of Crown (or Executive) privilege in Australia. These claims of privilege were subsequently referred to the Committee of Privileges for examination,[13] but in the supercharged atmosphere of that year in Canberra, the examination became an adversarial and party-political exercise of limited value.

So there I was, recalled to Parliament for a unique sitting of the Senate, watching as the whole thing appeared to fizzle out. The very senior witnesses were refusing to answer—and we were calmly letting them get away with it! What

---

11 Senate Hansard, vol. S64, 1975: 2,730.
12 Senate Hansard, vol. S64, 1975: 2,741.
13 Senate Hansard, vol. S64, 1975: 2,781 ff.

I had not understood was that the course taken by the Government was unwise and futile, and that it was seen to be unwise and futile by my seniors. Sufficient information was still becoming available to the Opposition to make certain the continuation of the loans affair to the great disadvantage of the Government. Senator Steele Hall called for the attendance of another witness, a Mr Karidis,[14] who attended with his counsel and revealed little to the Senate; he made no claims of privilege but played a very 'straight bat' to all questions.

Using our numbers, we passed a resolution asserting that the action of the Government in directing officers not to answer represented a 'massive cover up', that we still demanded a royal commission into the matter and, as mentioned above, that the actions of ministers giving instructions to officers not to answer questions be referred to the Committee of Privileges. It is worth reflecting here that, if the Government had appointed a royal commission, it might well have survived past 11 November 1975.

The Senate finished the examination of witnesses on 22 July 1975 and adjourned until the Budget about one month later. The interlude in Canberra at its coldest and least welcoming had seemed to me unproductive politically and played havoc with my program. I had been forced to cancel many visits, party meetings, flag presentations, and all the other activities that go to make up the daily round of a working senator. But I was able to use the rest of July for solid work back in New South Wales, and to spend as much time as possible with my family.

There was one other major event during that winter recess. Following the double dissolution in 1974, the new Senate, as one of its first acts, divided senators into two 'classes': those deemed to have six-year terms and those deemed to have been elected only for three years. Having been the last person elected, I fell into the latter class. So it was that I would have to face another election when next the House of Representatives went to the people and there would be, in normal circumstances, an election for my 'half' of the Senate. Accordingly, the Liberal Party arranged for a preselection for its Senate team. I nominated as a sitting senator and, as Senator Sir Kenneth Anderson was not continuing, there was a vacancy for a new candidate and I could anticipate selection in the top position.

The preselection took place on Saturday, 9 August 1975 at the Menzies Hotel near Wynyard in Sydney. I travelled in by train rather than driving my car in a rather tense and nervous state—preselections are always tense affairs. I had booked a room at the hotel so I could rest, and shower and change my clothes as necessary.

---

14 Senate Hansard, vol. S64, 1975: 2,806.

The rules of a Liberal Senate preselection are complex. First, the electoral college was made up of one preselector from each active federal electoral conference plus all the members of the state executive of the party. In New South Wales this resulted then in a college of about 90 people, although on that occasion in 1975 the college was much smaller.

Each candidate has 15 minutes and the order of appearance is determined by ballot. Eight minutes are allocated for a speech on any subject. I have seen one candidate who used his eight minutes to read the Bible for the edification of preselectors, another who lectured on abortion law reform (she joined the party only to provide the opportunity to address that electoral college) and a third candidate who, in a fine rhetorical flush, cut a large paper rooster to pieces to illustrate a dramatic point. The remaining seven minutes are allowed for questions on any subject, ranging from questions about one's political past to questions on arcane and complex issues of policy. Questioners bid for the call and the chair can exercise great influence by choosing or ignoring certain potential inquisitors. Voting is by exhaustive ballot, which means that one votes only for the candidate of one's choice. In 1975, any candidate with an absolute majority was declared elected to the first position (this rule has since been changed). If no candidate obtains an immediate majority then the field is reduced to six 'finalists' who speak and answer questions again, after which exhaustive balloting recommences. At that stage, candidates with the fewest votes are eliminated progressively, and ballots are repeated until one candidate obtains a majority. This is a prolonged process; on one occasion, I was present for 20 hours while we selected candidates for positions in the Legislative Council of New South Wales using the same procedure.

My speech was well received at the Senate preselection and Terry Metherell congratulated me on its content later over celebratory drinks. The questions were odd but were not too difficult. After I had made my appearance it was a matter of waiting for all the other candidates to have their turn. It was hard on preselectors and candidates alike. At one stage, the president of the Werriwa Conference collapsed just before Michael Darby spoke; I was called to give him some medical care and then sent him off to Sydney Hospital. I went for a walk around Wynyard Park with Misha Lajovic and then went to my room and watched football: North Melbourne versus Richmond in Melbourne and Gordon versus Randwick in Sydney.

There was a large field but I was well regarded in the party then and won first position on the Senate team on the first ballot, obtaining (so I was told later) all but seven of the votes cast. This was one of several occasions when Bronwyn Bishop and I have been opposed directly in a contest. As has always occurred in such confrontations, I beat her. On this occasion, she was not even selected when the final six were invited to speak again. For the record, the final six candidates were Bill Bridges-Maxwell, Richard Croll, Robert Holland, Joan Pilone, John Matthews and Misha Lajovic.

I was then invited to join the preselectors and watch the second speeches of the final six candidates trying for the other winnable position. This was an unusual and much appreciated compliment to me. Such a course of action was possible under the rules for preselection then applying; today the rules of the Liberal Party in New South Wales are different and I would not have been selected as cleanly or as quickly as I was then. I remember coming back into the room to a big ovation and then sitting at the head table and listening with interest to the six final candidates. Eventually, the ballots were over and Misha Lajovic was successful. I remember coming down to embrace him, just ahead of his wife, Tatjana, who rushed into the room; we had a good and very productive working relationship both before and after the 1975 election.

We all retired to the bar for drinks and then I went off with John Dowd for a pizza, after which he drove me home. I was late but it is hard not to be late home after such an ordeal. My diary recorded: 'Lajovic will sell well.'

With preselection behind me a great load was gone and I could look with confidence to the next sitting and to the next election. I spent the days before our return to Canberra in frantic busyness but able now to assume with confidence that I did have a career in politics—a career that would last at least a few more years.

The parliamentary Liberal Party and the parliamentary National Country Party met in Canberra on 12 August in preparation for the Budget due to be presented a week later. At the meeting, we considered our view on some government Bills, discussed some tactics and looked at some policy. My diary records:

> Kevin Cairns was sat down by Malcolm when he attempted to speak for the third time in a row. He was contributing little. Kevin was angry. He deserved it. Reg Wright gave a passionate address (again) holding on to the back of my chair and my head! I moved before he spoke again.
>
> Dined with Magnus Cormack and Peter Sim.
>
> It is fascinating to see Magnus examining life in retrospect—events and memories. Spoke of himself as a Parliamentarian—said he had twice refused places in the Ministry. Was this correct or was it self justification?

The next day, still in Canberra, an ad hoc group met to determine our position on the Compensation Bill and the Senate report on it. Reg Wright dominated proceedings, supported by Fred Chaney and Alan Missen. Don Chipp was in the chair and Tony Street was present.

Later I ran into Syd Einfeld by chance. He congratulated me on 'conquering the machine so quickly'—a reference to my success at preselection:

> We discussed the likely Labor tragedy in Tasmania and local problems with Lewis in New South Wales. Took Syd to lunch—he is well remembered and liked. Joined by Arthur Hewson from McMillan—a dolt and a fool—at least he did not move his dentures about today. Surely the National Country Party could do better.

In the evening, back in Sydney, I had my first experience with B'nai Brith. This Jewish organisation is named in translation 'Sons of the Covenant' and is the nearest thing to Rotary that the Jewish community has. It also has an honoured function fighting anti-Semitism. Today I belong to the Alfred Dreyfus Unit of B'nai Brith—the anti-defamation unit—but in 1975 I had not met the organisation before. I was the guest speaker and discussed the role of opposition and preparation for government. It was all received very well.

There were two notable occurrences the next day in Sydney. The first was lunch with Professor Bob Walsh and with Professor Byrne, president of the Royal College of General Practitioners. What made this memorable was that this doctor knew of plans I had made with a charismatic Englishman named John Stevens for a medical school at the University of Wollongong. I recorded: 'He described John Stevens as "derivative" which is not really a surprise but is a thought which I had not allowed myself to entertain.'

Let me recount here the tragic story of John Stevens. This outstanding English general practitioner first came to Australia as a Nuffield Travelling Fellow in the late 1960s. I was so impressed with him that I proposed that the RNSH should do something unprecedented: invite him, a general practitioner, to be its guest professor at its annual refresher week. The hospital, to its great credit, took a deep breath and then issued the invitation. What followed was the most memorable of all the North Shore reunion weeks I ever attended. For John Stevens' final address, the lecture theatre was packed to the ceilings with excited, fascinated and appreciative people. He not only described family medicine but also inspired people with what it offered.

While he was here, we discussed at length the need for another medical school to complement what Newcastle was offering and promising. We worked with a gentle medical genius named Wilson Corlis and prepared a submission for a faculty of medicine at Wollongong—a proposal that failed as a result of other political considerations.

Some time later Stevens suffered a disabling stroke in England. His patients and his partners could not cope with his disability and he left his Aldeburgh practice. Later he decided to sail a boat single-handed to Australia and was lost at sea somewhere in the Pacific. His memory remains with me as one of the greatest men I have ever known, a friend and an inspiration *nonpareil*.

The other memorable event on 14 August was a function for Malcolm Fraser. We met for a drink at 5 pm and then went to the home of Arnold Newhouse, a citizen prominent in the Jewish community. Asher Joel was already there and we all had 30 minutes of private discussion before dinner with a group of leaders of the Jewish community. We had a little problem with Justin Jones, who was argumentative. Malcolm listened attentively to a historical discourse from Joachim Schneeweiss and then handled questions very competently. As I had worked with Newhouse to set the whole thing up, I was delighted that it went so well.

The next day, 15 August, we started our Liberal Party Convention, an annual gathering at which there was a lot of breast-beating and some display of our wares. John Atwill made a good speech, then Puplick and Fraser spoke and there was a good question time.

On the next evening, in Penrith, we received 12 debutantes—yes, they still do this in some places. On Monday evening, Misha Lajovic attended a Parramatta Federal Electoral Conference meeting with me and was no better or worse than new candidates when first they are thrown in off the deep end and told to swim. I wrote at the time: 'The Parramatta Conference is grey and drab and very conservative—our image seems hopeless. How to improve?'

How to improve indeed! We were to be back in Canberra the next day for a new sitting and for an opportunity to take the battle once more up to the Labor Party.

4

BUDGET 1975

The 1975–76 Budget was brought down on the evening of 19 August 1975. It was Bill Hayden's only Budget and was rather less irresponsible than those of his predecessors. I flew to Canberra that morning and had an argument with an unusually surly hire car driver. I am normally equable and to have an argument was unusual. I had lunch with various staff members and John Carrick. Then, as usual, we filed into the Senate in the evening to hear the Budget read by the representative of the Treasurer in that chamber.

The Budget is an enormous challenge to any parliamentarian. There are some 10 or more printed books crammed with a mass of financial statistics, projections, analyses and explanations. These books contain programs, details of government outlays by functional area, payments to the states, government borrowings, and so on. They are more than I have ever been able to digest quickly and probably more than any parliamentarian can master in a moment. The Budget speech is merely a summary designed for public consumption; to understand the Budget, one has to go to the mass of detail. When our experts came to do that detailed examination, they concluded that the Budget itself was still sufficiently flawed to make it unlikely to work. I recorded:

> Poor Budget, I listened to [Senator the Honourable] Ken Wriedt deliver it in the Senate. I doubt it will work. I suspect that we will now have a double dissolution in April or May—there will be great pressures for an election. Labor men were despondent and the Senate rose early at 9pm.

These comments were indicative of the thinking even then prevalent in the world of politics. Not only did I raise the possibility of a forced double dissolution in that diary note, but also I acknowledged that there would be great pressure put on us to force an even earlier election. In the light of subsequent developments, these observations were prescient.

On Wednesday, 20 August, we had a party meeting at which we made our first collegial analysis of the Budget of the previous evening. Michael Baume (then a staffer with Fraser and my cousin) was brought in to give some detailed criticisms. I have recorded:

> There was a brief and unsatisfactory Coalition meeting at lunchtime. Doug Anthony was quite unregenerate—objects to the idea of tax credits as against tax deductions—he was big on eloquence but not on facts. The Budget was criticised piecemeal—not coherently as a whole. Michael Baume spoke on the details—there was too much detail and proper criticisms of the whole Budget seem obscured.

But we were having our own fights, too, especially on a number of issues relating to social justice and associated values. I learned on the Thursday that our side was likely to abandon the Social Welfare Commission, and I was upset at this foolish decision.

Colin Benjamin of the Victorian Council of Social Service phoned, angry about the treatment of the councils in the Budget. It had all the marks of political retaliation against them, possibly because they had given advice on policy to the Liberal Party. I was to pursue the question of funding for the Councils of Social Service in the Senate and later in the estimates committees. I recall the then minister John Wheeldon saying eventually, in paraphrase of Napoleon's famous statement, words to the effect of 'when they look at my heart they will find the word ACOSS [Australian Council of Social Service] written across it'.

On Friday, 22 August, we had a meeting of our 'campaign committee' in Sydney at which John Atwill and I had to await the arrival of Carrick and Cotton, who were late. It was of course a committee related to an election for half the Senate, but it did exist, it was working and it could be upgraded should circumstances change. Later we had a function for Dan Aarons, the long-time Liberal Party Treasurer who had turned 90, and then went on to the Liberal Party State Council.

I got home to find Jenny ill in bed with influenza. I did some tidying up to give her a hand and managed to get our daughter, Sarah, away from the television and to bed by 10 pm. The next day, I took Sarah with me to meet seven candidates in western suburbs seats, where we all agreed on a program of joint work and cooperation. After that we came home and I built a billycart for the children. It was great fun but the damn thing was so heavy it scarcely moved.

In the evening, Jenny and I joined the Carricks and travelled to Punchbowl for a celebration of St Stephen's Day. It was memorable in more ways than one. The microphones did not work, the girls forgot the bottle for the bottle dance and then a male choir member attacked a woman (possibly his wife).

The next day Jenny was still ill so I took Sarah riding. I met Charles Curran at the nursery, and I recorded that '[h]e says Michael Baume in real trouble. Feels Patricks are in a very bad way and the publicity is bad. I agree.'

I took the children with me in the afternoon to Ingleburn to a meeting of mushroom growers. We had a good barbecue and I drank a fair bit of slivovitz. Jenny remained ill on the Monday and eventually I got our family doctor, Bruce Glass, to see her. He said I looked awful, too! Sarah had been 'a little mother'. She went off to dressmaking at Abbotsleigh and our son, Ian, went to craft. He had never used a return ticket before and threw away the return stub, but Sarah sorted it all out.

I went to the office and shifted a mountain of paper.

On Tuesday, 26 August, we were back in Canberra for more of the usual activities. Malcolm Fraser made an excellent reply to the Budget and Labor prepared to 'bucket' Michael Baume as we had expected. It came the next day from Fred Daly in the House and John Wheeldon in the Senate. I recorded it as follows: 'Michael got a terrible bucket from Fred Daly. Savage and dirty. It seems to be getting worse.'

I then made an interesting diary record:

> Magnus Cormack seems to be duchessing me—drinks last night. He still fights the fight of Charles I vs the Parliament. Pym, Hampden and Speaker Lenthall and all that stuff. He told us that he called on O'Byrne yesterday and told the president he would get support if he asserted control of the chair over people like Jim Webster. Webster had behaved disgracefully yesterday on a personal explanation. This is intolerable from a chairman of committees. Webster is unregenerate and extreme in views and behaviour. It will come to a crisis and if O'Byrne plays it well we will support him. O'Byrne told Cormack he had not known he would get support. It is important for the chair to have support.

This was most interesting. Cormack was really an 'institutional' person and his approach to O'Byrne (and the reassurance he offered) was an important one for a minority president to receive. Webster was a nice man who was always friendly to me and good to my children, but he was always a party 'warrior' and the behaviour described above is typical of the hardline approach of some of the 'warriors' of that time.

On Friday, 29 August, I became a medical examiner again and took part in examinations into physical diagnosis at RNSH. It was good to be there again. In addition, I addressed an ACOSS conference and hammered at the unfairness of the cuts that had been imposed. Later I had dinner with Michael Baume:

> Dinner with Michael Baume. First good talk about his troubles, and about the attack yesterday in Parliament by Daly. Fraser's office holds an undated resignation. Clearly if ... called in he will be in trouble in Macarthur. He was open and cheerful. Agreed the business was hurting me too. Feel sorry and on his side at last.

Cousin Michael was then the endorsed Liberal candidate for the seat of Macarthur, which he won eventually from Labor's John Kerin. Michael had been briefly a partner in an ill-fated firm of stockbrokers and had never drawn a cent from that partnership. On the contrary, he entered the partnership almost at the time it went into liquidation and accrued only obligations and trouble. An independent investigator subsequently absolved Michael of any responsibility in the matter.

That week Don Chipp was 'suckered' into refusing to allow Senator Ruth Coleman to take part in a Parliamentary cricket game on account (so it was alleged) of her gender. 'He should have asked her to open the batting and bowling and to field at mid-off,' I wrote.

Chipp also said that we would dismantle Medibank and was not supported by Fraser in the furore that followed.

I returned to Canberra on Monday, 1 September for the next sitting week. On 3 September, we learned that the Queensland Parliament had not replaced Bert Milliner with a Labor senator, but had instead appointed (Albert) Pat Field. This was one of the most significant (and disgraceful) acts of 1975. I recorded in my diary:

> Queensland senator selected. It is disgraceful that ALP's Colston was by-passed. Thank God Liberal Leader Chalk led many Liberals to support ALP. The Queensland [Liberal Party] State Executive has given a firm indication of its view. But Chalk could not take all his own men with him. Clearly a grave mistake in Queensland. [Senator James] Keeffe [ALP] spoke about it on the adjournment and Greenwood responded very well.

On 4 September, I learned a lesson about parliamentary tactics. A point of order was taken just as lunch came and the determination of the matter was stood over until after we resumed. Without any leadership guidance, I did a deal with Merv Everett that met both our needs, but was told later that I should have done nothing and forced the point. It would have helped if a senior colleague, any senior colleague, had given me some advice at the time.

On 5 and 6 September, we celebrated Rosh Hashanah. I had an Aliyah Torah at the main Rosh Hashanah service at the North Shore Temple Emanuel. That evening we went to Dapto with Misha and Michael Baume for a very successful meeting. I drove home again—no wonder the doctor said I looked tired—and had a 'family day' the next day, which happened to be Father's Day. We did some garden work, repaired a fence, felled and burned an old tree, visited our neighbour and her new baby in hospital, took Ian to a birthday party, took Sarah to a football game, went to a Monty Python film, picked up Ian and, finally, called in on my brother-in-law and his family at Wahroonga. Ian turned eight a few days later and my present to him proved one of the best ever: an electronic kit. It was a good gift because it was something he really wanted, it accentuated one of his strengths, and it allowed him to construct things that people admired. I well remember going to the Sydney Cricket Ground with Ian a few months later. He produced a radio he had constructed from the electronic kit and incredulous cricket lovers around us all took turns at listening to the ABC commentary, while Ian sat there looking pleased and proud. He was not half as proud as I was.

The next day, 8 September, I received some good treatment for any inflated sense of self-importance. A branch that had attracted 400 people when Andrew Peacock came to speak provided just 10 people to hear me. It was good for me, I suspect.

Tuesday, 9 September was an infamous day in the Senate. It was the day on which Pat Field was sworn in as a senator for Queensland and on which a move to refer the matter to the Standing Committee on Disputed Returns was defeated. Senator Field was granted leave of absence from the Senate on 1 October[1] and did not sit thereafter. My diary recalls the scene as follows:

> New senator sworn in—[Albert] Pat Field from Queensland—sent by Queensland Premier Bjelke-Petersen when Dr Mal Colston should have come. Am horrified by it.
>
> The poor man is not equipped for the job in any way—he is a fool who will be destroyed. Withers caught short at the start of Senate sitting when ALP moved that the new senator not be seated. Standing Order 1(g) which clearly covers the

---

1   Senate Hansard, vol. S64, 1975: 2,801.

situation was brought to the attention of the president in time. Withers had not examined the Standing Orders and did well from this weak basis. Eventually Field sworn but only after a Division—question of a challenge to a court of disputed returns remains to be settled. I shook hands with him on the basis that he had been properly sworn, had come with a proper certificate from the Governor of his State, and had entered the Senate. I fear that some people might read into this some acquiescence in the event.

Alan Missen refused to speak to the man or otherwise deal with him—and I did not blame him.

We started the estimates examination on Thursday, 11 September. ACOSS was very professionally organised. Philippa Smith was up from Sydney and attended to brief me with Julia Hayes from the Australian Capital Territory. I learned that day to do what I have since refined to an art form—namely, to have questions organised with care and precision to elicit matters of fact. The Department of Social Security was horrified at my material and presentation and clearly saw its role as protecting the good guy (Minister Wheeldon) from the bad guy (me). I recorded: '*c'est la vie*!' I did obtain a promise that the ACOSS decision would be reviewed.

It was on this day that I was asked to join the backbench group drafting some of Fraser's replies to the masses of incoming mail. It was not unduly onerous and I accepted it as an act of minor patronage, although I did demand equipment with which to dictate draft replies; it was provided.

On Monday, 15 September, I went to the Yom Kippur service with about half the world. Sarah tried to fast with me and almost succeeded; most other kids her age did not even try.

It was now just one month before we moved to defer votes on the various Loan and Appropriation Bills. From here on the issue of deferral became more pressing and that period leading up to the crisis itself is the subject of the next chapter.

5
PRELUDE TO CRISIS

This chapter covers the month before the deferrals of Loan and Appropriation Bills on 15 October. During this time I faced and resolved my own doubts about deferral, discussed the matter with Malcolm Fraser and with Carrick and Cotton, and became outraged at the serial revelations wrung out of the desperate Government until, finally, I was ready for what we did.

We had an 'up' fortnight in our electorates in mid-September. It began with a trip to Newcastle, which was noteworthy because it was Misha Lajovic's first trip in a small plane. Our contacts in Newcastle were very old and very dangerous drivers, so we endured a certain amount of terror while they drove us unsteadily from place to place. But generally this was a time to do a mass of those electorate things I have described elsewhere.

One trip worth recording was the annual general meeting of the ACT Council of Social Service (ACT COSS), at which I was appointed returning officer by the meeting. I became aware that multiple voting was occurring and asked to see the ballot papers, discovering eventually that one person's handwriting appeared on eight ballot papers. It sure is rough at some of those meetings!

On another evening, we had a dinner at the Carricks' for NSW senators and for the Lajovics. Everyone opened up; it was so animated that Tatjana wondered what had hit her. One other matter was a field trip to Eden with the senate standing committee investigating the effects of clear felling and woodchipping. We found more damage than the woodchip company Harris Daishowa had admitted to and less than the conservationists claimed.

It was during this time that I flew to Canberra for my first meeting of the Institute of Aboriginal Studies, at which I represented the Senate. This is a body with a record of solid achievement. Many years later, I was able to obtain amendments in the Senate to save it from amalgamation with the Aboriginal and Torres Strait Islander Commission (ATSIC). But my impression at that first visit was not promising. I wrote: 'Found committees were hard at work trying to exclude Aboriginals. Confirmed my worst fears.'

Today I can no longer recall the reason for that harsh judgment; neither can I reconcile it with the very good impression I gained of the institute later on. But there it is: I was not impressed that first day.

On Friday, 26 September, I came face to face with some of the pressures for deferral of the Appropriation Bills. There was a campaign committee meeting of which I recorded: 'I argued with Jim Carlton against rejecting the Budget. Carrick and Atwill were strongly for. I felt then the pressure was mounting.'

The pressure was certainly mounting for us to deny Supply to the Government and that is why I was so vehement with my state general-secretary and with my senior Senate colleagues. I was determined to let them know that I did oppose the course being bruited so widely in the press. This exchange was the cause of their suggesting I should see Fraser just a few days later.

October was the crisis month in Australian politics. For me, it began on 30 September, when I waited on Malcolm Fraser. I had acceded to the suggestions of my senior colleagues John Carrick and Bob Cotton that I should do this, once they had learned that I was reluctant to consider the refusal of Supply.

I had some difficulty getting an appointment but was taken eventually to Malcolm's office by Tony Staley so that I could have a drink with the Leader of the Opposition. There was a large group of people in his office drinking and talking when I arrived but he separated from them, guided me over to a bench near one wall and then spent between 10 or 15 minutes with me. We discussed in detail my objections to any radical course, including my concern that our policies were not ready, that an election in May would be better timed, and that Malcolm's popularity and acceptance were on the basis that he would not force an election as the press was discussing so widely and so freely. I recorded in my diary: 'I see no real impropriety tho' I recognise wisdom will depend on circumstances.'

Malcolm outlined to me his view on the two competing principles involved. I recorded: 'A useful discussion over one whisky.'

On 1 October, both Carrick and Cotton told me that Malcolm Fraser was pleased I had talked to him. I recorded: 'One more head counted off.'

5. PRELUDE TO CRISIS

Later that day I had lunch at the Department of Health—a private lunch hosted by Gwyn Howell, the Director-General. Many years later, when I was acting minister, Gwyn was still Director-General. He and I disagreed about the number of ministerial letters for signature, about the content and length of those letters, and about many other matters. Gwyn used a medical metaphor again and again, pointing out each time I complained that my relationship with the department was like that between a locum doctor and a principal—that is, my job was to maintain what I found in good working order ready for the return of the substantive minister. Then that minister was forced to resign and Malcolm Fraser decided that I should be sworn in as minister in his place. When Gwyn came that day and I renewed my complaints, he started once more on his tale of how I was like a locum, and so on and on. I was able then to point to my desk and ask what he could see there. 'A Bible,' he replied, and then quickly, 'My God, you are no longer a locum!' He was right; the Bible had been given to me that morning at Government House when I had been sworn in. We had quick attention to the problems I had raised after that—after all, I was now the principal and no longer the locum.

At lunch on 1 October the officers were trying to sell me the departmental line on a current controversial issue while we ate a pleasant meal. I tried to get some answers on one matter of policy still before the Government. It concerned possible compulsory acquisition by Fawnmac and CSL of licences to manufacture drugs held by other companies. Very properly, they would not be drawn.

Back at Parliament House, I chaired a meeting of our unique parliamentary group of Amnesty International and got the work completed quickly.

On the Friday morning we had a meeting of my senate standing committee in Sydney where we held a public hearing on our current reference on woodchips. That evening I went to Sydney Hospital to a mess dinner, held by the medical staff, particularly by the resident staff but including some older and more senior doctors. My diary records:

> Made the best speech I have made for ages—jokes very well received and also some serious talk. Lots of questions. Very pleased. It is as Royal North Shore Hospital used to be ten years ago with a fine corporate spirit.

The next day, Saturday, 4 October, I took the family with me when I went to Broadway to visit Theo Skalkos. He gave me a translation of some allegedly defamatory material that he wanted me to see. He was very aggressive about a Greek communal argument related to radio 2EA. Later that day I put on a medical hat again when Jenny and I visited Bernie and Helen Amos to meet Eric Andrup, the guest professor at RNSH for 1975. This all seemed like an idyllic interregnum before the crisis that was to come in a fortnight. The mood continued on 5 October when I attended a seminar on Israel at Shalom College at the University of New South Wales. Monday, 6 October was a public holiday in Sydney and the next day I returned to Canberra by plane.

On Friday, 10 October, we finished the examination of the estimates of expenditure for social security, repatriation and health. I was then able to fly back to Sydney and went to RNSH for the traditional mess dinner that preceded North Shore Reunion Week. The jokes were very poor. The general medical superintendent Roger Vanderfield took me aside and advised me that RNSH would invite me to join the council of its Medical Research Institute. I told him I would be delighted (but it never happened). I was delighted partly because they were now coming to me in a spirit of friendship and support.

I sat at a bottom table with Martyn Sulway, who has always been my friend but who, like me, has made some of the 'heavies' uncomfortable because he is slightly unconventional. Martyn and his wife, Rosie, have always been close friends of ours. We have had some wonderful boozy evenings at their home with former quiz kid Chris Ringstad. On one of these occasions, in between food, poetry recitations and Gilbert and Sullivan, they advised us that their bitch had been spayed a week earlier and that the vet had advised them 'to keep her quiet' for a couple of days on return from the dog hospital. They alleged that they complied with this instruction by telling the dog solemnly 'not to climb trees'. She climbed no trees and prospered.

On 11 and 12 October, a weekend, we embarked *en famille* on one of the most ill-fated family outings ever. We had with us in our old Mercedes our dachshunds, Barnaby and Rusty, and a friend of Sarah's named Nicky Israel, as well as Sarah, Ian, Jenny and me. The plan was to travel to a state forest beyond Central Mangrove and camp there overnight. This plan had been inspired by the beauty of the forests as I had seen them with our senate committee and the particular forest had been made known to me by John Yarwood, a Forestry Commission officer who gave evidence to us.

We got to Olney State Forest by late morning and to the spot marked on the map by John Yarwood. Ian was delighted and was quite prepared to pitch camp there and then, but Sarah in particular was not impressed as she wanted us to find a spot closer to a creek so that she could swim. With some reluctance, we drove on from the marked spot. We passed a group picnicking on Wollombi Creek and then, two kilometres further on, we became hopelessly bogged when some apparent puddles turned out to be deep ruts into which the Mercedes sank. I spent almost two hours trying to get rocks under the car wheels to enable it to get moving but the differential was resting on the solid centre of the track and I failed totally. The dogs and the children were milling round and all were covered in leeches in no time (as was I). Eventually, I broke the car jack and so, drying off the sweat and pulling off the leeches, I walked back to the group at Wollombi Creek. A Dr Timms from Avondale College (who recognised me from my time at the Sydney Sanitarium and Hospital in 1967) pulled us out. Ian was so upset by it all he wanted to go home.

Instead we drove down to Kilcare Beach and found Bouddi State Park. Unfortunately, no dogs were allowed into the camping area proper so we parked in a depression out on a dune area, pitched our tent and let everyone relax. Even Ian was happy and the dogs were able to run around and establish territorial rights over the area.

It began to rain so Jenny cooked some food over a primus and by 7 pm we all retired to sleep. Jenny and Barnaby were sensible and slept in the car. That Barnaby always did know where to find comfort! Rusty, Sarah, Ian, Nicky and I slept in the tent. With the rain, some water began to run in the slight depression in which we had our tent. Somehow we remained dry enough to sleep the sleep of the dead and the virtuous. We woke next day to glorious weather at Kilcare Beach. Jenny and the girls went off to swim after we had cooked a legal breakfast on our primus (no open fires were allowed outside the designated camping area). Ian and I struck camp and packed up the car. We all left Kilcare after lunch and were home by late afternoon. We cleaned the car and unpacked, cleaned mud from ourselves and got Nicky home. I went back to work on papers.

I have recorded in my diary: 'Weekend was really a great success in spite of dogs, mud and bog.' Perhaps it was, but reading the account almost 40 years later, I wonder.

John Atwill had won the federal presidency of the Liberal Party: 'So much for that vaunted numbers man Reg Withers. We did him in! 27 votes to 15 each for Sampson and Wing. Puplick as active as ever.'

On Monday, 13 October, I saw patients, all of whom wanted to talk politics: 'Indeed everyone wanted to talk politics. Just the one question.'

I arrived in the city and met an office bearer from the Cook Federal Electorate Conference with whom I talked too frankly about Don Dobie and problems he had within the parliamentary party. It was probably dangerous to be so frank. Happily Don Dobie became a senior and very respected member of the parliamentary Liberal Party but at that time we had to exert real effort to stave off some marauders who wanted him out. At lunchtime I joined an impromptu syndicate at the American National Club and came away with some profit from the poker machines.

I then met Terry Hillsberg, who told me that social security people were saying that I was trying to knock off Don Chipp. I decided that I would have to clear this up with Chipp directly, as it was untrue. As part of my communal duties, I attended the Malcolm Gillies Lecture and annual cocktail party at RNSH and then a meeting at the North Shore Temple Emanuel.

On arriving home late and tired, I learned that Rex Connor had met Whitlam following the release of documents in Melbourne papers, provided by Khemlani. Connor seemed to be resisting. This was stunning news: it meant that Connor had been lying, too, that the assurances we had all been given were of no value, and that Labor was much more vulnerable than ever to the charge of 'reprehensible behaviour'. My diary records: 'Election now looks imminent. My own doubts recede as the government's lies on Loans Affair catch it up.'

6

THE CRISIS DEEPENS: OCTOBER 1975

The constitutional crisis of 1975 began formally when, on 16 October, the Senate deferred any vote on the Appropriation Bills (that is, the Budget) until the Whitlam Government agreed to submit itself to the people at a general election. Most observers had predicted the event, and pressure for it had built up inexorably over a year or so. The Labor Government had, by a series of errors, sackings, demotions and unpopular decisions, made the course easier to take and to justify.

In the previous chapter, I recounted how we had prepared ourselves, and been moved by our leaders, to the position where, as a political group, we were ready to agree to take this extraordinary and unprecedented course. In this chapter, I will set out the events as they unfolded during the first fortnight of the crisis, how they appeared to a backbench senator, how the pressure built up, how it was manifested, how the main protagonists seemed at the time to be presenting themselves to the public and how each was trying to justify his position and gain maximum support for it.

The first day of the first sitting week of the crisis period was Tuesday, 14 October, and I flew to Canberra on an early plane. There was suppressed excitement at the airport. Headlines shrieked the story of the Khemlani telexes and the story was carried in detail. I recorded: 'Clearly the web of lies is tightening around Connor and Whitlam too.'

At our party meeting, Malcolm Fraser had trouble—which was unusual for him—getting and keeping silence to start the meeting. The excitement was palpable. He asked for discussion on Connor and the prime minister but not on an election. He invited any person with a particular view to come and see him. Then we went on to deal with legislation seriatim, after which Margaret Guilfoyle presented an education policy document. I then took Senate candidate Misha Lajovic with his wife, Tatjana, to lunch.

In our Senate party room, Reg Withers was calm and reasonable. Reg Wright was all for 'action' and for once made sense:

> At question time I popped in an innocent 'fishing' question to find Govt tactics—they probably do intend to hold back the pension bills.
>
> Finished estimates, played four sets of squash with Fred Chaney and then had dinner with Sid Sax. Had phoned home to find everyone very excited about a new bird.

Children have a way of getting their priorities right—the deferral of Supply was over within a month but the new bird lived with us for some years. It was a budgie but we solemnly called it Bob—short for Bob Hawke. It was, incidentally, an undistinguished budgerigar and never sang for us.

Rex Connor resigned that morning. There was only a brief statement made by the Government and our questions in the Senate were parried. I spoke on the Loans Bill for about half an hour after dinner and then went to see Fraser to offer him my support. I recorded: 'Election is on!'

I reviewed some of the Connor papers for Carrick and concluded that Connor had been lying; I read and suggested alterations to the social welfare policy for Don Chipp, and did not get to bed until after midnight.

Wednesday, 15 October was the day of the formal start of the constitutional crisis of 1975, the series of events that culminated on 11 November in the dismissals of the prime minister and the Government and, on 13 December, in the landslide election of Malcolm Fraser and the Liberals.

I woke very early. My diary records: 'Now quite ready and any doubts concerning proper procedure resolved. Phoned Jenny to warn her.'

Many years later I had a personal crisis when I had to resign from the Shadow Cabinet. But on that occasion too I phoned Jenny as soon as the crisis was upon me to bring her into the picture, to allow her to warn our two mothers and our children, and to get the views of family, all of whom were totally supportive of my position and my action. On that later occasion, Jenny joined me in Canberra; in 1975, we kept in touch by telephone.

6. THE CRISIS DEEPENS

John Carrick talked me through the likely procedures. I slipped out to see three home units and selected one in Lyons near the Phillip offices. That purchase was completed by the end of the year and we owned the unit until 1989, when we sold it to help finance the purchase of our apartment in Mosman.

There was a secret Senate party meeting at 9.15 am for which no notices had gone out. At this meeting, people expressed clearly their views on the imminent deferral of supply. Alan Missen, Don Jessop, Condor Laucke and Neville Bonner all expressed to the meeting their reservations about the course proposed.

After Senate question time, I finished my contribution to the Loan Bill and ended it with Cromwell's admonition to the Long Parliament, repeated by Leopold Amery to the House of Commons during the debate that forced the resignation of Neville Chamberlain.[1] That quotation was picked up the next day in *The Australian* as follows:

> You have sat too long … In the name of God, go, Labor is told.
>
> The disgraced remains of the federal Government should take a line from Oliver Cromwell and get out, a Liberal senator said yesterday.
>
> Senator P Baume (NSW) quoted what Cromwell said when dismissing the Long Parliament: 'You have sat too long here for any good to have been done. Depart, I say, and let us have done with you. In the name of God, go.'

A day or so later, I received in the mail an anonymous typed comment above a copy of that item from *The Australian*. It said: 'This was a splendid idea when first quoted by Duff Cooper to Chamberlain. It has now become an overworked political cliché.'

I noted at the bottom that someone seemed not to like me and, anyway, it was Amery and not Duff Cooper.

Labor speakers were enraged by some of our speeches (including mine) on the Loan Bill and took to us in their subsequent contributions. We had a joint parties meeting at 1 pm, at which Missen again spoke out but at which the others (including Jim Killen) just stated their views. Lynch took Missen out to Fraser's office. I recorded: 'I doubt they used rope + water + fire but they probably tortured him. He agreed to go along.'

A press conference followed the meeting—then a sense of let down. I recorded: 'It's here! It's on!'

---

1   Journals of the Senate—56th Session, 1975: 905.

When the time came for a vote on the Loan Bill[2] in the Senate, we caught Labor out by moving to delay, rather than voting to defeat the Bill. We caught the press, too, with this unexpected tactic and Whitlam had to delay his press conference for a while. Withers announced our intentions in the Senate soon after 4.35 pm in the following terms:

> The Opposition will attempt to delay this Bill and the Appropriation Bill (No. 1) and the Appropriation Bill (No. 2). I will delay them because we have decided that the people must be given a chance to express their will. The only way to force the Government to submit to the people is by this device. The Opposition is not rejecting the Budget. It is not taking action that will cause anyone to suffer. We will pass legislation providing social service and repatriation payments, State grants, and any other legislation of a similar nature. We will give that sort of legislation a speedy passage. Let there be no mistake. We are not cutting off the flow of money to the people. We are merely adopting the constitutional method of giving the people a choice. Immediately the Government agrees to hold an election the Opposition will pass the Loan Bill and the Appropriation Bills. There will then be no delay[3] ... In order to bring that about I move:
>
> Leave out all words after 'That', insert:
>
> this Bill be not further proceeded with until the Government agrees to submit itself to the judgment of the people, the Senate being of the opinion that the Prime Minister and his Government no longer have the trust and confidence of the Australian people because of—
>
> (a) the continuing incompetence, evasion, deceit and duplicity of the Prime Minister and his Ministers as exemplified in the overseas loan scandal which was an attempt by the Government to subvert the Constitution, to by-pass Parliament and to evade its responsibilities to the States and the Loan Council
>
> (b) the Prime Minister's failure to maintain proper control over the activities of his Ministers and Government to the detriment of the Australian nation and people and
>
> (c) the continuing mismanagement of the Australian economy by the Prime Minister and this Government with policies which have caused a lack of confidence in this nation's potential and created inflation and unemployment not experienced for 40 years.[4]

The amendment was agreed to using the fortuitous majority caused by the failure to replace Bert Milliner with a Labor-voting senator.

---

2   Journals of the Senate—56th Session, 1975: 928.
3   Senate Hansard, vol. S66, 15 October 1975: 1,125.
4   Received from the House of Representatives on 27 August 1975; Journals of the Senate—56th Session, 1975: 885.

6. THE CRISIS DEEPENS

I dined at Maggies Restaurant in Civic with Alan Missen, Kathy Martin, Eric Bessell, Don Jessop and a friend of Missen's. A note about that dinner appeared in a subsequent edition of the *National Times* newspaper[5]—which just emphasises how much on public show one is all the time in Canberra. Back in the Senate we had the then president of the Australian Council of Trade Unions (ACTU) Bob Hawke in the gallery. He was certainly noisy and called out loudly; we thought he could have been drunk. We all chose to ignore him and the standing orders that regulate the behaviour of 'strangers'; we did not want a major story about Hawke being tossed out of the Senate. What a day that was!

On Thursday, 16 October, we had one of those strange artificial days that make up part of parliamentary life. Here we were with a major crisis upon us, arguing in the Senate about supply for the Government—about its very survival—and then adjourning to hold a state luncheon for the Prime Minister of Malaysia, at which we moved into a 'time bubble' of truce, sitting together, and listening to formal and banal speeches (there was a general instruction to try not to drink too much at the luncheon). If I found the speeches hard to take, I have no doubt that Whitlam and Fraser found them harder to deliver. I sat near the pathetic Patrick Field, who told me he would stand as an independent at any election. I was also seated close to Race Matthews MP, who was 'very brittle and brilliant'. The tension was getting to them, too. Later I made a good and strong attack on Rex Connor for 2WL.

During the morning some of our senators had, without warning, exercised their right to speak on the first reading of the Appropriations Bill (a particular Senate right under the Standing Orders of that chamber) and Bob Cotton was furious. We eventually got to the vote on the Appropriation Bill by late afternoon after excellent speeches from Greenwood and Wheeldon. The motion moved was in identical terms to that moved on the Loan Bill the previous day. We had to cross from side to side to vote. As we did so, I had to pass Don Grimes physically as he was passing the other way to oppose us. He called me a 'cunt' as we went past each other. I have recorded:

> McAuliffe called me a 'liar' and Wheeldon screamed, 'Go, go, piss off, piss off.' The bitterness is more than palpable—it charges the atmosphere. There are no friends any more.

---

5   Senate Hansard, vol. S66, 15 October 1975: 1,152.

Greenwood also tabled legal opinions from two learned counsel on the power of the Senate to reject Appropriation Bills and on the lack of power of the prime minister or Attorney-General to advise the Governor-General to give assent to any Bills that have not passed the Senate.[6] These documents were important in the public debate then under way about the legality of what was occurring.

I missed the plane and therefore a Sydney function, and made it home by 9 pm. Someone had already talked to the press about Alan Missen holding out.

Friday, 17 October was a working day in Sydney. This was my first day in Sydney since the battle had formally been joined. The press was unfriendly. I heard from Chris O'Connell that the High Court had upheld the validity of federal funding of the Australian Assistance Plan (AAP). Terry Hillsberg spoke to me, too. He told me that my questions at the recent senate estimates had caused a lot of comment in the Department of Social Security. He said it was 'favourable comment and some "fame" for me—especially on my knowledge of the AAP'.

At my regular Rotary meeting at the St Leonards Club, I got some inkling of the depth of the fears people held. My old friend John Dalton was incredibly agitated, saying, 'It's going to happen here. It's going to happen here.' His memory is of Europe in the 1930s. I wrote in my diary: 'I do hope he is wrong.'

In the afternoon I chaired a session at the North Shore Hospital Reunion Week. The title of the seminar was 'Permissiveness and the Media'. Mungo McCallum contributed and was terrible, and said Fraser had been drunk each night that week. I let it go; it was untrue as far as I know.

Freda Brown did well; Russell Prowse did well enough; John Singleton was unashamed Workers' Party. After the session was over, I picked up Jenny and we went to the Hospital Dinner Dance. Harry Cumberland, a conservative senior surgeon at RNSH was worried about what Mungo had said about Fraser; I was amazed that he believed rubbish like that.

I heard of Fraser's bad reception in Hobart that evening; for him, television was better than public rallies. I recorded:

> I am depressed by the bitterness and tension—no fear or resiling—just depressed. Agree with Chris Puplick that we are moving to an American situation where only numbers count. Needed Daricon to sleep.

Daricon is the trade name for an anticholinergic agent, and the entry would indicate that I had troublesome epigastric pain. Jenny recalls that only during this time in my political life did I walk in my sleep.

---

6   Senate Hansard, vol. S66, 15 October 1975: 1,156.

6. THE CRISIS DEEPENS

The weekend that followed was fairly typical of the period: some little time for family and relaxation, more time for rallies and for work. On the Saturday I worked in our garden, did some cleaning, got into trouble with Jenny for trimming the wisteria (again), helped Ian to cover some of a model aeroplane, and so on. Later we travelled to Wollongong to our good friends the O'Malleys to help Sue celebrate her fortieth birthday. Sue's sister Kerry was aggressive about our course (but knowledgeable about what she was saying):

> Very tired indeed on our way home to Sydney. No doubt it is getting to me a bit. Whitlam is winning the battle of the press and public. Fraser needs to get away from public to more private functions.

On Sunday morning, I went to the office with our dachshund Barnaby for three hours' work. I just could not afford to fall behind in routine work if I wished to concentrate fully in Canberra on the constitutional crisis.

I then went out to Horsley Park in Sydney's far west with the dog to speak to 200 Liberals at a barbecue in the rain. Again doing my reassurance act, I recorded: 'It's up to Sir John Kerr—hope I'm right.' I saw film of a Fraser rally in Melbourne and felt better and more secure.

On Monday, 20 October, my neighbour Ken Perkins drove me to the North Shore Medical Centre. He complained that:

> [M]y dogs had upset his rubbish ('impossible naturally') and told me that we are being done in over the present crisis. He does not help my self-doubts—after all it is a balanced situation. Feel clearly Fraser needs now to get to TV and away from large rallies where Labor disruption attracts the highlight.

Later that morning, still in Sydney, I did normal constituency things. In the afternoon I went back to RNSH to open a new animal house for the Research Institute. I had done my training and my doctorate there and was quite at home.

After some more work in the city, I flew to Canberra, worked in the office there and then fell into bed.

On Tuesday, 21 October, we were back in the Parliament, back in the confrontation and back in the midst of the unresolved constitutional crisis. The mail was running against us but the press was less vocal, less knee-jerk and more thoughtful. We had a revealing meeting of the joint parties. I observed: 'A gathering of weak hearts needing reassurance. JMF [Fraser] good in face of some puerile contributions. "Carry on. Be of good heart etc."'

At the Senate party meeting, Ian Wood again wanted us to call some of his witnesses but would not reveal in detail who they were or what it was they might say if called. We had an unsatisfactory rally outside the Parliament; I got two questions in at question time, had an interview with Merle Hurcombe and Charles Chambers about Sydney City Mission problems, and negotiated acceptable contributions for my column in the *AMA Gazette*.

We had a long scheduled meal with the Pharmacy Guild and learned that they had seen a draft health policy not yet seen by the relevant backbench committee of the parliamentary Liberal Party. This was an unfortunate discourtesy on the part of our front bench, and, sadly, this kind of thing happens still. After dinner I spoke in defence of pharmaceutical companies in a debate on the National Health Bill No. 3. It was well received on our side, with compliments from Carrick, Reg Wright, Bonner and Webster. Labor hated it; they shouted and yelled.

Fraser saw the Governor-General at Yarralumla that evening and Sir Robert Menzies issued a good statement.[7] I wrote: 'This will be interesting. Will watch the papers in a.m.'

The Appropriation Bills were returned the next day with the assertion that the Senate lacked the power to do as we were doing. The words of the motion were:

> That the House of Representatives having considered Message No 276 of the Senate asserts that the action of the Senate in delaying passage of the Appropriation Bill (No 1) 1975/6 and the Appropriation Bill (No 2) 1975/6 for the reasons given in the Senate resolution is not contemplated within the terms of the Constitution and is contrary to established constitutional convention, and therefore requests the Senate to re-consider and pass the Bills without delay[8].

There was then a bitter argument in the Senate when we sought time overnight to consider the message and prepare our rebuttal. The procedure we used to achieve delay was to adjourn debate on a motion: 'that resumption of debate [on the Government motion] be an Order of the Day for a later hour this day.'

We finally had to vote and adjourn that procedural motion, after which the Government moved again to bring on the matter and we amended that motion so that, in the end, it was held over until the next day. To achieve all this required seven bitter and time-consuming divisions. It was a taste of what was to ensue in the next several weeks.

It was on this day, too, that the Leader of the Government, Senator Ken Wriedt, advised the Senate that he had become Minister for Minerals and Energy, that Rex Patterson had become Minister for Agriculture and that the then young Paul Keating had become Minister for Northern Australia.

---

7   See National Times, 20 October 1975: 6.
8   Senate Hansard, vol. S66, 21 October 1975: 1,289.

6. THE CRISIS DEEPENS

On the next day, 22 October, I dined with Stephanie and John Jorritsma at their home; it was all very pleasant. They had been friends since I had attended Stephanie's father, Douglas, during my doctoring days. I was also trying to be a father—something that is more difficult when one is 300 kilometres from one's family. Sarah and I had an argument by phone; she wanted (at the age of 10) to attend a concert by Suzi Quatro and our conversation was acrimonious and difficult. I compromised by offering her a record by the same singer. I saw Sheila Kellock from Tony Street's office, who was angry and depressed about our deferral of the Budget Bills.

In the Senate we voted eventually to assert the rights of the Senate and to send the Appropriation Bills back to the House of Representatives. The Pension Bills about which I had been worried finally arrived and we took them straight through all stages. The actual motion moved by Senator Withers on the Appropriation Bills was as follows:

> Leave out all words after 'That', insert:
>
> the Senate having considered Message No. 380 of the House of Representatives asserts:
>
> (a) That the action of the Senate in delaying the passage of the Appropriation Bill (No. 1) 1975/6 and the Appropriation Bill (No. 2) 1975/6 for the reasons given in the Senate Resolution as communicated to the House of Representatives in Message No. 276 is a lawful and proper exercise within the terms of the Constitution of the powers of the Senate.
>
> (b) That the powers of the Senate are expressly conferred on the Senate as part of the federal Compact which created the Commonwealth of Australia.
>
> (c) That the legislative power of the Commonwealth is vested in the Parliament of the Commonwealth which consists of the Queen, the Senate and House of Representatives.
>
> (d) That the Senate has the right and duty to exercise its legislative power and to concur or not to concur, as the Senate sees fit, bearing in mind the seriousness and responsibility of its actions, in all proposed laws passed by the House of Representatives.
>
> (e) That there is no convention and never has been any convention that the Senate shall not exercise its constitutional powers.
>
> (f) That the Senate affirms that it has the constitutional right to act as it did and now that there is a disagreement between the Houses of the Parliament and a position may arise where the normal operations of Government cannot continue, a remedy is presently available to the Government under section 57 of the Constitution to resolve the deadlock.

(2) That the Senate reaffirms to the House of Representatives its resolution set out in Senate Message No. 276 in respect of each of the Appropriation Bills, namely: That this Bill be not further proceeded with until the Government agrees to submit itself to the judgment of the people, the Senate being of the opinion that the Prime Minister and his Government no longer have the trust and confidence of the Australian people because of—

(a) the continuing incompetence, evasion, deceit and duplicity of the Prime Minister and his Ministers as exemplified in the overseas loan scandal which was an attempt by the Government to subvert the Constitution, to by-pass Parliament and to evade its responsibilities to the States and the Loan Council

(b) the Prime Minister's failure to maintain proper control over the activities of his Ministers and Government to the detriment of the Australian nation and people and

(c) the continuing mismanagement of the Australian economy by the Prime Minister and this Government with policies which have caused a lack of confidence in this nation's potential and created inflation and unemployment not experienced for 40 years.

(3) That the foregoing Resolutions be transmitted to the House of Representatives by Message.[9]

These messages—in identical or almost identical form or meaning, or in response to responses to messages—passed backwards and forwards across Kings Hall daily, between the Senate and the House of Representatives, during the remaining weeks of the crisis.

Thursday, 23 October, was the third day of this second crisis sitting week. My diary records:

> Feel quite depressed—am getting a lot of 'iron in the spine' advice but no tactics. Either the Governor-General will side with Reps or with Senate (and that will settle the issue) or one side will back down without the Governor-General. Peter Durack supports me and so does Ken Anderson that the Governor-General will need to be supported … Am holding on.

I recorded a radio segment for Wollongong, finished drafting letters for Fraser, presented a petition and asked some questions. I took the Israeli Ambassador Michael Elizur to lunch at the Lobby Restaurant, which was an awful rush at that hour. I had been worried about some anti-Israel moves within the Inter-Parliamentary Union (the international umbrella parliamentary association)

---

9   Senate Hansard, vol. S66, 1975: 1,231.

but he advised me not to press the matters. Bruce Lloyd and I met Harry Jago and people he had brought up on behalf of the Proprietary Association. Then Jenny arrived and we saw and finally settled on a unit to buy.

> Missed a party meeting. I am to do an urgency motion next week with Bonner and Bessell on unemployment. Apparently Withers and Greenwood had a real ding-dong in the meeting—Marriott said please go elsewhere—it all arose out of an urgency motion in the morning.

After a rest, we went to a reception at the Israeli Embassy and then to a parliamentary reception for Princess Margaret. We sighted the princess only distantly. We saw and spoke to Malcolm and Tammie Fraser at supper.

And so another parliamentary week finished. On Friday, 24 October, Jenny and I flew to Sydney on the 7 am plane; looking back, I realise just how much she must have hated getting up so early. We got home to Gordon by 8.45 am and I raced off immediately to a scheduled meeting of our senate standing committee only to discover, on arrival, that the meeting had been called off and neither Naomi nor I had been told. Eventually, I went to Rotary and found them more supportive and more receptive to encouragement than they had been one week earlier. Chris Puplick records in his own diary that he and I spoke at length about the current situation and that he agreed with my assessment 'that things are on the way up'.

> Granny is feeling the strain—aren't we all?—everyone is a bit short. Labor rally today in Sydney. Sarah says she will 'vote' Labor—she is more aware at ten years than many at adult age and I listen with respect to her views. Labor PR is based on lies and is very effective.
>
> Rocky McEwin informs me of projected very successful conclusion to Medibank arrangements with New South Wales.

On Saturday, 25 October, I attended a meeting of childcare associations representing Malcolm Fraser and debated Labor MP John Armitage. During this day, I saw state Liberal MP Steve Mauger, my diary recording: 'Argued with Steve Mauger about the significance of John Waddy being refused re-endorsement. Mauger was angry and unresponsive. Where is this kind of inward liberalism going?'

The papers contained a story in which Jim Cairns asserted that Whitlam was lying. I recorded: 'This is the kind of break we needed. This could, just could, open the nut.'

My brother Stephen and his children visited to play with models for a couple of hours and then Jenny and I went to dinner with Russell and Helen Price.

Sunday, 26 October was another mixture of family and political activity. I spent the morning with the children but in the afternoon attended a rally. It was quite a rally—there were 20,000 people at Randwick Racecourse. It was well done and a credit to Alan Viney and Jim Carlton. From there I flew to Melbourne to attend a fundraising event for the Jewish Welfare and Relief Society. John Seleznikov, who met me at the airport, was Labor but most friendly and courteous under the difficult circumstances created by events in Canberra. Because of spending Sunday evening in Melbourne, I had to catch a dawn plane back to Sydney on Monday, 27 October to see my patients. Later I lunched with Professor Bob Walsh, John Morris, Helen Bashir and Gordon Archer. We discussed problems associated with the availability of blood-clotting factors and I arranged to have some questions prepared for the Parliament.

I went home early with Chris Puplick and slept for an hour before taking Sarah up to Bruce Glass; she was just not well and I did not know why. After that I went to the Wentworth for dinner with the Private Hospitals and Nursing Homes Association, with Richard Thompson in the chair and accompanied by his wife, Kim: 'Gave a very political speech. We were stiffening people's backbones.'

On Tuesday, 28 October, I returned to Canberra for the third sitting week of the supply crisis. The stakes had increased progressively, the community was more and more polarised and there was less and less room for any compromise. I knew before I reached Canberra that this would be another week of high drama and of the unfolding of great events:

> Enormous amount of mail, almost all against us. The party meeting was disorganised and slightly less direction to it. Ian Wood hinted that he might vote for Supply 'if we did not do things better'. I sneered at him and asked him to be more positive: he was not happy.
>
> The strain is now starting to tell. Everyone is edgy, tired, and on a hair trigger. Senate party meeting concerned with Khemlani—should he appear or not. Left unresolved until we got more detailed information.
>
> Ian Wood then failed to appear for two divisions on the Loan Bill.[10] We think he slept through—I believe him this time. After all he is a very old man.
>
> I went to dinner with Kathy Martin, Fred Chaney (whose birthday it was) and Alan Missen, Eric Bessell, Peter Sim, at the 19th Hole Restaurant. We also saw Tony Street dining with Sheila Kellock and Les Johnson and Reg Bishop dining together.
>
> Felt very tired, worried and flat.

---

10   Senate Hansard, vol. S66, 22 October 1975: 1,335, 1,377.

6. THE CRISIS DEEPENS

Wednesday, 29 October was a very difficult day for me. It began with another senate party meeting where we agreed on some procedural matters. Rumours were flying that certain vital telexes were available in Sydney—at a price. It was early in the day that some trouble occurred for me. When Labor senators began to present petitions identical to one I had presented earlier in the week, Ivor Greenwood took what I described as 'a very evil point of order'. He drew attention under Standing Order 87, operating at that time, to the fact that a particular petition referred to matters (namely, the Appropriation Bills) on the notice paper and for that reason should not be received.

Alan Missen objected, pointing out that petitions on family law had been received without objection during debate on the Family Law Bill a few months earlier. He also made clear that the point of order was a personal one and not an Opposition view. I spoke on the same point to observe that an identical petition had been received without objection from me just a day or two earlier.[11] I joined Missen in opposing the point of order and received 'Hear! Hear!' from all around the chamber.

The press was hypersensitive to any crumb, any small event, and reporters were ready to blow anything out of all proportion. So it was that I was then besieged by reporters asking if my objection to Greenwood's point of order meant I might be signalling personal distress about deferral of the Appropriation Bills. They really were clutching at straws and I told them so. Nevertheless, Fraser was asked on the ABC program *This Day Tonight* about Baume and Missen attacking Greenwood.

In order to clarify my own mind, I saw Alan Cumming-Thom, the Clerk Assistant, and received assurances that one could reject one only of the Appropriation Bills. He went further and assured me that one could restore an Appropriation Bill to the Notice Paper for a second vote, which was an interesting possibility. He promised to prepare for me some words that might form the basis of an address to the Governor-General from the Senate inviting him to intervene and determine the crisis. I thought it could be 'a' or 'the' way out.

I attended a Rotary meeting at Woden where all the members were worried by events and by the crisis. I reported:

> Worked at the House to 10pm. Saw Reg Withers on the way out. He was furious with his colleagues, possibly over Khemlani. He too is tired. Shared a car home with George Georges—he is worried. Perhaps Labor will crack. My ulcer hurts and I am tired.

---

11   Journals of the Senate—56th Session, 1975: 995; Senate Hansard, vol. S66, 29 October 1975: 1,523.

I slept better that night but then found no access to breakfast at the Parliament: 'The bastards are contracting all services.'

It was a quiet day, although everyone was very tense in the chamber and there was a rather ugly flare-up between James McClelland and Jim Webster in which Webster uttered an aside inaudible to most of us but heard by McClelland, who responded, 'I will fix you for that'.[12] 'Ian Wood threatened again to cross the floor—he is tricky and irrational. Demands we do things his way.'

I got out of Canberra on the evening plane and returned to Sydney. The next morning, I took a car at dawn and caught an early plane to Dubbo. I went to radio station 2DU, having travelled with the station owner, Janet Cameron, on the plane. I recorded some segments with John Mason and then inspected local industries and the Western Plains Zoo.

> Large Liberal lunch—spoke very forcefully (although with low volume) speech intended to assist people to stand firm. Amazed myself. Very well received.

I flew on to Bathurst and attended a dinner for 130 people at which I spoke on the same subjects and with the same aims of stiffening people's backbones. Misha Lajovic was there and spoke well.

At the end of October the constitutional crisis was well and truly joined and was gripping all political *cognoscenti* in Australia. There was still no sign of either side backing down; no clear sign of the likely winners and losers. It was a titanic struggle in which I was doing what I could to keep our community and branch supporters with us. It is a well-recorded feature of that time that all political meetings were well attended and all parties experienced great upsurges in interest and participation. The Liberal Party certainly displayed these features and I was frantic in Canberra as a member of the Senate, in the community as a busy Liberal, and at home trying to be a father and husband.

---

12   Senate Hansard, vol. S66, 30 October 1975: 1,607.

7

EARLY NOVEMBER 1975

At the beginning of November the constitutional confrontation had been under way for more than two weeks. Its outcome was still unclear and was certainly unforeseen even by that majority of Australians whose attention was riveted to the battle. As with all such matters occurring in the national capital, citizens distant from Canberra understood what was going on only as the events were interpreted by journalists writing for print media or presenting material on radio or television. And it was in this area that we were doing rather badly. To put it bluntly, I thought we were getting a pasting in the press.

Although I had entered the battle reluctantly, having first had to overcome some doubts about the wisdom of our course, once into the battle, I was determined that we should stay the course—and win. Nevertheless, I recorded in my diary for 1 November the plaintive note: 'We all continue to whistle in the dark. God help us!'

When November began we had just finished some drama-filled weeks of October sittings. We were eyeball to eyeball with the Government and tension was already apparent among our members. I had returned to Sydney on 30 October, went to Orange the next day, and 1 November found me in Bathurst with Misha and Tatjana Lajovic, with whom I had spoken the previous night at a dinner for 130 people. Misha was at that stage our preselected Senate candidate and was working well. We drove that morning from Bathurst to Sydney, stopping at Lithgow so I could do several radio spots on 2LT for Reg Gillard, our candidate for Ben Chifley's old seat of Macquarie. On this drive we had one of those rare chances to talk uninterrupted and at length. I have recorded in my diary:

> [R]eal concern with Misha's philosophies. Anti-communism is important but just not enough on its own. Seems to have little expertise in areas of other policy development—but then neither did I at the stage I was a candidate.

In retrospect, I smile at that comment and at that concern. For one thing, I was only just becoming aware of many of the matters against which I judged my soon-to-be colleague. But more importantly, I have come to understand clearly that the party founded by Robert Menzies was successful because it was so broad and inclusive. It had room for conservatives like Lajovic, whose thinking was dominated by anti-communism, just as it had a place for philosophical liberals like me. It is sad to see the party, in the late 1980s, early 1990s and early into the twenty-first century, being driven ideologically by people of narrower minds. They will achieve their philosophical hegemony but it is not likely that they will ever again enjoy sustained electoral support of the kind that Menzies enjoyed. Perhaps one difference between Lajovic and me was that while he has always known what he is against, I have struggled closer to knowing what I support. And the further I have gone, the more I seem to have returned to family roots—to the beliefs that would have sustained my grandfather, Frederick Baume KC MP, who sat as a liberal in the Parliament of New Zealand, opposite the conservatives in the first decade of the twentieth century.

But Misha was then, and has always remained, my close friend. In the election of December 1975 he entered the Senate and served there for 10 years before retiring. In his final speech, on 31 May 1985, he paid a generous tribute to me in the following words:

> It is impossible to name all of them, but there is one person I have to name—Senator Peter Baume. He guided me in my first days here and was constantly at my side, always willing to help. Thank you, Peter.[1]

On that first day of November 1975, I arrived home from Bathurst to find Jenny and her cousin Ros McTaggart planning a new layout for the living room of our Gordon home. Ros is a professional decorator and they kept at their task until I stopped them peevishly at 1.30 pm. It was at least a change from an endless diet of Canberra politics.

This was already the 'pre-campaign campaign' and I was frantically busy. On that day, I slept for a while in the afternoon and then we went to the Prospect Ball at Penrith. There were about 500 people there. We had a real turnout of candidates and MPs: Dorothy Ross, Philip Ruddock, Max Ruddock, Frank Calabro, Ron Rofe and Alan Cadman. My diary records for that day: 'people are not happy about the supply situation.'

---

1 Senate Hansard, vol. S109, 31 May 1985: 2,947.

That is where we seemed to be; people do not ever like uncertainty and we were the cause of great anxiety and uncertainty for them. Also, we were being painted as wreckers and obstructionists and were getting rather the worse of the public argument. The papers were not encouraging and I recorded my view on 2 November that 'they say we have clearly miscalculated. The issue had been moved away from the front pages to some extent.'

On that day, I recorded that I actually had 'only my second meal with the family for eight days or so'. Jenny's memory is that this was not unusual. It was part of the strain and imposition made by political life on families. It had also been bad in medicine. Our neighbour was also a doctor and Jenny overheard the children, when young, playing one day with the children of a third doctor. The game was 'families' and the text ran something like this:

> 'Mother, do you realise that Father is coming home to dinner tonight?'

> 'Coming home to dinner is he? Then we had better have a special family dinner. Children—Father is coming home to dinner tonight.'

For all those children, the chance to eat as a complete family was rare enough to be treated as special.

On the evening of 2 November, Malcolm Fraser was attacking Gough Whitlam's announced decision to explore ways by which he could continue to govern when properly authorised supply was exhausted. It raised serious questions of constitutional propriety, which Malcolm presented crudely but effectively as Whitlam attempting to 'set up a dictatorship'.

Even at this stage, three quite separate timetables were operating. One related to the determination of the Senate to press its course; how long could Fraser hold his senators before someone cried 'enough'? We had already had Ian Wood threaten (in a moment of pique) to cross the floor on 30 October in the Senate party room. How long would it be before Reg Withers lost a senator from the fold?

The second was the supply timetable itself. We know now, many years later, that the last date for securing passage of the main Appropriation Bills was the end of November. This was logical as the Supply Bills, passed at the end of the autumn sittings, provided money for five months (to the end of November). Withers, who was a master of the pithy statement, told me once that a government needed only six Bills annually to be able to govern—four Appropriation Bills and the two Supply Bills—and that all other legislation was a bonus. Today we have extra Appropriation Bills for the parliamentary departments, so the total number of 'essential' Bills rises to eight, but Withers' aphorism retains its force.

The third timetable in operation was the election timetable. If an election were to occur in 1975 it would need to be on 13 December—a practical necessity related to the imminence of Christmas. For this date to be chosen, an election would need to be announced early in November—no later than 11 November. It was this third timetable in fact that probably determined the date of the Dismissal itself.

Monday, 3 November was a typical day for that period. I was up at dawn and saw patients at the North Shore Medical Centre. They were starting to want to ask me questions about politics rather than about their health. I was having increasing difficulty keeping medicine and politics separate in my discussions with them—but still I tried to do so.

The press and editorials that morning were quite good—better than they had been—and I felt somewhat reassured. I flew to Williamtown, just north of Newcastle, and was met by Bob Scott and Bob Freeman, then president of the Shire of Port Stephens. My diary describes Scott as 'that marvellously competent organiser'. He had, on 12 August 1974, won a Liberal Party preselection for a place in the Legislative Council of New South Wales, and later served a term in that chamber. We did interviews for the Newcastle radio, television and print media in which I stated our determination with absolute firmness and vigour (having decided that anything less than absolute conviction was worthless). We had a lunch in Maitland for '70 people needing reassurance', which I gave them.

When, later that afternoon, I returned to Sydney it was to discover (from a taxi driver in fact) that Malcolm Fraser had offered to pass Supply if the House of Representatives would go to an election with half the Senate in May. I have written in my diary:

> Why not tell the Party Room first? I feel cheated and angry and hurt—egg on my face after all my strong statements. However I guess
>
> a) Whitlam will refuse so restoring the balance of virtue to us; and,
>
> b) Caucus meets tomorrow and so Fraser's statement needs to be in their laps.

I recorded in my diary that the tension was getting to me and I thought I would benefit from small doses of Valium that week. At the same time I wrote: 'But I feel much more on top of it all.'

The evening news confirmed that Whitlam had rejected Fraser's offer and so we were back to square one.

Tuesday, 4 November was just one week before the Dismissal, but my diary notes were written on the day—and therefore without the knowledge of events yet to occur. Early in the day, I snapped at John Carrick and made him quite aware of my concern about the lack of information given to us about the offer of the previous day by Fraser. Then I saw the papers, which were not negative for us. Mail was continuing to pour in—20 or 30 letters each day, many from old acquaintances, almost all arguing vehemently against our stand.

We had a party meeting at which Malcolm reported on what he had done but not on why he had done it or why he had done it as he had. Ken Anderson spoke with some heat about the manner and suddenness of changes in direction since the previous party meeting just five days earlier. I supported him and am reported in one book as emphasising that I heard of the changed direction from a taxi driver,[2] and that we had been caught short in public because we had not been told. We were told that because Whitlam's office had been preparing to distort what Fraser had done, an immediate statement was necessary.

Our Khemlani statement was now ready and we took it into the Senate. The Australian Labor Party (ALP) objected to it, took points of order, but did themselves no good with all their carrying on. The way we got the stuff into the Parliament was as follows: Reg Withers quoted from the documents and then Fred Chaney moved under the appropriate standing order that they be tabled. Withers then moved that the papers be printed. These motions were carried, Steele Hall and Cleaver Bunton exercising some of their rare votes for us;[3] Withers had not wanted the statement read to the party room before its presentation.

I am now led to believe it is a very good statement; it has been made available from John Howard to *The Age* and the *Australian Financial Review*.

Later on that Tuesday, I was able to have more relaxed conversations with Carrick. This was definitely a good day for us in the Parliament. I recorded several other matters on that day. One was that Fraser bested journalist Richard Carleton on television. Another referred to our horserace 'that stops the nation': 'Melbourne Cup—who cares?' A third was prescient: 'What will Kerr do? This is the crux. Whitlam too—he must do something. Perhaps it will be a half-Senate election.'

---

2 Ayres (1987: 288).
3 *Journals of the Senate—56th Session*, 1975: 1,011.

The next day, thinking more about the Governor-General, I talked with the Clerk Assistant, Alan Cumming-Thom, whose job included the drafting of Opposition amendments, about preparing an address to the Governor-General asking him to take decisive action and so on. The motion as finally drafted read:

> That an Address be presented to His Excellency the Governor-General praying that he exercise the power vested in him by section 57 of the Constitution to dissolve both Houses of the Parliament simultaneously.

The address itself read:

> To His Excellency the Governor-General and Commander-in-Chief of the Commonwealth of Australia.
>
> MAY IT PLEASE YOUR EXCELLENCY:
>
> We, the Senate of the Commonwealth of Australia in Parliament assembled, respectfully request Your Excellency to exercise the power vested in you by section 57 of the Constitution to dissolve the Senate and the House of Representatives simultaneously.
>
> We respectfully call Your Excellency's attention to the situation which presently exists as between the two Houses of the Parliament and as between the Parliament and the Government, a situation in which
>
> (a) the Senate has exercised its parliamentary and constitutional right to withhold from the Government the money required for it to carry on its normal services
>
> (b) the Government has not, as the Senate requested and as precedent has provided, announced a date for a general election for the House of Representatives
>
> (c) the Parliament is likely to become unworkable as a result of recent conflicting resolutions agreed to by the Senate and the House of Representatives and
>
> (d) the requirements of section 57 of the Constitution have been satisfied in respect of twenty one Bills,
>
> We respectfully ask Your Excellency to take the necessary action, pursuant to the provisions of section 57 of the Constitution, to dissolve both Houses of the Parliament simultaneously.

I took the draft to Fraser and then to Withers for consideration among the tactics open to us. I recorded then that Withers told me he feared that one particular senator (whom I will not name here) would crack.

On Thursday, 6 November, we had a long discussion in our Senate party room about different ways of handling the Khemlani matter. Some were in favour of a judicial inquiry. Clearly, Withers had shown my prepared form of words to no

7. EARLY NOVEMBER 1975

one, for Greenwood knew nothing about it. When Reg Wright heard of it he was attracted and was keen to see it activated. That day I spoke on the Income Tax Bills and then took the Cities Commission Repeal Bill through for John Carrick and on behalf of the Opposition.

This was the end of the last complete sitting week of the Twenty-Ninth Parliament, although we did not know that at the time. I returned to Sydney and spent most of the Friday in western Sydney looking at health facilities. People there told me that they were sick of the political crisis. I saw an old friend having dinner and he told me quite clearly and calmly that we would be done.

On Saturday, 8 November, we had a candidates' convention at the Boulevarde Hotel. Many of these candidates were soon to win seats in Parliament. Speakers were Bob Cotton, Bob Ellicott, John Carrick, John Howard and Chris Puplick. Cotton was prolix and not really to the point; Ellicott was superb; Carrick and Howard were good; Puplick was cynical; and Don Dobie was cool to me, which was too bad. Later in the day, there were functions, at one of which I was cheered to the echo by 300 Croatians.

I recorded that day that I was beginning to 'feel the Governor-General will intervene'.

The next day was Sunday, 9 November, and Jenny, Sarah, Ian and I went to Wollongong for a day with our dear friends Sue and Terry O'Malley. It was just what I needed. I recorded: 'Sun and relaxation and bridge—wives got lucky cards to trounce husbands!'

Whitlam made an address to the nation that I thought was defensive and weak. Some of the radio and television programs, I noted, 'were coming round to our view—at last'. I was able to write: 'I approach this week with a little more confidence.'

There was a strange phone call from Bill Wentworth that day giving me the name of another shadowy loans affair person. Why me? At that time, with the vanity and arrogance that go with the job, the question might not have crossed my mind. But there it was: one of the most experienced members of the Parliament and a former minister making contact with one of the newest and least experienced over a matter of great delicacy and moment. At the time I did not reflect on the strangeness of the contact, so great was my hubris; these days, I wonder. I made contact with the person and began negotiations for a meeting. He did not want another MP present but did want his lawyer. After more negotiation, we met the next day, 10 November 1975. I had John Howard with me and made an *aide memoire* of the conversation, which I signed the next day. The gentleman in question had with him a lawyer from Allen,

Allen and Hemsley. He presented for viewing a document indicating that he had played a small role in seeking funds and he made several hearsay statements about demands for part of the commission to be available for Labor Party funds. But he refused to let us hold any documents or do anything else to verify what he had said.

Earlier that day I had visited the Glebe Lands project with Chris Puplick and Misha Lajovic. This was an ambitious redevelopment of a working-class suburb in Sydney; it was done very well. We met the minister, Tom Uren, by chance during the morning. Considering the circumstances of the crisis, he was courteous and friendly.

On the evening of 10 November, I attended a meeting in Canberra of the medico-legal society in place of Bob Ellicott, who was tied up with the ongoing crisis. I told the group, based on the excellent account that Ellicott had given to our seminar two days earlier, that the Governor-General would resolve the crisis by intervening on our side. I remember quite clearly that my assertions were greeted with disbelief and amusement. The audience was almost derisory of my view in discussion time.

The Dismissal occurred the very next day. For weeks after the Dismissal, I kept meeting people who had attended that dinner—they all treated me with much greater respect! While they might have thought I had known something, that I had some inside information or foreknowledge, the truth was that I had spoken with more bluster and certainty than my firm knowledge could justify; it just happens that I was an accurate predictor of what happened the next day.

The mail at Parliament House now had some support in it for our position and our course. We now faced another scheduled three-week sitting period and the sure knowledge that the crisis had to be resolved in that time. We knew, too, that there were no second prizes—that we had gambled heavily and that we must win or lose everything. I came to Canberra that week somewhat more buoyant than I had been for weeks, somewhat sustained by favourable comment in the community, and hopeful that we could still win. In the event I was to be proven right.

8

REMEMBRANCE DAY

This was the most dramatic day in which I have played any direct part. Though I was merely a minor actor, an insignificant courtier, I was there. I was present. I played some role.

On this day all the events of previous weeks came together in one convulsive climax. On this day, the consequences of foolish and reckless ministerial actions came home to roost, the constitutional confrontation was resolved, Supply was obtained, prime minister Whitlam and opposition leader Fraser each saw in a historic confrontation the results of his respective gamble. While the crisis had begun much earlier—formally on 15 October—and while it would be finalised only at the general election of 13 December, this day was when the winning and the losing were determined decisively.

Looking back from a distance, the drama is less intense in memory than it was on the day. There is less thunder and lightning; less sense of *Gotterdammerung*. The harsh edges have gone. I remember the sweep of the events but have to search for those details that made each moment so memorable, so difficult, so frightening, so draining, so exhilarating.

Before me are the documents that bring back the day in such clear memory, which bring back so much that I had forgotten. My diary records the whole day; the journals of the Senate record the parliamentary decisions; the Hansard has the exact words spoken; the newspapers record the story; the cartoonist of that year, Larry Pickering, was able to summarise the events with the drama that only a cartoonist can bring. This day was a culmination.

The atmosphere was unreal, the emotions were white hot. This was the only time I could use that phrase accurately. We who had been part of the crisis saw events come to a climax that day. What followed was unpredictable in the morning, a matter of history by nightfall. We were stretched tight when we arrived, in despair at lunchtime, and triumphant by evening. The election on 13 December was no more than act five of a Greek tragedy, merely the acting out of the conclusion made inevitable by the events of that Remembrance Day.

Many other authors have described the crisis. Each of them has spent a lot of time on the events of 11 November, each from his or her own standpoint. Alan Reid, for example, describes where he was at each vital moment, to whom he spoke, and so on.[1] Sir John Kerr[2] does the same, as do Gough Whitlam[3] and each of the other major participants. There is no value in my repeating their accounts; there is real value in my setting out what a backbench Opposition senator was doing on this critical day, which produced a major consequence of actions of which he had been part. So this chapter will deal with what I did on that day, without apology, and in the hope that it will be read alongside the accounts of the great and significant figures whose careers were so affected by the outcomes.

As always, my diary was written up on that day or the next morning. I recorded it was 'a great and wonderful day', so it would have been written up late in the evening or early on the morning of 12 November. On Remembrance Day, I came to the Parliament from my unit—early as always—and attended a meeting of the joint parties at 8.30 am. For minor players like me, this was important as a source of information and an even more important opportunity to smell the atmosphere and test the wind. This early meeting preceded a vital meeting recorded by other writers as occurring soon after 9 am between Whitlam, Simon Crean and Fred Daly on the one hand, and Fraser, Philip Lynch and Doug Anthony on the other.

That meeting was recorded in my diary as involving an argument with Magnus Cormack and Peter Sim over the content of a press statement made the day before by John Howard. I cannot recall either what was in the press statement or why two such senior colleagues would get sufficiently upset to want to argue about it. But the episode demonstrates the extent to which we were all under enormous tension and likely to react to any irritant with unusual fierceness.

---

1   Reid (1976).
2   Kerr (1978).
3   Whitlam (1979).

8. REMEMBRANCE DAY

At the time I had, as already mentioned, a small extra task of dictating responses to some of Malcolm Fraser's heavy mail. Such a task is routinely given by leaders of the Opposition to backbench colleagues as a form of minor patronage, and as one part of efficient office management. It is not necessary for prime ministers to do the same thing, as they have public service resources available for tasks like that. So after the early party meeting, I did some of this dictation while Fraser met with Whitlam, after which the joint parties met again; it was scheduled originally for 10 am but was put off for half an hour.

This meeting served merely to heighten the tensions and the sense of crisis on what we now knew was the Day of Judgment. Malcolm asked us simply 'not to push' him, and said that 'developments were occurring'. It is indicative of the dominance of his leadership, and of the position in which we found ourselves on that day, that his request was not questioned and not pursued. How could it be? Our hopes rested with him totally. If he asked us for forbearance and time, he received both without serious question.

At 11 am we stood in the party room for the (then) traditional two minutes of silence—an unreal moment on an unreal day—and the meeting ended soon after. The Labor Caucus had met the same morning and Parliament House was awash with rumours. Soon afterwards, the House of Representatives sat and began a censure debate, which has been described in other books.

The Senate met at midday and proceeded in a desultory way with banal routine business, questions without notice and the introduction of a Bill to establish a Tertiary Education Commission. Somewhere in all this we broke for lunch, unaware of the drama being acted out at Yarralumla.

The midday news had announced the Labor Government's decision to ask the Governor-General to call an election for half the Senate on 13 December. In the Members' Bar, Labor MPs were taunting Don Cameron on our insistence that there be a double dissolution of the Parliament. I have recorded Keith Johnson as saying about 1.30 pm: 'Did you think you'd get it? You might as well have showed your arse to the moon.'

One anecdote—possibly apocryphal—concerning Paul Keating, is worth recounting here. He was sworn in as Minister for Northern Australia on 21 October, and had been a minister for only a few weeks on 11 November 1975. It is said that Whitlam, sacked before lunch, strode back into Parliament a little more than an hour later, saw Keating in the Government Lobby, still unaware of what had happened, pointed a finger at him, and thundered 'Keating, you're sacked!' The story is that the performance had a great effect.

At 2 pm the Senate reassembled for the most dramatic 24 minutes of my life. It was also the greatest failure by a government to retrieve a retrievable situation at the last moment, for had the Government not taken the course it did, we would have had the Budget held up for hours or days and Labor might yet have defeated us. It was as if Labor did all the unlikely things necessary to ensure that its ministers failed to retrieve the position in the Senate. Later in this chapter, I discuss some of the courses then open to Labor but not used because ministers did not know what the prime minister should have thought to tell them.

After we reassembled, Justin O'Byrne answered one of my questions on notice. Then a message came in to the Opposition and was passed orally down our side in something of the following form: 'Do not allow your expression to change at all, but Whitlam has been sacked, Malcolm is prime minister, and we are going to pass the Budget as quickly as we can.' Labor senators did not receive the news and we were told later that Labor members of the House of Representatives did not know until after we did.

The debate on the Tertiary Education Commission Bill was interrupted by agreement to allow the president to present again, as he had done daily, a resolution from the House of Representatives asserting that the Senate had no right to hold up the Budget, denouncing the actions of the Senate, and calling again on the Senate to pass without further delay the Appropriation Bill (No. 1) 1975/6 and the Appropriation Bill (No. 2) 1975/6.

Senator Ken Wriedt, Leader of the Government (and ignorant of the events at Yarralumla), then moved at 2.20 pm:

> That, responding to Message No. 406 of the House of Representatives again calling upon the Senate to pass without further delay the Appropriation Bill (No. 1) 1975/6 and the Appropriation Bill (No. 2) 1975/6, and responding to the Resolution of the Senate agreed to on Thursday, 6 November, on the voices and without division that the Appropriation Bills are urgent Bills, and in the public interest, so much of the Standing Orders be suspended as would prevent a question being put by the president forthwith—that the Bills be now passed—which question shall not be open to debate or amendment
>
> and I move:
>
> That the Question be now put.[4]

This is the standard motion of urgency (known in Parliament as a guillotine motion) with a closure motion (gag) attached. Ken Wriedt had moved it more in hope than expectation, just as he had moved motions like it day after day. The

---

4 Wriedt, Senator the Honourable Ken, Senate Hansard, vol. S66, 11 November 1975: 1,885.

Leader of the Opposition did not, on our behalf, raise any objection, though he opposed that motion on our behalf on previous days. I noticed that Reg Withers, sitting in his place as Leader of the Opposition opposite Wriedt, said some words. It was reported—although Alan Reid[5] has other words involved in the exchanges and his sources were renowned—that Wriedt asked Withers why we were caving in, and that Withers told him that Whitlam and the Government had been sacked. Withers had a habit of dropping laconic one-liners and Wriedt would not have known immediately how to interpret this.

But, without the benefit of briefing, Wriedt could scarcely believe his good fortune. The Opposition was caving in. The Budget would be passed. The crisis would be over. Some of his ministers could not understand what was happening and were not comfortable. Their professional political instincts screamed to them that something was wrong—but they did not know what it was.

The president then put, in quick succession, the three questions involved: first, the gag motion, and then the guillotine motion itself, and finally the consequential motion agreeing to the passage of the Appropriation Bills. They were agreed to on the voices and without dissent. Even as the questions were being passed, ministerial advisors were rushing in and trying to get to their ministers (particularly Doug McClelland) with the critical news—but all too late. Labor had failed to play its last and best card properly.

The president, still unaware, then declared: 'The sitting of the Senate is suspended until the ringing of the bells.'[6] The Senate was suspended at 2.24 pm. That Senate did not meet again as the Parliament was dissolved two hours later. The new Senate met in early 1976 with a membership determined by the election of 13 December, but it was a different Senate with a clear majority for the Liberal/Country Party Government and without Senators Cleaver Bunton or Pat Field.

For the record, the Senate was far more resistant to government legislation during these three months than during the sitting periods that had preceded it. During the period from 9 July, there were 71 government Bills introduced, of which 31 were passed by both Houses, 11 were negatived, two were laid aside in the House of Representatives, seven had consideration deferred in the Senate and 35 lapsed, still on the notice paper, at prorogation on 11 November. There were 201 non-government amendments moved and agreed to, 30 clauses of Bills negatived, three schedules negatived and 10 amendments to amendments agreed to.[7]

---

5   Reid (1976).
6   Senate Hansard, vol. S66, 11 November 1975: 1,885.
7   *Business of the Senate 11 February – 11 November 1975*, The Senate, Canberra.

Let me now explain how Labor could have won the day even at the very end. Had Whitlam thought to brief his Senate leader (Ken Wriedt), or the manager of government business in the Senate (Doug McClelland), the obvious tactic would have been to delay passage of the Budget. If this had happened, Fraser would have failed to deliver to the Governor-General one of the elements in the solution that he had been commissioned to deliver that day.

Since the Government controlled the business and a Labor president occupied the chair, delay would have been possible. Without a president willing to take the chair (or a president who suspended the Senate 'until the ringing of the bells'), or without a minister to move for their passage, the Appropriation Bills could not have passed the Senate. There was no Liberal or Country Party Senate minister until the next day. The addition of a 'gag' to the motion or urgency was a device added deliberately to truncate and prevent debate. Without it senators could have debated the proposition that the Bills be declared urgent and could have done so each for an hour.[8] In retrospect, the gag was unhelpful to Labor, and a long debate—as long as possible—would have suited Labor's tactical needs much better. Even should the debate on the Appropriation Bills have commenced (in the absence of a guillotine and gag of the type moved by Senator Wriedt), the procedures of the Senate allow for detailed examination of the Budget at second reading stage and in Committee of the Whole. Odgers sets out some other readily available ways in which the ALP could have frustrated proceedings had Labor senators known of the situation, and I make reference later to ways in which Senate practices could have been used by Labor senators.[9]

Had Labor done even some of these things, Fraser would not have been able to deliver what he promised to the Governor-General, certainly not by that afternoon when David Smith read the proclamation that dissolved the Twenty-Ninth Parliament. The Senate chamber itself would have become the crucible and Labor might have regained an initiative. Any Labor leader with the competence of Wriedt or McClelland could have strung out the proceedings while we would have required a regiment of soldiers around Parliament to protect us from angry mobs.

But Labor did none of the things available to it. That it did not is a reflection of the style and priorities, on the attitudes and values of Edward Gough Whitlam. His failure of judgment at lunchtime on Remembrance Day cost his party dearly.

---

8   In fact, the Senate Standing Orders operating then provided (SO 407B) that the motion that a Bill be declared urgent 'shall be put forthwith—no debate or amendment being allowed'. But another motion is necessary to allocate the times for the various stages of the Bill and that motion could be debated for up to one hour.
9   Odgers (1976: 69–70).

8. REMEMBRANCE DAY

We came out of the Senate about 2.30 pm. As I left the chamber, I found an elderly couple who had come into the Senate to see some of the drama that had been reported in such detail by the papers. Instead, all they had seen was low-key agreement from all sides and the suspension of the sitting! To put them into the picture, I told them that we had just passed the Budget and that Whitlam had been sacked. They were stunned! I always tell people that the Senate does dramatic things quietly; it was never better demonstrated than that afternoon.

Just as everyone can remember what he or she was doing when John Kennedy was assassinated, so everyone can remember where he or she heard the news of Whitlam's sacking. It was reported to me that the news was shouted in cafeterias and factories, that it was taken into classrooms and meetings, into offices and shops. There was further drama in the House of Representatives. But it was just that: drama. The real action, as always, takes place in the Senate, where the votes are balanced and the results less predictable. Whitlam never understood this and it was this, more than anything else, that defeated him in the end. I needed a pass to get into the House as the box reserved for senators was full of colleagues who had got into it ahead of me. Only when I heard what was happening did the full import start to sink in. Malcolm Fraser was now prime minister! Labor did him in quickly and efficiently on a motion of no confidence but it did not matter. Malcolm already had the double dissolution well in hand.

We had another meeting of the opposition parties at 3.30 pm. This time there were cheers for the new prime minister. Later in the afternoon, I was at the back of the crowd on the front steps[10] when David Smith came to read the proclamation proroguing the Twenty-Ninth Parliament and setting 13 December as the date for the general election. It was an ugly scene on the steps. There was a large crowd out in front, a lot of police and some violence of mood and action. David Smith was booed as he read the proclamation. My diary records: 'Labor rowdies turned on a poor show—Whitlam a disgrace.'

I walked back into Kings Hall with Doug Anthony and Ian Sinclair, who had been on the front steps with me. Staff of the Parliamentary Library lined the railings above and booed us. My two tough Country Party colleagues seemed less concerned by the reaction than I was. As I moved across Kings Hall, a senior parliamentary reporter who was standing quietly by the now closed main door to the Senate chamber called me over and said softly, 'They're booing you here, Senator, but Hansard's with you!' God bless him, I thought.

---

10   I am so recorded in the photograph of that occasion that was reproduced in *Good Weekend* magazine of 2 November 1985: 1.

We had a party in the Opposition Senate Party Room at 6.30 pm. By now a large crowd was gathered outside and we were hissed and booed when we appeared on our balcony. Somebody had turned on champagne for the troops. Prime Minister Malcolm Fraser was happy. John Carrick was exhausted but happy. I went back to my room and did a little more work. I drank some more alcohol and was home by 10 pm. There was a very ugly *Lateline* program on ABC TV. My diary contains a note that the ABC went overboard that day. The diary note goes on to say finally:

> Fraser has defeated Whitlam face to face. The Governor-General has issued a marvellous statement and has destroyed Whitlam. And I have been part of it all. It will sink in—to me, to each of us, and to the community. I was able to sleep well again.

9

THE ELECTION CAMPAIGN

From the moment Gough Whitlam was dismissed, the election campaign was under way. His famous appearances on the front steps of Parliament House on 11 November—once when David Smith prorogued Parliament; the other with his colleagues later that evening, to sing *Solidarity Forever*—were both early campaign activities. The election campaign lasted until the day of the general election on 13 December 1975 when, in the face of an unprecedented electoral disaster, Whitlam had finally to recognise that '*La commedia è finita*'.[1] During this time, Malcolm Fraser was prime minister, heading a caretaker government that made no new policy and no appointments. There are grey areas in knowing what is 'new' and what is the continuation of 'existing' policy; my friend John Wheeldon fired off several telegrams to the Governor-General alleging that Don Chipp had taken action that transgressed the 'caretaker' convention.

In order to present the material with some logic while at the same time avoiding the mere setting out of a series of diary entries, I will discuss the election period under thematic headings. The diary entries made each day remain the primary material and are available; however, one writes an account with the reader in mind and a straight diary record is sometimes boring and sometimes repetitive.

---

1   The last line of Pagliacci by Leoncavallo.

The Aftermath of the Dismissal

One of the less well appreciated characteristics of political life is the suddenness with which cataclysmic events occur and are concluded. These include most 'institutional' events with major impacts on the lives of individuals. On the morning of 11 November 1975, all members of the Twenty-Ninth Parliament were active participants in a life-and-death political struggle unequalled in the history of the Federation. By that evening the Parliament had been terminated, all members and senators were out, power had shifted to a new prime minister, the president and speaker had effectively been terminated as power brokers and an election campaign was under way. Many of those now out of Parliament would never return—some because they were retiring, some because they had been stripped of party endorsement, and many more because they would be defeated at the forthcoming election.

It was not unlike the situation facing players in a football grand final. All season they have worked towards this day. The press has followed each step of their journey and that press coverage has intensified as the event has come closer. In the days before the final game, it is the one subject discussed in all football circles and the players are feted and known and welcomed everywhere. After the game is over, instantly, all interest in it goes. Each player is nothing. The losers are not the only ones who feel let down; the winners do, too. The sense of let down is felt by many sportspeople after the finish of important events; it is the same for politicians in the situation in which we found ourselves on 12 November.

While Parliament itself continued to function after prorogation, it now did so on the much leaner basis of an 'out of session' structure than it had the day before, when it was fully staffed and the hub of a national conflict. All staff employed just for the duration of the sittings—cooks, waitresses, attendants—found themselves suddenly and unceremoniously out of work. Stunned and despondent Labor ministers were busy moving out of offices, archiving papers and telling ministerial staffers that they had to look for new employment.

Not only that, but the Parliament, which until then had been in the public spotlight continuously for a year, suddenly ceased to matter. The notices on the doors confirming that the Parliament was dissolved gave mute testimony to this. The public neither knew nor cared about the multiple human tragedies that had been precipitated within Parliament the day before and that would occur later when this campaign was concluded and the votes counted.

9. THE ELECTION CAMPAIGN

For us individually it was a sudden change, too. No longer were we the centre of press attention, of pressure, of importance, of interest. We were now junior campaigners in a great election—a contest, to be sure, but a different phase of the contest that had gripped the nation for almost four weeks and in which the Senate had been central to the outcome.

So it was that on 12 November I began to prepare myself for the next phase. First, I packed up and closed my flat as I would not be returning to it during the campaign. Then I came into Parliament—I had to get a taxi as the Commonwealth drivers had gone on strike, as had many others, in protest against the Dismissal. The taxi driver, however, made no secret about his delight at the Dismissal or the opportunity it gave him to vote. I had reason to talk to my solicitor and to a Canberra building society about my imminent home unit purchase; they were equally delighted.

The ABC was running a line very sympathetic to the Whitlam cause; on the other hand, the *Sydney Morning Herald* had a magnificent editorial setting out some of the issues well. Pickering had an unforgettable cartoon to finish the series he had run during the crisis.

We met as joint parties at 10 am and saw our senior colleagues leave for Government House to be sworn in as ministers in the caretaker government. We then did those things necessary to let us get out of Canberra and begin the campaign in earnest. I packed up my office, did my last Fraser dictation (which he now did as prime minister), said goodbye to Arnold Drury (Labor, South Australia), Ellis Lawrie (Country Party, Queensland), Dudley Irwin (Liberal, Victoria) and Nigel Drury (Liberal, Queensland), all of whom were retiring.

I caught the early afternoon plane to Sydney and received a splendid reception at the Ansett Lounge. At my office building in Chifley Square, Gough's photograph had already been taken down from its place of honour.

The suddenness and completeness of the change caught our selected candidates and our conferences on the hop as well. Although they had been on alert, although they knew we had been pressing for just this election, many of them were still ill prepared. I made some campaigning plans at work and was home early. Our neighbours were delighted by the outcome. I had a call from Joan Sookee, our candidate in Chifley, who was terrified by what had happened and by what it might lead to.

A week later I returned to Canberra to do some more of the settlement on the purchase of the new home unit. On this visit, I went to sign the visitors' book at Government House and was pleased to note that activities in Canberra were very much back to normal with no apparent 'maintenance of the rage', as Gough had asked for.

Personal and Family Pressure

Pressure on senators who had been part of the refusal of supply continued. Many old friends let me know throughout the campaign that they disapproved of what we had done, and that they disapproved of me for being part of it. Some of our friends and relatives made their concerns known to Jenny and not to me, which made her life more difficult. They were a damn nuisance.

Labor people who were bitter about the events did not try to hide that bitterness. It was not always easy to cope with. One example occurred when, before a dinner to honour Judge Adrian Curlewis given by the Surf Life Saving Association on 29 November, I reminded the organisers that, although I had accepted to represent the Leader of the Opposition, I was now representing the prime minister. The organisers rearranged things so that I had precedence over Bill Morrison, who represented Gough Whitlam—no longer the prime minister. The Morrisons had in previous encounters been proper and pleasant to Jenny and me, but on this occasion they cut us completely. It did not really matter as we were engaged in a war, but it is sad whenever people carry matters to those lengths.

I found, too, that I was manifesting physical signs of some of the unremitting stress. I reacted badly to this early phase of non-activity, getting a nasty and persistent bellyache, which responded to anti-ulcer medication although I did not ever have it properly investigated. The treatment worked and was simple—and I am an expert in that area of medicine anyway.

During the campaign period we still had to maintain a normal home, see the kids off to school and riding, attend to homework, and so on. Our car decided to give up the ghost during the month, so we had to rent a vehicle to keep up the work and domestic schedules. It was not always easy to keep things running. For example, there was a good Liberal literally going mad with grief over the death of his wife in a car smash and the failure of police subsequently to charge the young driver with any serious offence. In his grief, he was harassing Jenny, which made life just a bit more difficult than it was already.

At one stage we had a row. I was rushing from point to point and Jenny was bearing the brunt of a million aggressive phone calls. When I finally got home from one of the rallies, I found a nice note: she took the blame for my being angry ('I am sorry that I was so grumpy') when it was scarcely her fault at all. Added to our lack of a car, she was a saint to cope as she did.

Even the children felt the strain. We went to Wollongong for campaigning in the last week. There was heavy fog on the tollway and we were held up. I have recorded in my diary that Ian was fascinated by the fog lights. But then at the

9. THE ELECTION CAMPAIGN

Wollongong end the car that was supposed to pick us up (easily identifiable because of the candidate's decorations on it) just drove past without seeing us, and Ian began to weep. He has always been a time-conscious person and this event was too much for him. But it was quickly corrected and the tears were quickly forgotten.

The pressure got to all of us. I showed scant interpersonal tolerance when James Darby complained to me, one day while we were driving round on his fire engine, about his removal from the Werriwa Conference of the Liberal Party. My diary records that I asked him in return whether the Werriwa campaign books (from 1974) had ever been audited. This was a very aggressive response made with inside knowledge. My diary then records: 'Strained my back on the bloody fire engine.'

Then on 4 December, we had Bob Scott ring us from Newcastle, where he was working miracles, to say that he had just had a bad day. He had run into the car in front of him and now had decided to give it all up—just nine days before polling! I did my best to get him to delay a decision, which I recorded as 'immature—will cost him dearly'.

The weather was difficult, too, as one would expect in November in Australia. We had heavy rain some days and extreme heat on others. I just had to keep driving on, trying to stay fresh and looking fresh—although it was not easy. At one evening rally in a packed hall in Liverpool, we estimated that the temperature was about 40 degrees; it must have been difficult for the audience, too.

The 'Phoney War'

The first few months of World War II were quiet for the British. Germany was active elsewhere and the full fury of its assault was yet to be turned westward. This brief period of respite became known as the 'phoney war' and the phrase is appropriate for the first few days after the Dismissal.

For it was not as if everything moved suddenly into top gear as far as campaigning went. It was not as if there were suddenly rallies, meetings, campaigns and candidates needing advice and help. On the contrary, things moved up from low to high gear at what seemed to me a snail's pace. The first few days were particularly slow.

For me, there was a period of about five days when I had almost nothing to do. I cleared up a backlog of correspondence and did all the routine work that Naomi had ready for me. But I work quickly and we both had this done in no time. On Friday, 14 November, I recorded in my diary: 'I have nothing to do. No campaign. No meetings. No real work. Attending to trivia and details only.'

I even attended my normal Rotary meeting and managed to get home early, entertained my sister to lunch, attended the theatre with my wife, and attended some receptions and conferences arranged long before. One of these was a conference arranged by the Council of Social Service at which a speaker tried to link the achievement of social goals with the re-election of the Whitlam Government. I had to intervene hard to stop that line.

I found I was reading signals into everything. At a nursing home in Blakehurst where I represented the minister there was a warm reception and I felt good. On the other hand, the newspapers in that first week treated us quite roughly and I recorded for Sunday, 16 November: 'The press is not friendly. I feel depressed and unsure. We are being done in both the press and the public is uneasy and unhappy.'

It was not like this everywhere. A day earlier I had attended a meeting of Liberal workers in Chifley, a safe Labor seat in Sydney's west based around Mount Druitt and Blacktown. With just 24 hours' notice, there were 60 people who attended the meeting, planned a campaign, allocated tasks and showed some enthusiasm. This was due to the fact that we had Max and Dulcie Harrison running the show in Chifley; if we had more people like them we would be unstoppable.

I realised that we still had an election to win and that we had only a finite time in which to do it. I was worried that we were not gearing up or proceeding with an appropriate sense of urgency or with appropriate speed. Because of the slowness with which things hotted up, it was possible for me to keep seeing patients for two hours early on Mondays. I continued to see patients each week, although the number decreased as the campaigning intensified. John Lyons, our campaign manager in Chifley, had his phone cut off. The relevant department then claimed that he had never had a line on! It took some sorting out and probably involved some funny play by someone. Don Dobie reported that a bugging device had been found in his campaign rooms. Incidents like this were most common during the early 'phoney war' period but continued to occur sporadically and did not make our job easier.

9. THE ELECTION CAMPAIGN

Active Campaigning

By the morning of 17 November, the Monday after Gough Whitlam was sacked, we had some semblance of a program of activities. I was to concentrate my time particularly in Labor-held 'hard-luck' electorates, and in some marginal seats we hoped to win. Within days, I was to record that there was enormous and well-organised activity in hard-luck electorates, which was very encouraging. From that day on our phones ran hot all the time. By Monday, 24 November, my program was very crowded and required adjustments as urgent calls poured in. While I was concerned with motivating candidates and helping campaigns on the ground, I was also monitoring our national presentation continuously. Philip Lynch continued to come across unclearly and our press was mixed at best as the second week began.

What did I really do over the next four weeks? Almost everything—some of it at a measured pace, some of it frantic. There were rallies, meetings, dinners, street meetings, home meetings, lunches, school visits, flag presentations, press conferences, citizenship ceremonies, cocktail parties, instructional meetings for scrutineers, regular radio segments, private meetings with trusted advisers, looking after visiting colleagues, and so on.

There were a number of large rallies. Some of them, especially later in the campaign, were of doubtful value. Some others actually frightened me with the passion and vehemence of the audience. It was clear to me that electors were polarised more than I had ever seen, and that they were showing support for the side they had adopted just like supporters at a grand final support their football team. I recorded in my diary on 28 November about the large rally at Ashfield:

> Drove Jenny *et al*. to ballet. Then to Ashfield. Enormous crowd—hysterical—JMF [Fraser] *et al*. got a very emotional reception. It worried me by its fervour. Home by 11pm. Very tired. Lost all my notes for Saturday dinner speech.

One busy two-day period I remember very well. As recorded in my diary, it began on Friday, 21 November with Jenny and me getting a car at 5.30 am and a plane to Merimbula at 7 am. We were met there by Murray and Janet Sainsbury and by David Barton, Secretary of the Eden branch of the Liberal Party. We went down to the wharves and got a very good reception from fishermen at the co-op and the cannery. It was a very good trip down the coast, with visits to the newspapers in Eden, Bega and Bombala. I was also able to record a segment for Bega radio. We ate a hurried and public lunch at the Bega RSL Club. We were driven from Bega to Bombala at about 130 km/h by the field officer, Peter Mazengarb, who told us casually as he drove at high speed and turned to look at us while still careering along that he had suffered a coronary just six months earlier. It scared the hell out of us!

We reached Bombala late in the afternoon and were met by Peter Smith, president of the Bombala branch of the party. We did a 'soft sell' in the RSL club there to conform with the 'non-political' policy of the club—talking to foresters and truck drivers, and so on. In the evening there was a rather wasted and pointless function at the home of a local Liberal, Mrs Chirnside, a widow who made us welcome and in whose home we stayed overnight. I use the word 'wasted' only in the sense that it was a function for committed Liberals and so did little to win hearts and minds, although it might have made some money for the campaign.

The next morning, Saturday, 22 November, we made an early start from Bombala for Cooma. There was clearly much more support here for us than there had been in the previous election. Murray and Janet Sainsbury performed well: she did a street walk with Jenny. I saw an Italian supporter quietly hand a $70 donation to Patrick Litchfield, a local Liberal official.

Our charter plane had been unable to get out from Sydney so I chartered a local plane from Cooma to Nowra. When we arrived, there was no one to meet us (as had been arranged) so I conned a man into driving us into town by truck. We arrived at the rally there for the electorate of Macarthur and I made a rousing speech in support of my cousin Michael Baume. Then I went off to lunch with the group, including Bid (Brigid) Baume and the boys. Then I caught a light plane with David Connolly back to Sydney and then home. I had a rest and later set out again to two barbecues, one in Woollahra, and one at Woolaware! That evening the car was not at all good and it broke down the next day. Not surprisingly, Jenny was pooped. There were some memorable confrontations during the campaign. One occurred on 27 November, when a group of us held a street meeting outside the Billabong Hotel in Merrylands in Sydney's west. My diary records:

> Immediately trouble started. One man revved his motor bike beside our microphone to drown us out. Then 15–20 men with Labor badges began to shout and swear and harass us. Several punches were thrown, there was jostling, some drink cans were thrown, and water was poured over us. Then the microphone was torn out of the car. Ten police arrived. We carried on and gained a lot of sympathy from the (by now) large crowd. I was angry and defiant.

Another marvellous day occurred on Tuesday, 2 December, in Newcastle with Ivor Greenwood. Among the many things we did was go to BHP, where we were turned away from the main gates and then abused by busloads of workers. Television cameras were there and the story appeared across the country that evening. In the afternoon, we joined Phil Lucock for a meeting at Raymond Terrace and saw a young heckler carrying a sign 'Graziers for Gough' with subtext objecting to the 'diary [sic] subsidy'. It transpired that he was not a grazier at all. That evening we had a meeting in Newcastle in support of Liberal Party candidates, with 750 people present. It was magnificent, and the marvellous organisation was the work of Bob Scott. We finished with a party after the rally, which is recorded in my diary because a policeman tried to run off with one of our attractive workers!

On 4 December, I visited the Yeshiva College at Bondi and its charismatic leader, Rabbi Pinchas Feldman, with Jack Birney and Chris Puplick. Jack won the seat of Phillip in the election and served with us until 1983. Feldman was an amazing person. I remember well that Jenny and I were struggling to make ends meet on a senator's pay, yet this man talked me into buying for myself a Hebrew reading course for $150 that I could ill afford. Needless to say, the Yeshiva has prospered under his leadership.

The Tide Turns

By the beginning of the second week of the campaign it was clear that we were ahead in the public opinion polls. My worry was that we had been ahead at that stage in 1974 and had seen Labor storm home. This time, however, the press was concentrating increasingly on the economy rather than on the events leading to the calling of the election; this was very encouraging as we would win any sustained economic argument or any argument based on capacity to manage things well.

It had not always been so during the campaign. A poll in the last week of October showed that Labor would have won 49.2 per cent of the Senate vote Australia-wide.[2] On 12 November, Maximilian Walsh wrote in the *Australian Financial Review* of the likely outcome in the Senate that 'it is probable that the actual balance of power will be held by senators elected on tickets other than that of the Liberal and Country Parties'.[3] He was only five years early! A Gallup poll in early November indicated that Labor's electoral stocks had been rising rapidly;[4] the *National Times*[5] reported that Labor had been making a rapid recovery before the sacking but it was still behind the Coalition. Morgan Gallup polls taken serially showed Labor support was at 47 per cent in a poll taken on 8 November, but fell to 41 per cent in the week before the election. A series of McNair Anderson polls showed Labor support at 44 per cent on the weekends of 1 and 8 November, but then progressively falling to just more

---

2 *The Age*, 5 November 1975.
3 *Australian Financial Review*, 12 November 1975.
4 *The Advertiser*, 11 November 1975.
5 *National Times*, 17–22 November 1975.

than 40 per cent by the end of the campaign.[6] At lunch on 24 November, the American consul-general Norman Hannah told me that he saw the election as 'balanced'—but that is not what the polls were saying, even then.

Malcolm Fraser gave his policy speech on Thursday, 27 November, and was very well received by early commentators. At this stage, the polls showed us well ahead and drawing away with 51 per cent of the popular vote. Then we drew well (number two position) for the Senate ballot in New South Wales. The editorial writers started to go our way and I was able to record on 28 November that 'it is all starting to hang together', and on 30 November 'we are now gaining strength and momentum'.

On 2 December, Don Edgar, then reader in sociology at La Trobe University, reported that 18 per cent of voters in a Victorian electorate were still undecided in their voting intentions.[7]

On 5 December, I was eating a hurried lunch at a Chinese restaurant when the owner recognised me and showed me the afternoon papers. They predicted an enormous swing away from Labor and a majority of 51 seats.[8] I just did not believe it; but results were to confirm it all.

On the Tuesday before the election, we had a meeting for those who would scrutinise the counting of votes. There were 700 people at the meeting; I have never seen anything like it. By 6 December, a Gallup poll showed that Malcolm Fraser's approval rating in the electorate was rising in line with rising support for the Liberal and Country parties.[9]

We were now on a roll and were looking and feeling like winners. The run into election day was almost anticlimactic. Activity lessened during the last week. There can be no doubt that Whitlam's pollsters were giving him accurate and depressing news, just as ours were telling us the opposite. We had a so-so rally at Kogarah on 7 December, at which I recorded 'it is now almost too late to hold effective meetings'. But messages were getting through. My diary records that the next day in the Hunter Valley coalfields, at Kurri Kurri, a policeman produced one of our campaign pieces that had been given to him and which he had read and kept.

---

6 *The Australian*, 13 December 1975.
7 Edgar (1975).
8 Most polls at the end of the campaign were predicting a massive Coalition win. See, for example: *National Times* (8–13 December 1975); *The Age* (13 December 1975); *The Australian* (12 December 1975); *The Sun* (Sydney) (10 December 1975); *Northern Territory News* (3 December 1975).
9 *The Advertiser*, 6 December 1975.

My last campaign activity was on the Friday afternoon, just 18 hours before polling began. I went into Marrickville to help Johnathan Fowler, who was our candidate there. I have recorded 'no activity of any worth'. This is not a criticism of Johnathan; people were exhausted and were heartily sick of politics. I remember, too, that it was humid, hot and heavy—a thoroughly unpleasant afternoon. I was able to finish by going to synagogue that Friday night; it was a tiny congregation I joined as part of my own 'winding down' process.

Election Day

Election Day 1975 was 13 December. By that time I was almost exhausted but, on the day, still managed to visit polling booths in 14 different electorates, visit party headquarters and vote in Caringbah in southern Sydney. It was good news everywhere. We had booths manned well and received a good reception from voters everywhere. Luckily it was less hot than it had been during the final days of the campaign. I got home in time to take Jenny, Sarah and Ian out for an early dinner. We got home by 8.30 pm and watched some of the second cricket Test in which Australia was taking a pasting. Then on to the results.

The election results were staggering. The newspapers and polls had been right. We gained votes everywhere. John Gorton lost in the Australian Capital Territory as voters polarised to the two main parties. Whitlam, pale and tense, tired and still angry, was forced to concede, which he did as gracefully as possible. Max Harrison phoned me from Chifley three or four times and I spoke to Bob Scott in Raymond Terrace about their excellent vote. I did two segments on Wollongong radio. I finally got to bed at 1 am.

Dimensions of the Victory

The election result was shattering for Labor. It represented a complete rejection of the Labor position by the people. We gained votes everywhere, won 91 of the 127 seats in the House of Representatives and 35 Senate places. The Liberal Party could have governed alone but chose not to break the Coalition. Whether or not Australians had wanted an election, once it was forced on them they had no hesitation about how they would vote. The next day it was more or less back to normal. I did swimming pool duty like other parents at the local swimming pool and later took Sarah with me to the Lajovics' home. I noted that 'Tatjana Lajovic is so excited she is dangerous'.

If the Dismissal was a sudden end and loss of interest and public attention, the election was more so. I began the long clean-up and wondered what would be the road ahead.

10

LOOKING BACK AT THE DISMISSAL

No event in Australian political history has so stirred or excited or angered people, including people who otherwise make an effort to avoid any interest or involvement in politics. The Dismissal has been described variously as a 'coup d'état',[1] as 'a political revolution',[2] as 'a coup'[3] and so on. In the Senate, it was described by many pejorative words, including 'jackboot tactics'[4] and 'reprehensible',[5] that it 'jeopardise[d] the defence of the country'[6] and as an 'impropriety'.[7] The events of that period polarised people as has no other event I have known. It caused lasting bitterness, it entrenched a sense of injustice in the minds of a part of the Australian community—bitterness that was not resolved until Labor won again at the polls in 1983. I had not imagined, when we acted in the Senate, just how deep or prolonged would be the sense of wrong within sections of the Australian community as a result of our actions.

Many eminent constitutional lawyers have analysed the issues of legality and constitutionality raised by the events between 16 October and 11 November and, as Tom Hughes and S.E.K. Hulme set out in opinions tabled in the Senate,

---

1   *Time*, 24 November 1975: 10.
2   *The Australian*, 13 November 1975: 1.
3   Ayres (1987: 297).
4   Senate Hansard, vol. S66, 1975: 1,629.
5   Senate Hansard, vol. S66, 1975: 1,643.
6   Senate Hansard, vol. S66, 1975: 1,757.
7   Senate Hansard, vol. S66, 1975: 1,870.

have concluded, generally, that the Senate acted within its powers, as did the Governor-General.[8] It is not necessary for me to repeat or canvass their arguments. Since then there have been several questions put to the Australian people at referendum. None has sought to limit or remove any of the powers of the Senate, nor would such a referendum question succeed were it to be put.

But the issues raised by the deferral of Supply and the Dismissal go much further than merely the legality or constitutionality of what was done. They include questions of propriety, of judgment and of wisdom. There is also the question of whether Labor was robbed of its rightful chance to resist its opponents in the Senate by wrong Senate replacements—that is, whether in fact it was deprived improperly of its chance to exercise the mandate of the election of April 1974.

It is to these that I will now address some thoughts.

First, to the question of the irregular (and later forbidden) breaches of established practice associated with the replacements of Labor senators Lionel Murphy and Bert Milliner. I have no doubt that there were some notable breaches of propriety, but believe too that Labor cannot assert that it was beaten just because it was deprived of its rightful Senate numbers.

As a parliamentarian, I was upset by the behaviour of Tom Lewis in New South Wales, and outraged by that of Joh Bjelke-Petersen in Queensland, in not replacing Labor senators with the nominees of the Labor Party. In New South Wales the one-time Mayor of Albury Cleaver Bunton replaced Lionel Murphy, who went to the High Court from the Senate. Bunton described himself (as did Tom Lewis) as a 'political neuter' and he voted with the Labor Party, especially in the matters of deferral of Supply.[9] After Murphy's resignation, the Senate had made known its view that convention called for a replacement from the same party as the retiring senator and in a resolution:

> The Senate commends to the Parliament of all the States the practice which has prevailed since 1949 whereby the States, when casual vacancies have occurred, have chosen a senator from the same political party as the senator who died or resigned.[10]

Tom Lewis ignored this expression of Senate view in the choice he made.

---

8   See, for example, Odgers (1976: 58, 61 ff.), which summarises succinctly that the Senate did possess the power to act; White and Kemp (1986: 135–9).
9   See, for example: Reid (1976: 326).
10 *Journals of the Senate—56th Session*, 1975: 505.

Christopher Puplick has provided me with the following account of the response of the party organisation in New South Wales to the decision to appoint Bunton:

> When Lewis decided to appoint Bunton to the Senate (vice Murphy) there was considerable hostility within the party. A meeting was held of senior members of the State Executive, including Philip Sidney-Jones (president), Dr Peter Solomon (VP), Mr John Atwill, Sir John Pagan, (federal Executive members) and myself. It was decided to convene a special State Executive meeting at which Lewis would be asked to explain his decision. This was held at Ash Street. The meeting was attended by virtually all State Executive members. Lewis was present as was John Maddison, Minister for Justice. By agreement I spoke on behalf of the State Executive and was supported briefly by Peter Solomon. Maddison spoke at length to outline the law, precedent, and the constitutional position. Lewis then launched a tirade against me personally for my remarks and was exceptionally abusive. At the end of his tirade Jock Pagan told him he was a disgrace and owed me an apology. An even stronger rebuke was administered to him by Albert Hurley. At this point Lewis walked out. Discussion continued and State Executive resolved, without recording anything formal, that it believed that Murphy should be replaced by another Labor appointee. Sidney-Jones was instructed to convey the Executive findings to the Premier formally (John Maddison was still present) and later did so. The Executive decided not to make any formal statement on the matter. Subsequently Lewis wrote to the State Executive, noting its views and at the same time apologising to me for the nature of his remarks which he agreed had been intemperate and improper. I believe that this incident in fact commenced the breakdown in relations between the party and Tom Lewis which eventually led to his replacement by Willis.[11]

The Journals of the Senate show that on the divisions crucial to the constitutional crisis Bunton voted consistently with Labor, as did Liberal Movement Senator Steele Hall. Each of them declared on or before 15 October that he would not be a party to any move of the kind that was eventually taken.[12] To that extent the presence in the Senate of Cleaver Bunton seems not to have affected adversely efforts by the Labor Party to obtain Supply during the critical days. In short, the appointment of Bunton, however wrong it was, seems not to have altered adversely the balance of Senate numbers against Labor.

But Cleaver Bunton was not a member of the Australian Labor Party and should not have been imposed on the Senate. His appointment by the Government of New South Wales was morally wrong whatever the legal niceties might have been. Bill Snedden, then still leader of the Liberal Party, deplored his appointment and was right to do so. The will of the people in 1974, expressed at the polls, had been to elect a definite number of Labor Party senators and to establish a certain balance between parties in the Senate. By refusing to

---

11 Written document held by the author.
12 Senate Hansard, vol. S66, 15 October 1975: 1,178, 1,183.

reappoint a Labor nominee, the Lewis Government besmirched itself and acted wrongly. In its defence, it was carried along by the anti-government fervour of the times and was genuinely outraged that Lionel Murphy should have been elevated to the High Court of Australia. Tom Lewis is reported to have said: 'I am aware that tradition favours election of a member of the same party, but in the case of Senator Murphy's resignation I am not going to be bound by hidebound tradition'.[13] Looking back now, it is hard to see what the fuss was about; Lionel Murphy was a competent, qualified and respected justice.

But if the Bunton appointment was bad, the appointment of Patrick Field was outrageous. This was an appointment to replace an elected Labor senator who had died in office. To my mind now, in calmer retrospect, there could be no possible justification for doing other than appointing the nominee of the Labor Party to replace him. It is an absolute indictment of the honour and judgment of the then Country/Liberal Party Coalition Government in Queensland that it refused to send Mal Colston to Canberra, deciding instead to send a nominee of its own. The character assassination of Colston within the Queensland Parliament under privilege merely made matters worse.[14] This thoroughly discreditable appointment sickens me now, as it always sickened me. Field should neither have sought nor accepted nomination, he should not have been chosen and he most certainly should not have taken his place in an elected chamber. In the Senate during the period of the crisis one of our amendments restated the principle and the convention that senators should be replaced from the same political party.

Although arrangements were made for Field not to sit, Labor lost the vote that Colston would have brought to divisions, and we on the Liberal/Country side gained a fortuitous and vital majority. The division lists show that Field voted only twice, on 10 September, and thereafter did not vote at all. Since the lists show that 59 senators were voting subsequently, it follows that Field was not paired, that Labor was disadvantaged as a result, and that we enjoyed a majority to which we were not entitled.[15] We could, and should, have offered a pair to Labor to offset the appointment of Field.

It has often been asserted that without that fortuitous majority the non-Labor parties could not have engineered the constitutional crisis. This assertion might be convenient for Whitlam apologists and Labor propagandists, but it is not correct.

---

13   Reid (1976: 326); Oakes (1976: 143).
14   Oakes (1976: 146).
15   Senate voting lists from 10 September are contained in *Journals of the Senate—56th Session* (1975), and confirm these figures.

At all times the Liberal and Country parties together (with Michael Townley, who had now accepted the position as Liberal whip) had enough Senate votes to negate any proposition of any kind put up by the Government. During the debate on the Loan Bill in October 1975, we demonstrated that we could run and maintain a filibuster and could negative any attempt by the Government to force a vote (should it have moved the standard closure, or 'gag', motion 'that the Question be now put'). We could, and did, negate any other procedural motion that the Government might run whenever we wished to do so. We could, and did, arrange a long list of speakers on any Bill; we could and did put down long lists of questions as we did on the Loan Bill; we could encourage each senator to speak for the maximum time allowed (then one hour)[16] and could under the same standing order then move for a substantial extension of time at the end of the hour (although we could not debate that motion); we could move amendments to the main question to permit every senator to speak again to the amendment even if that senator had spoken already to the main motion.[17] So it was that I made my speech on the Loan Bill in two parts between 14 and 16[18] October and could have spoken again if needed. We could have encouraged our speakers to exercise a right of reply in closing debate on any motion they had moved.

Further, the Standing Orders of the Senate provide a number of ways in which oppositions can take over business. Some of these include debates on matters of public importance and motions of urgency;[19] motions to suspend standing orders;[20] long speakers' lists on motions of condolence; debates on the first reading of any Bill that the Senate may not amend;[21] and long debates on the committee stages of any Bill. This last is a particularly powerful weapon for any opposition since one is permitted to speak many times (as many times as one wishes) in committee.[22] Finally, Odgers has set out other means by which our numbers would have been sufficient to achieve the end we sought.[23]

In short, we could have maintained our position of deferring the Appropriation Bills in 1975 without ever voting to defer them by:

a. using every opportunity to advance our own business

---

16   Senate Standing Order 407A in force at that time.
17   Senate Standing Order 407 in force at that time.
18   Senate Hansard, vol. S66, 1975: 1,091, 1,123.
19   Senate Standing Order 64 in force at that time.
20   Senate Standing Order 448 in force at that time.
21   See Senate Standing Order 189 in force at that time, which read: 'Except as to Bills which the Senate may not amend, the Question "That this Bill be now read a First time" shall be put by the President immediately after the same has been received, and shall be determined without Amendment or Debate.'
22   Senate Standing Orders 407 and 407A in force at that time.
23   Odgers (1976: 62 ff.).

b. speaking to maximum length on every motion brought forward by the Government

c. speaking on every available first reading

d. filibustering on every second reading and in every committee stage debate

e. prolonging every second reading debate with amendments moved after most senators had spoken and at all times using our numbers to defeat any government motion of a procedural kind.

I was later the government whip for three years, between 1978 and 1980 (and deputy whip for two years before that), and have no doubt about the feasibility of the tactics outlined above.

So, it is possible to be quite definite that Labor was not beaten just because two non-Labor state governments had acted improperly in not sending Labor replacements to the Senate. Those actions were improper and unjustified and they did give us a fortuitous and unexpected advantage. They did allow us to use simpler tactics to achieve our end. But we could always have achieved our goals, albeit with much more difficulty, even had Labor senators replaced the two who left.

As a result of the actions by the Governments of New South Wales and Queensland, the people agreed in 1977 at referendum to alter the Constitution to ensure that, for ever after, a replacement in the Senate should be the nominee of the same party of the departing senator.[24] In the late 1980s, premier Robin Gray of Tasmania sought to oppose the particular choice of the Labor Party (John Devereux) as a replacement for Don Grimes, arguing that the choice of the member of the appropriate political party was one for the Parliament of the state, not for the political party concerned. He wanted a choice of nominees from the party from whom the Parliament would choose one person. No political party should accept such a situation. The position taken by Robin Gray did not, and does not, represent the wishes of the Australian people expressed in that 1977 referendum, nor does it express the spirit of that constitutional amendment.

I have explained earlier that we could still have pursued our policy of deferring Supply in the Senate had these two Labor senators been replaced 'properly', as they should have been. We had numbers sufficient to block any affirmative motion by the Government and so could have continued to deny passage of any affirmative proposition (for example, that the Budget Bills be voted on)

---

24 At a referendum on 21 May 1977, the people of Australia agreed to amend Section 15 of the Constitution to ensure that the Bunton/Field appointments could never again occur. The first senator to be elected after this amendment was Austin Lewis and we always referred to this particular amendment in the Senate as 'the Austin Lewis amendment'.

while ever our numbers held. The process would have been more difficult to initiate and maintain. Also it would have been more difficult to present and sell than the course we actually took.

Many people have asked me since 1975 whether our numbers would have continued to hold as they did for the 27 days of the crisis. I have already recorded my own disquiet early on, and it is common knowledge that Alan Missen, Don Jessop, Eric Bessell, Neville Bonner, Condor Laucke and probably others were unhappy at our use of Senate power to deny Supply to an elected government.[25] Withers had told me (and it is recorded earlier) that one of those named above was ready to crack.

There seems no doubt to me that our numbers would not have stood firm for more than another day, or two days at the outside. The pressure on senators was enormous, with highly targeted campaigns against some of us thought to be unhappy with our course and against the wives of others; I know, for example, that Barbara Jessop was under a lot of pressure in Adelaide. My own mail was enormous, with old friends assailing me with demands that I vote (or abstain) to allow for the early passage of the Appropriation Bills. Of all these doubters, Missen was the one of greatest clarity of view and experience. He was a man of courage and determination and I wonder how long it would have been before he, or one of his colleagues, would have cried 'enough'. But we will never know.[26]

The Senate stayed the course. Reg Withers and his whips did a masterly job in marshalling the senators, in stroking those who needed it, in staying close to all with doubts, and generally giving an exemplary display of the management of people. As one of those who had to be cossetted, I can say that I received a lot of invitations during that time to drink whisky with the leader.

In the foreword to this manuscript, I asserted that I was—now from a distance—relatively dispassionate about the events of which I was part in 1975. Critics might well argue that I am not dispassionate, that I have a position to protect, that I wish to 'justify' what we did and to present it in the best possible light. Such critics might like to examine my later history.

In 1987, when it was necessary, I resigned from the Shadow Cabinet over a matter of principle[27] and have never returned. For a long time I was not wanted and was not asked. Then I was invited to rejoin the front bench but declined to accept. Following that resignation in 1987, I voted for the government measure over

---

25 Oakes (1976: 155, 159); Kelly (1976: 224, 225); Reid (1976: 360).
26 Alan Missen died in 1986. See my parliamentary eulogy on his passing in part two of this volume.
27 See my daily diary from 1987.

which I had resigned,[28] crossing the floor to vote with Labor and against my colleagues for the first time in my career in the Senate. In 1988, I abstained from votes on some referendum questions; that same year I crossed the floor to vote with Labor on a resolution related to immigration, and in 1989 I abstained from voting with my party and colleagues against the Government's War Crimes Bill.

I have written and spoken out in recent years, since my perceptions became clear, on a 'liberal' rather than a 'conservative' philosophical agenda and have been an editor of the Liberal Forum Occasional Papers series as well as contributing to books produced by the Liberal Forum. My reputation is secure from these activities and I have no fear about analysing honestly the merits and weaknesses of what I did 40 years ago. If I reach a different conclusion now, it is simply that I see things with the advantage of more experience and more political wisdom. I hope any critics will accept this.

There seems to have been an inexorable movement that swept all the actors towards those cataclysmic events of late 1975. The press was interested in the possibility of Senate deferral of Supply for the entire duration of that Parliament. Questions about possible deferral were among the first thrown at Malcolm Fraser when he became Leader of the Opposition. Those questions continued almost daily. They produced their own dynamic: if the journalists and leading television interviewers continued to pursue this matter, perhaps it was a matter to which we should have been directing more serious consideration. But of course the press did not do this alone. Input from impatient and ambitious figures in the Opposition was part of the daily interaction that produces press stories and in which journalists are briefed. It was as if we backbenchers were getting briefing from ambitious leaders via the press.

There is no doubt that as a groundswell of interest in the matter increased, it was handled quite delicately within the parliamentary party. First the leadership group took a view that, according to some commentators, was heavily influenced by Country Party fears of a possible redistribution. It was then taken, not once but several times, to the Shadow Executive, which was gradually locked in. Those of us with doubts were encouraged to see Fraser individually and efforts were made to listen to each of us. By the time the matter came to the Coalition parties for approval, almost all resistance had been removed or dealt with. It was a fait accompli by the time our party room considered it formally—so much so

---

28 The measure was the Equal Employment Opportunity (Commonwealth Authorities) Bill, which became Act No. 20 of 1987. I crossed the floor together with six colleagues: Senators Robert Hill, David Macgibbon, Christopher Puplick, Baden Teague, Michael Townley and Reg Withers. Together we made up one-quarter of the Liberal Party senators.

10. LOOKING BACK AT THE DISMISSAL

that when Alan Missen objected in the party room, he was invited to withdraw (with Philip Lynch) to consider the matter further. He gave way only in the interests of collegiality.

Missen was never happy with what we did. This is well illustrated by some events in 1985, 10 years after the Dismissal. Peter Rae produced a memo that was signed by nine of us who had been part of the events. The memo read:

> OFFICE OF SENATOR PETER RAE, SENATOR FOR TASMANIA
>
> 11th November 1975
>
> Remember the day when the steadfastness of Coalition senators was rewarded.
>
> Remember the overwhelming vote of confidence given to us by the people in the ballot which followed.
>
> 11th November is the anniversary of the day when democracy prevailed—when Whitlam failed in his plan to 'smash the Senate.'
>
> To commemorate that occasion, the following, who all participated in voting in 1975, and are still in parliament, are gathering for lunch in the members' guests dining room at 12.45pm on the 11th November 1985:
>
> Senators Baume signed
> Carrick signed
> Chaney signed
> Durack signed
> Guilfoyle signed
> Jessop signed
> Missen refusal
> Rae signed
> Sheil signed
> Townley signed
> Withers signed
> and Kathy Sullivan apology

Alan Missen's refusal was typical of the man. Instead of signing Rae's missive as the rest of us did, he wrote the following message beneath the proforma document:

> Peter Rae,
>
> Although I said I would attend a luncheon, as you suggested, it was when I understood it was a reunion for those who went through the 'fires' of 1975. I now find that you are arranging a cheap function to glorify your cause.

> As you well know I regard the Opposition's conduct in Oct/November 1975 as indeed the nearest thing to wrecking democracy and I am determined to see that no such selfish venture occurs again. It has taken the Senate ten years to live down that event.
>
> In view of your invitation and particularly the terms in which it is couched, I would not be seen dead at such a function.
>
> Alan Missen

Missen then circulated an article from the *Melbourne Sun* of 9 November contrasting the giant wake to be held by the Labor Party with the 'celebration' of the Liberals—that is, the luncheon referred to above. Missen added the following note to Jessop and me only:

> This will show you the reasons why I objected so vehemently to the invitation. I do not blame Peter Rae. I do not think he would perpetrate such a dirty trick. One of the conspirators of 1975 has obviously leaked this false information.
>
> Alan Missen[29]

It is proper here to make some observations about the Senate as an organic entity, an entity separate from the people who make up its membership. During my time there I sat with some of the longest-serving senators ever. Justin O'Byrne served 34 years; Reg Wright and Ian Wood served almost 25 years each.[30] Yet each of them once was a new senator entering a functioning and powerful Senate. When each of them left, he left behind him a functioning Senate. What is more, the day after each person leaves it is as if he or she has never been there. The corporate memory is for the institution and not for the individuals who sit in it.

Each of us has to live with this knowledge of our own transience and unimportance compared with the continuity and power of the Senate itself. Some cope with this by avoiding all thought at all. They glory in their own temporal and temporary power, generally unaware of how momentary it all is. Some just put the thoughts aside as they knuckle down to the work of the day in the chamber or in one of the many senate committees. A few, however, having realised the message of history, dedicate themselves consciously to the institution—to the Senate—and become what are called 'institutional' senators. They do have a reputation that continues within the Senate itself even after they are gone. But they are few, and the price they pay is that they make the

---

29   All these documents are in the author's possession.
30   Justin O'Byrne served from 1 July 1947 to 30 June 1981; Reginald Wright and Ian Wood each served from 22 February 1950 to 30 June 1978.

'institutional' decision at the cost, too often, of advancement within their party. They often forgo advancement towards executive government because their commitment is less to the party and more to the Senate.

Even during the crisis I was aware that some of my colleagues were 'institutional'. Sadly, my appreciation of their contribution grew only with the passage of time and with increasing wisdom. During my first Parliament I was too new, too unaware and too caught up with the great power struggle into which I had been thrown.

One other question has been asked more and more as we have distanced ourselves from that turbulent time. It is whether we were wise, whether we were prudent, to act as we did when we did. Was it a premature act by impatient people? Was it unnecessary as the Government self-destructed? Why did we not wait patiently for the elected government to serve out the miserable time left to it, taking the high moral ground in the meantime? Whether or not the Senate will ever take such a course again, one matter of interest should not be overlooked. The people seemed to disapprove of what we did in the Senate to defer Supply and so force a general election. But, that having been done, the people did not hesitate to vote the Government out decisively. So we see a paradox: distaste for what we did, but an avidity to act decisively on the results of that action.

There seems little doubt in retrospect either that the Whitlam Government was damaged irretrievably by the events of 1975 or that it would be defeated soundly whenever an election was held. By waiting it would have been possible for Malcolm Fraser to have been installed with a legitimacy he was never able to achieve. His premiership was forever tainted by the events of 1975 in the eyes of a significant minority, and the question arises of whether this was either wise or necessary. But none of us realised that in 1975. None of us thought ahead clearly enough to foresee the terrible legacy that the Dismissal left in the minds of too many Australians.

Too many people either have forgotten the temper of those months or were never close enough to experience the atmosphere. It was something I had never known before and I have never met since. Events, disclosures, developments, statements burst upon us daily. Titans in the forms of the prime minister and the Leader of the Opposition seemed to be engaged in some gigantic struggle that simple backbenchers like me struggled to follow and to understand. We suffered from information and emotional overload, from unbearable tensions, from unsustainable heat, battle and smoke. We experienced more ministerial casualties than I have ever known before or since. We had media attention and comment unparalleled in my experience.

It was almost impossible to maintain a calm and studied judgment and I believe we lost our collective judgment as the weeks progressed. Some writers have concentrated on our fear of the outcome of a half-Senate election in the special circumstances of that time. In retrospect, it is clear that such an election for half the Senate would have gone heavily against the Government, just as the general election did in December 1975.

I believe now that my original reticence to defer Supply was correct and that we should not have embarked on the course we did. Not because it was illegal—for it was clearly legal and clearly within the scope of powers properly available to the Senate. Not because it was improper—for it was clearly not improper for the Senate to act as it did. My objection then, as now, was that the action was premature, foolish and unnecessary, and that the costs of acting as we did outweighed the benefits we obtained. Government with legitimacy could have been ours had we waited another year and a half at the most. There is little possibility that the Whitlam Government could have recovered the ground it had already lost; there was little likelihood that Gough Whitlam could have bested Malcolm Fraser in a head-to-head contest, and the vaunted dangers from Labor's proposed redistribution were potential advantages at best. An election held within a normal time frame would have seen a legitimate Liberal/Country Party Coalition government installed under calmer circumstances and possibly for a longer term.

Steele Hall raised these questions in a letter written to Malcolm Fraser on 1 October 1975. He urged Fraser not to take the course we eventually took, and predicted accurately some of the less pleasant consequences of any grab for power. He said:

> It would be extremely difficult to develop a popular base for your leadership in a community which contained the bitter and growing discontent of Labor supporters who believe the ballot box had lost its democratic function. Strategically, our non-Labor side of politics must surely be better served by planning to win a significant number of years of office at a normal election rather than by prejudicing the length of that office by grabbing at 16 or 17 months of Labor's remaining term.[31]

I changed my mind and agreed to the course for several reasons. First, as a freshman senator, I was dragged along by great events before I had become politically mature. Second, peer pressure on me from within the party (but not from Fraser directly) was enormous. Third, I was outraged at the serial revelations of misconduct by minister after minister. It was after the dismissal of Connor that I told Fraser finally that I was ready to support deferral of Supply and,

---

31 Quoted in Oakes (1976: 153).

having told him that, I was prepared to see it through. But now, from a vantage point 40 years on, I think that I was wrong on balance. If I was now called on to make a similar judgment it would be against deferral of Supply as we did in 1975. Not that we have a great deal to worry about there; Reg Withers told me,[32] almost at the time, that the Senate, in spite of its undoubted power, would not refuse Supply again to any government in our lifetimes. I think he was right.

---

32 Withers, Rt Hon Reginald Grieve, Personal communication with author.

SPEECHES & OTHER PRESENTATIONS

PART 1: PERSONAL PHILOSOPHIES

LIBERAL BELIEFS AND CIVIL LIBERTIES (1986)

In October 1986, I was invited to address the annual general meeting of the NSW Council for Civil Liberties in Sydney. This was before I resigned but after the Liberal Forum group had begun (too late) to fight against an emerging conservative tide. The council reprinted the address in their newsletter in March 1987.

My late father first introduced me to the Council for Civil Liberties [CCL]. He supported it strongly and supported strongly much of the work it did and the issues it pursued in the 1940s, 1950s, and 1960s.

Indeed his support was sometimes practical and important. In Don Watson's book *Brian Fitzpatrick: A radical life*, complimentary reference is made to my father in the following terms: 'the time on [radio station] 3XY was arranged by a friend with a public conscience and an advertising business, Sidney (Bill) Baume.'[1]

There are so many things which could with advantage be raised tonight. The merit of some of the burning contemporary issues—some new, some continuing. The appropriateness of some of the issue selection by the CCL. The difficult balance needed by an organisation like CCL to maintain its credibility as an impartial and issue-oriented organisation.

They are not my choice tonight. I wish to discuss not issues but values, and in particular some liberal values for which I have been taken to task and which are coming under attack from both extremes of the political spectrum.

---

1 Watson (1979).

At this point some of my own relevant values should be identified clearly. Because you are entitled to understand clearly my prejudices and values—values relevant to my political activity and relevant to my interest in this council.

My vision, my ideal, is of a society of autonomous individuals each able to make his or her own critical decisions and to determine individually those critical matters that determine her or his destiny.

I supported—and do support—the Government's recent legislation for employment equity for women, because it empowers individuals to compete more equally than has been possible in the past.

I supported—and support still—legislation to prohibit discrimination on grounds of sex, marital status, race or pregnancy, because these measures too seek to empower individuals to compete more equally and to outlaw practices which prevent them from so doing.

To the extent that conservatism as a philosophy or state corporatism now represented in power are both underpinned centrally and essentially by a belief in the status quo as regards the distribution of power, and of access to power, then I am in philosophical terms neither a conservative nor a state corporatist. Nor do extreme manifestations of so-called economic rationality hold attractions for me.

Central to my vision are pluralism and the value of tolerance. To paraphrase Harold Macmillan, who expressed it well in 1966, we do not stand and have never stood for collectivism or the destruction of private rights. We do not stand and have never stood for laissez-faire individualism or for putting the rights of the individual above his duty to his fellow men. We stand today, as we have always stood, to block the way to both these extremes and to all such extremes, and to point the way towards moderate and balanced views.

I am a philosophical liberal, an endangered species some say—wrongly— precisely because liberalism seeks to enhance the capacities of individuals, to enlarge the liberties, the rights and capacities and opportunities for individuals, to share to the maximum degree possible in the decision making about events that affect them and their lives, and not to have third parties making those decisions—even better decisions—on their behalf. To that extent my passion is ideological.

Part of my world view, part of my philosophical liberalism, and the goal of enhancing independence and individual autonomy, is even more important to me as a liberal than are the passing political crises of the moment.

And it is critical, in the society of which I dream, that two attributes are valued highly and protected jealously. They are the quality of tolerance and the acceptance of pluralism.

And why do I value tolerance?

Well, first, because I acknowledge the sovereignty of the individual in making decisions about oneself for oneself, while ever certain obligations towards others are accepted and discharged. Even if we argue about the details and limits of that proposition, the proposition itself seems to have merit.

Secondly, tolerance is valuable because on many contentious matters, we might be wrong and others might be right. Holbrook Jackson said: 'suffer fools gladly; they might be right.'[2] And Sir Arnold Lunn wrote:

> [T]he modern theory that you should always treat the religious convictions of other people with profound respect finds no support in the gospels. Mutual tolerance of religious views is the product, not of faith, but of doubt.[3]

Bertrand Russell recorded that 'a characteristic of Locke, which descended from him to the whole liberal movement, is lack of dogmatism'.[4]

And thirdly, we need tolerance in society because of the enormous dangers of any alternative course. History is replete with examples of cruelty and oppression, carried out by regimes motivated by doctrinal zeal but unwilling to accept diversity of view or practice as part of that zeal.

What concerns me today is that more and more, in more discussions, in more decisions, in more value systems, pluralism is being rejected and tolerance is criticised.

I am certainly criticised by close and old friends for being 'too tolerant', for accepting the autonomy of people and the choices they make rather than requiring them or actively desiring them to conform to one preferred set of values and priorities. Our forebears fought in past years against the absolute tyranny of the Crown. Even with the act of settlement and even into the nineteenth century ideas of democracy and the sharing of power in society left much to be desired. It is hard to remember now that while the United States wrote religious freedom into their Constitution in 1776 there was not religious tolerance within the structures of British society until a century later.

---

2   Available from: www.brainyquote.com/quotes/authors/h/Holbrook_Jackson.html.
3   Lunn (1933: 101).
4   Russell (1948: 630).

For example, Mr O'Connell, Roman Catholic, elected for County of Clare in May 1829, refused to take the oath of supremacy—so a new writ was issued.[5] Baron Lionel Nathan de Rothschild, Jewish, upon in 1850 being elected as one of the members for the City of London, took oaths of allegiance and supremacy but omitted the concluding words of the oath of abjuration 'on the true faith of a Christian', adding instead 'so help me God'[6]—he was not allowed to sit or vote but no new writ was issued as the Act did not so provide. Mr Alderman Salomons, 1851, returned for Borough of Greenwich—same process, but returned on a later day and sat in the House and voted until removed by the sergeant-at-arms. The House determined he was not able to sit or vote.[7]

It was the liberalism of the nineteenth century, the reform bills, the ending of slavery, the factory acts, the religious tolerance acts, the empowering of women, free and compulsory education—all of them promoted by liberals against the opposition of conservatives; all of them civilised society and made it more generous, more tolerant, more diverse, more interesting, richer and more democratic. We cannot do better here than look to the battle women had to achieve tolerance, to achieve opportunity, to achieve choice and fairness. That battle has been a microcosm of all the battles over centuries, of the battles which we now face and which we must fight.

Let us look just at women's battles in a few areas. Every attempt to empower women to participate in society has been opposed, and every advance has been won with difficulty. First, let us look at equal opportunity in education, vitally important because it provides a capacity for women to participate. Denied much education at all, women's attempts to enrol, to graduate, and to use education were all opposed during the nineteenth century. It was 1880 before women were permitted to graduate from Australian universities—and Adelaide was the first. Oxford and Cambridge universities resisted completely the equal recognition of women students for decades; Elizabeth Windschuttle has recorded that the theme of most opposition to women gaining full educational opportunity was that they would lose their femininity if educated and reject the role of wife and mother. In this way it was argued that education of women would lead to a breakdown of the family and so of society as a whole. It was an objection based on the desire to maintain an unequal society.

Indeed, Dean John William Burgon in a sermon at Oxford in 1884 argued that allowing women to study mathematics and natural science was 'a proposed reversal of the law of nature which is also the law of God governing woman …

---

5   Available from: en.wikipedia.org/wiki/Daniel_O'Connell.
6   Available from: en.wikipedia.org/wiki/Lionel_de_Rothschild.
7   Available from: www.jewishencycopedia.com/articles/13038-Salomons.

so far at least as women's education is concerned'. He ended the sermon with the following sentiment: 'inferior to us God made you, and inferior to the end of time you will remain.'[8]

Indeed, Cambridge University only admitted women to full honours degrees with complete equality with men in 1948. We all know of the recent and continuing inequalities in school offerings and in the different expectations and ideology of schooling for girls.

Yet there has been progress. Today women students represent 45 per cent of total higher education enrolments, but they still represent only 7 per cent of engineering undergraduates. While women represent 45 per cent of the most junior academic staff, they represent less than 3 per cent of those at professorial level and less than 5 per cent of those at the level of associate professor.

And let us consider some milestones of progress—using South Australia as a convenient example—which reveal other discrimination which has made it impossible for women to compete as equal members of the society. Women had been little more than chattels through most of the nineteenth century. In 1884 the South Australian *Married Woman's Property Act* gave women some rights to own property, and to continue to own their own property after marriage. In 1911 women were allowed to practise law, and in 1921 they were allowed to become public notaries and justices of the peace. Not until 1940 did women gain equal parental guardianship rights. South Australian women gained the right only in 1948 to have individual nationality, not necessarily the same as their husband. Not until 1965 did women gain the right to serve in juries—though they had appeared as defendants before male juries for centuries. They were still barred from serving in the public service if they married and could not buy drinks from the front bars of hotels.

And the story of the winning of electoral equality for women was equally slow. Women were given the vote in South Australia in 1894 and federally in 1902. But the Bill granting women the franchise was itself bitterly opposed by some conservatives. For example, part of the contribution of Senator Simon Fraser in the Senate in 1902 read thus:

> Woman naturally and properly clings to man. Naturally and properly, by an instinct born in her, she seeks the advice of man, and looks up to him for advice and guidance ... I say that woman should not enter into the arena of politics, the turmoil of it, and the chicanery of it. I say that if she enters into the arena of politics herself: if she is a unit, as has been contended here; if she uses her own judgment and discretion in politics, she throws away all the advantages which have been extended to her from time immemorial. I say the one thing involves

---

8   Available from: www.guardian.co.uk/books/209/sep/06/bluestocking.

the other, and were I a young woman, I would infinitely prefer the position of looking up to man as my director, my guide and adviser, to that of having the privilege, the sham privilege, of entering into politics and fighting and elbowing my own way in spite of man.[9]

His grandson, Malcolm Fraser, let me hasten to add, had very different views. In 1914, South Australian women were permitted to become municipal councillors. It was 1943, however, before a woman was elected to the Federal Parliament. Indeed, the gap between the right of women to stand for election and the successful election of a woman—more often than not a liberal—was often considerable.

May I digress and say something about my own family. My grandfather—and the grandfather of Senator Michael Baume—was Frederick Ehrenfried Baume KC MP, Liberal Member for Auckland City and then for Auckland East in the Parliament of New Zealand. He died while a Member of that Parliament in 1910.

In 1919, the first occasion on which women were permitted to offer themselves for election in New Zealand, his widow, our grandmother, Rosetta Ida Baume, an early woman university graduate and feminist, was a candidate for the Auckland seat of Parnell. She was unsuccessful.

Australia's first woman MP was Edith Cowan, elected in 1921. During her first campaign, Edith Cowan was accused of being a disgrace to women and heartlessly neglecting her husband and children. Her youngest child was then 30, and her husband was out canvassing for her.

While the issues change in detail, the themes do not alter. On the one hand, those seeking to impose conformity of action, to narrow available choices, to preach and seek to enforce orthodoxy, to limit acceptable behaviour in line with a particular form or view of society, and to control access to resources in so doing. On the other, those groups in society who welcome diversity and who tolerate difference, who value pluralism and who seek to see power with individuals rather than with organs of state or church or establishment.

And the reason that I am fearful of state corporatism, just as I am fearful of moral absolutism or of extremes of the right or the left, is that each of them works from a collective starting point—either the organic societal whole of the conservative or the competing and antagonistic classes of the socialist—and because each of

---

9 This was Senator Simon Fraser, the grandfather of Malcolm, in the early years of Federation. (Malcolm has a different view!) Fraser, S., Speech on Commonwealth Franchise Bill, Senate Hansard, no. 15, 10 April 1902: 11,558.

them seeks to accrete power at the expense of individual citizens, and to lay down what others should be doing, often in areas which are no business of the state, rather than letting them do it for themselves.

I am fearful of those who feel a passionate need to prevent homosexuals living their lives without harassment, just as I am fearful of those seeking through a variety of strategies today to achieve a monopoly in education, just as I am fearful of those of extreme views who want to gather power into sectional groups of the right or the left and away from individuals.

And I believe it is worsening. A corrupt and opportunistic State Labor administration has little regard for diversity or for individual choice. Neither do those conservatives, ever more vocal and extreme who would try, so far unsuccessfully, to hijack the non-Labor side of politics.

This council does a lonely job. It is misunderstood—sometimes it seems deliberately—by people who should know better. It was not pleasant to hear the assault on the CCL by a Premier at a gala dinner not so long ago. It is not pleasant to hear the CCL smeared with some collective taint because it has as valued members people from all strands of political belief, people not always in the mainstream of power and influence.

To your president John Marsden—congratulations on a task well done. It just shows that a liberal candidate can achieve greatness even if he doesn't win at the polls. To your volunteers go our grateful thanks, for without you the CCL could not function at all. To your committee, our gratitude. It has to be better than that committee on which Dick Klugman and I served as a kind of balanced and neatly neutered political duo, along with George Petersen, about whom neither of those adjectives are even remotely appropriate.

You are and remain the guardians of essential elements of our liberal and democratic heritage and tradition. Whatever your individual political preferences, you are, almost by definition, by your active membership in this council of civil liberties, the successors to Locke and Mill, and to classical liberal philosophy.

Your success is critical to the health and future of our liberal democracy. I wish you well as colleagues, as comrades and as friends.

THE MUD OF PREJUDICE (1989)

In April 1989, I gave this address to graduating arts students at the University of New South Wales. I had already resigned from the Opposition front bench. That I was invited was in itself a political statement by that university. The speech, arranged months before, was given during a strike by airline pilots. The Senate was sitting and I had to drive (at the last minute) from Canberra to Kensington in a rented car because there were no aeroplanes to catch.

This graduation is a recognition by this university of several things.

It is an opportunity to congratulate you individually for your persistence, your exam cunning, and your success. It is an opportunity to congratulate your spouses and your families for their part in that success.

It is an opportunity to acknowledge that this graduation day is a day of celebration and happiness.

It is an opportunity too, to welcome each of you, formally, to the community of scholars. To welcome you to the rights and to the obligations that go with membership of that community.

In the United States occasions like this one are not called graduations. They are called commencement. If words are bullets in the war of ideas then this choice of name is both deliberate and revealing. Commencement emphasises the concept of starting anew, of using the qualifications you now possess to do something new, to achieve something more, of setting out rather than of having arrived.

Each one of you has now had some months since you knew of your success and graduand status here. Most of you have moved into your own communities to work, with new standing and new status. You will continue to do so for the rest of your working lives, as contributors, as leaders, and hopefully, as exemplars.

Let us together spend a few moments on that last point. Let us think a little about just what you will be able to offer to the society that has chosen to educate you.

As graduates in Arts you have the advantage of a generalised degree. You are likely to reap the benefits it offers—the wider and extra options, the extra opportunities, and also the rather wider view of society that made graduates like you the main recruits to positions of eventual power in the greatest bureaucracies in the world. With those opportunities, however, there are extra and onerous responsibilities. You, and particularly you graduates in Arts, become the trustees of community values and the defenders of those values.

Today in Australia we find ourselves in one of those ebb phases of political life. The tide of liberalism—lower case spelling at a university occasion—is retreating before a new and different force. You will know that the ebb tide is not always attractive, for example, if one lives on Pittwater and sees that body of water at low tide. And in this ebb tide of our political times we find that the mud of prejudice is everywhere; it is not good to walk in; it clings to you; it is worse to smell; and one cannot walk in it without becoming soiled.

So it is in Australia today.

The values that in my generation were accepted as proper starting points for policy are now discarded, sneered at, and rejected. Tolerance of those of other religions, of other political persuasions, of other value systems, of other races, is no longer automatically accepted as proper or even desirable. My mail now contains more hate letters based on race or religion than ever before. The old liberal balance of rights balanced by obligations is now threatened on one side by those who call for rights but reject any idea of obligation, on the other by those prepared to deny to others rights that they claim for themselves.

Some politicians, aware of their capacity to alter the legitimacy of values, have promoted policies based on matters beyond the control of individuals—matters like the colour of their skin—instead of insisting that it is the value and worth of the person that should determine our views and our decisions. You will know that the little skirmish last year turned that issue aside, but you will also realise that it was only a temporary stay, a momentary victory.

The attack on values like tolerance, like pluralism, on our traditions of valuing and profiting from diversity, is gathering force. A creed of self and selfishness, a lack of care and concern for others, blindness to what we might be leaving to our children, are all of them present, and accepted, and even valued.

Which is where you become vital.

You are not the people you were when first you came here as undergraduates. You have had some glimpse of the history of human thought and achievement, you have shared in some of the ideas that have inspired and led societies, you have examined, analysed and understood some of the enduring values that have led humans to create a better world. You have studied philosophy. You understand history, its themes and messages. You have a love of our language and many of you have capacity in other languages too.

You are not narrow technocrats from some professional faculty as so many of us were. You are the trustees for the accumulated culture and wisdom of millennia. In this harsh time you are also, like it or not, those who must be advocates and participants in the unending battles about values and purposes and directions.

In a famous quotation, Thucydides put the following words into the mouth of Pericles as he stood over the bodies of those who had died in the defence of Athens:

> We do not think that a person who takes no part in politics is minding his own business. We think he has no business in a democracy at all.[1]

Thucydides was right. If those who can contribute choose not to do so, then the civilisation of which they are a valued part is in peril.

So today, here at your graduation, your commencement, your formal acceptance into the community of scholars, each of you must decide whether you will be a passenger or a participant, an inspiration or an incubus. You have seen the signs with the ugliness of debate and disputation in 1988.

Congratulations again on all you have done and on all that you have achieved so far. This society is now yours. You hold it in trust. This is commencement day. Your real task now lies before you, and the way in which you discharge that task will be the society you bequeath to those who follow.

---

1   Thucydides (1972: 147).

PURPOSE IN POLITICS (1990)

In May 1990, the Labor Government presented its Budget and, at the same time, an Address in Reply debate was instituted in the Senate in which a formal address was made to the Governor-General. In such a debate, senators may speak on anything they wish. In the context of the Budget that had just been brought down, I made the following remarks about purpose and politics. It was actually a speech about an important aspect of philosophical liberalism. I also spoke about evaluation.

My first task is to congratulate the mover and seconder of this Motion and to thank them for their maiden addresses.

This contribution will draw attention to the poor state of political debate in Australia. The debate today is too personal, too trivial, too technical but above all too little attention is paid to matters of purpose, of goals, objectives.

As a result people have been moving to support third parties and independents. They have been moving away from the main political parties that enjoyed their support traditionally. An independent member won a seat in a formerly safe Liberal area offering no specific policies but projecting hope, integrity, concern and involvement.

There are lessons in these voting movements. Either we move to understand them or else we will continue to see support moving to third parties and independents.

It is sad that so little of the public statements of the major political movements so far has related to the lessons of this phenomenon or to the ways in which we might seek to respond to a new and deeply felt public demand that things be done differently.

Let me return to the assertion that political debate in Australia today is too technical, too personal, too trivial and too little addressed to matters of purpose. We should be determining the strategic goals first, providing the inspiration, exciting our young, inspiring all Australians. That we do not achieve this is the greatest indictment of the current Australian polity. That too much of debate is too detailed and too technical is sadly borne out by yesterday's speech by the Governor-General.

Most people do not understand it. Most feel it does not touch them or their lives. Almost none is inspired by it. Programs are not presented in terms of goals, but in terms of activity and structure, or in terms of inputs.

Senator [John] Button came close to getting it right when he told a camera crew that it would be another expletive deleted boring speech. It need not be so. It is possible to communicate between politicians and people.

Great crises have occurred throughout this century. One characteristic of leaders during those times is that they have been able to articulate goals with which the majority of people could identify. The most recent example that comes to mind is the case of Václav Havel. This man has been chosen as the ninth President of Czechoslovakia. He is a poet. His skill is to communicate brilliantly. He communicated the aspirations of a nation crushed by dictatorship. His speech on his election was one of brilliance and passion—not one of dreary detail.

It has been said of Churchill that, in a time of greatest crisis for the United Kingdom, he made of the English language a weapon of supreme clarity and power, and used it to gather the people of his country with him in a noble common purpose. He did so without being overly specific as to details, but by being quite specific as to purpose.

We have no such common purpose in Australia today. None is offered to us by our national leaders. We are offered instead statements of inputs, of structures to be established, of things to be done. Being busy, being active, doing things, seems now to be enough for tired governments.

But one can be busy on quite ignoble things. This Government, for example, decided a few years ago to withdraw the supporting parents' benefit from a particular class of beneficiaries. The proposal saved money and disadvantaged some needy and vulnerable women and families. At no time did the Government present any logical statement of the social purposes behind its action. It did not because there was none. What it did was to meet a financial objective—to save outlays—and there was no defensible social purpose at all. On the contrary, that decision made inevitable the emergence of more latch-key children and more difficult the task of single parents wishing to be home-makers.

But that is but one example of myriad actions. While I criticise this Government for its program as we heard it yesterday, I have to say that the Labor Government, in another area, has taken action that is to its credit. It has moved the Public Service towards program budgeting and requires that the budget be presented in program terms. This means that spending is grouped under programs, that for each program there must be stated objectives, objectives which can be examined and tested and challenged and that there should be performance measures related to those objectives.

What I ask is that the same government apply to itself in what it proposes to do what it now requires of those who work for it. We must judge the speech of the Governor-General against these benchmarks.

Did the speech point the way towards a better nation? Towards a fairer future? Towards new opportunity and hope?

These tests are what are important today. Not the specific programs. Not just busyness. One can be so busy doing quite ignoble things in which there is no virtue.

So let us now look at the speech of the Governor-General. First, let us acknowledge that it is the Government's speech uttered faithfully by the Governor-General on behalf of the Prime Minister and the Ministers. So, if it is deficient in any way, the deficiency must be sheeted home to those who wrote the message, not to the man who delivered it on their behalf.

Recently I re-read Alan Reid's book *The Whitlam Venture*.[1] In it he recounts the night of the election of 13 December 1975 when Labor suffered a massive election defeat. As he left the tally room he reports that he had the following thoughts:

> As I left the tally room I wondered what that victory would mean for the future of Australia and the futures of the average, ordinary Australians of whom I was one.
>
> Australians who really did not ask for much but only for the right to work in jobs that would keep themselves and their families in reasonable comfort, for a bit of leisure, for homes that they owned and could take a pride in, for being left alone and in peace and not pushed round by government and bureaucrats; to know that they and their fellow citizens were getting a 'fair go' and that the underprivileged and vulnerable were being helped so that their lives became more bearable and their children had some opportunity to escape the harshness that their parents had known and to achieve a better life style.[2]

---

1   Reid (1976).
2   Reid (1976).

These are noble goals. They describe an Australia in which I would like to live; an Australia for the achievement of which I would fight and strive; they are purposes which promise the enrichment of the society which embraces them.

But the Labor Government has chosen not to do so. Worse than that, it has done the opposite. It has trivialised the opportunity presented by the opening of Parliament. It failed to set visionary goals; it was content to identify actions.

We have seen, not the enhancement of work opportunity but increasing evidence, now becoming apparent, of less jobs being advertised, of pessimism about future prospects for work, of longer periods out of work, of longer periods between jobs, of less jobs where they live. As for Alan Reid's goal that Australians should have jobs which would keep them and their families in reasonable comfort, Labor has a lot to answer for and a lot to explain.

Family living standards have fallen and continue to fall. We are having more trouble paying for food for our families, more trouble buying shoes and clothes for our children, and so on. Individual living standards have fallen too. It is harder to afford small luxuries, to continue today to do what we could do readily seven years ago. As for getting a home that we can own and in which we can take pride, all the movements in Australia are in the wrong direction. It is almost impossible for young people to afford homes anywhere near their parents. My son is despondent about ever being able to afford a home in Sydney at all. He is a qualified person with good earning prospects and yet he has no hope, no optimism, that he will be able to own a home in Sydney. Many more decent, caring, responsible Australians are finding it impossible to continue to pay mortgages on the homes they have acquired. More and more are losing those homes. Others are spending larger and larger parts of their income on mortgage payments swollen by record high interest rates. For most it is harder and harder to keep that home as they would wish, harder and harder to maintain it properly, harder and harder to furnish it, and harder and harder to enjoy it.

This after seven years. There is nothing in the speech to offer hope. Nothing to inspire. Nothing to lead.

As for ensuring a 'fair go' for the vulnerable (as Alan Reid sought), we should be ashamed of what we see in Australia today: more and more alienated people; more and more homeless young people; more and more people living below the poverty line; more and more giving up the struggle. More and more unmet need.

Look into people's eyes. Listen to them when they weep, when they tell you how it is, when they tell you how hard the struggle is, only then can we begin to understand. And while all this is happening to real people we have to listen to government rhetoric that seems not to understand and to government ministers who seem not to care. Harshness is all around us and increasing, so that, far from achieving what Alan Reid had sought, we see more and more people condemned to experience and continue in poverty and misery, and condemned to repeat the cycle of dependence.

This is not a new or a young government. It has had years—the best part of a wasted decade—to deliver a better life for Australians, to deliver better prospects, more opportunity.

I looked to the speech of the Governor-General for some hope and direction. For some noble goals. For a vision to lead and inspire our young. For some message to draw people back to contribute to the mainstream of politics. But I looked in vain.

There is just one phrase on the first page of a 12-page speech. Otherwise it is a technician's document—good for accountants or bankers or economists perhaps; good for technocrats who fiddle and adjust without knowing what it is they seek to do for people. Not only that but it will accelerate the flight of caring people from the main political parties to third and fourth groups and to independents who seem to identify with their needs, and hopes, and aspirations.

I would like to dedicate myself to achieving those purposes identified by Alan Reid so eloquently almost 15 years ago. To assert for individual Australians both rights and obligations. To reject those libertarians who would argue on the one hand for rights without corresponding communal obligations, and on the other to reject those socialists who would identify obligations but grant no rights to individuals, just as I reject that increasing number who would replace the government of people with the administration of things.

In order to achieve the Reid vision we must allow the energy, enterprise and vigour of Australians to be released. But we must at the same time ensure that our duties as members of a community of caring people remain committed to those principles of care and compassion, and of action to achieve good outcomes, which characterised so many administrations of my political persuasion in the past.

It is only by identifying objectives that we can see where the Government wishes to travel, where it seems to be going, where it has been, and only by identifying objectives can we judge the performance of the Government. To the extent that this or any other government continues to avoid setting noble, visionary, admirable, defensible, testable, objectives, so long will it sell short, to a lesser or greater degree, the community in which it operates, and in so doing it will continue to oversee alienation and cynicism. So long will it remain irrelevant to the problems blighting the lives of so many, and so long will it contribute to the flight of people away from the mainstream of politics.

VALEDICTORY SPEECH: THE SENATE (1990)

On 21 December 1990, I enjoyed my last day in the Senate, going from that institution to the University of New South Wales as a professor. Newspapers made gracious and positive reference to the occasion. The Senate made me honorary president for the day, so that I opened proceedings, and then the whole afternoon was taken with goodbyes from many senators. I made the following comments in what is called in Parliament a 'valedictory address'.

Many colleagues have been kind enough to be in the chamber for this small event, and to all those senators, thanks. Some other senators have been kind enough to speak, and I apologise to those who would still like to speak but I am conscious of the time and of the nearness of 3.45 pm. To you, Mr President, to the clerks, to the Hansard staff, to the committee secretaries, to the Senate officers, to the waitresses—thank you not just for what you have done this year, but for what you have done over the long period since 1974 for me personally. You have all been very kind.

I want to thank my colleagues, too, for their friendship, for their tolerance, for their collegiality and their kindness. I want to thank you, Mr President, and the Senate for the great honour you did me this morning and say how much it was appreciated. I would like to thank the attendants in this place for an event earlier this week where they made a presentation to me that moved me very much. To all who have contributed—thanks.

Valedictories while the person is alive have something of an anticipatory quality. It is the kind of occasion where only the good is remembered, where people's attributes are magnified, and where faults are conveniently forgotten. It is an important occasion for the individual—one that should occur once only and, in my case, Senator Teague, it will be once only. I will probably take the advice of some of my colleagues and not return.

However, it is an opportunity for a look back and a retrospective view of one's parliamentary career, and what one has done. On that score, let others judge. I do not care to do so. I just mention that when I was whip and we brought down the guillotine, we did not just bring down a guillotine, we brought down a guillotine with a gag attached.

But, in any case, Mr President, I came here with less understanding than I have now. I have taken part in some great events—some of them quite painful to those dear to me; and some have been mentioned today. The thing about it is that one grows in the process of moving through those events, whether it is 1975, 1987, or whatever. I have grown in terms of passion and in terms of clarity of view. I have grown because of the crises and I would not have avoided them.

This question of growth and understanding—perhaps it is the same with all honourable senators. Honourable senators should leave this place with no apologies and they should remember that senators are generally of better quality than people outside generally acknowledge even if they are not always of the quality they give themselves. There is a story about General Douglas Macarthur, to whom an apology was made by a newspaper, I think in San Francisco, in which it said that it had made the great error of underestimating him simply because he overestimated himself. That is a good story.

Perhaps honourable senators might consider that we sometimes lack a sense of historical perspective. We sometimes ignore the lessons of those who built up the Senate over 90 years since Federation. If we do forget these lessons, Mr President, we know that we are doomed to relearn them in a painful way.

Retirement from Parliament is such a matter. There are people who have been here previously who have given some very good advice about retirement. Senator the Right Honourable Reg Withers advised me, not once, but three times, and twice in writing, to get out. He made the point that those who leave voluntarily do so with much less bitterness than those whose retirement is forced on them. Dame Margaret Guilfoyle has probably told Senator Kemp the same thing. She told me that she has not missed the place once since she left. Sir Robert Cotton made a complete break when he left, after a very distinguished career here. And, of course Senator Powell, your predecessor, Senator Michael Macklin, having made his own decision, spent the next three months urging me to follow him—which I am now doing.

VALEDICTORY SPEECH: THE SENATE (1990)

Honourable senators often believe that the institution began when they arrived and that it will end when they leave, that its existence is for that brief period when honourable senators are here. Because I am leaving today, I do not have that view. Honourable senators sometimes think they are immortal and invincible. They know in an intellectual sense that they will go sometime, but that is something to be put off. The Senate only exists because they are here.

Well, in medicine we sometimes talk about the process we call denial. It is quite useful sometimes but it can be difficult if taken too far. 'Golden lads and girls who read *Cymbeline* might care to remember their inevitable association with chimneysweepers.'[1] It is the institution, Mr President, that is continuous. It is the Senate that continues; not the senators. It is the Senate that outlasts presidents, clerks, officers and senators.

Since I have arrived here, I have seen some amazing characters leave this place. Senator Justin O'Byrne was a senator for 33 years. We have only had the Senate existing for 90 years. He served for a lot of that time. Then there was Senator Sir Reginald Wright and also Senator Ian Wood, who served 27 years. Senator Douglas McClelland and Senator Peter Rae each of whom had served more than 20 years. Yet when each of them left, they were forgotten one day later: it was as if they had never been here. That is as it should be. The view of the Senate is resolutely towards the future. There is little time for any regrets or any farewell. There is almost no time for a backwards glance.

It does not matter how long honourable senators serve; their role is in helping the institution. It does not matter, Mr Clerk, how long you are here; you are but the present clerk in a line that stretches from the past into the future. It does not matter, Black Rod, how long you are here; you are the link between the black rods past and present. It is the same for all honourable senators. So I look forward, with some pleasure, to knowing who it is that my division will eventually choose to replace me and who will come here next year in my place.

I mentioned the General of the US Army Douglas Macarthur. As an old man, he returned to the US Military Academy at West Point, of which he had been commandant, to receive the highest honour that the academy could confer.[2] And he made an amazing speech—he used no notes at the age of 82. In the peroration of that speech he mentioned that wherever he was his mind would always come back to 'the corps, and the corps, and the corps'. The best testament to the service of any individual senator in this place will not be what rank he or she achieved—whether that senator was a minister, whether that senator

---

1 'Fear no more the heat of the sun; or the furious winter's rages, thou thy earthly task hast done, Home art gone and ta'en thy wages; golden lads and girls all must, as chimney sweepers come to dust.' *Cymbeline*, Act 4, Scene 2.
2 MacArthur (1964: 422 et seq.).

got into Cabinet, whether that senator did this or that. The best testament will be through his or her part in sustaining and developing the Senate itself; in contributing to the vigour of the Senate, in contributing to its procedures, to its capacities and to its role and to determining whether the senators have contributed towards the strength of the Parliament.

I remind honourable senators that a former senator, Fred Chaney, was once asked whether Parliament lacked power. Chaney's answer was that the Parliament lacks no power, what it lacks are parliamentarians to use the power it has. Each of us has a duty to think about our contribution and our role in the Parliament. I say to officers: I have set these things out so that you can know what my objectives are and if you wish to question me later we can go into performance indicators and performance standards. When Arthur William Edgar O'Shaughnessy wrote a very famous poem with the lines 'For each age is an age that is dying, and an age that is coming to birth',[3] he could have been talking about the Senate, and its progress, movement and change. I leave now, in line with the advice of Reg Withers, at a time of my own choosing, to go to a career of my own choosing—to a third career: to a position of value and worth to teach medical students in a fine university. Of course, there is sadness and loss, particularly with regards to the friendships and the company of significant people. But I go to do more work, to contribute to the education of young doctors, to lead an important school in a fine university. So, Mr President, I will not be here when you return in February, but always there will remain in my mind the Senate and the Senate and the Senate. I wish you all good fortune for your remaining time here and for the work you undertake on behalf of this institution and this nation.

Responses to the speech

> You should be proud of your years of service to the Senate, the Government and to Australia. Because of your intellect, honesty and integrity, you will leave a space in the Senate which will be hard to fill in more than the usual sense.
>
> —Murray Hanson, Parliamentary Liaison Officer, 1975–77, 1990

> When I spoke to the hundred outstanding year 11 students at the Queen Elizabeth Silver Jubilee seminar [that week] they were at pains to tell me how much they had been impressed by Senator Peter Baume who had spoken to them the day before. They drew the contrast between the impact Senator Peter Baume had on them and what they thought politicians were actually like.
>
> —Senator Janet Powell, Leader of the Australian Democrats[4]

---

3   Available from: wonderingminstrels.blogspot.com.au/1999/02/ode-arthur-o.html.
4   Senate Hansard, 21 December 1990.

VALEDICTORY SPEECH: THE SENATE (1990)

Today the spotlight is on the human face of Parliament. On the motion of Senator Bourne, a NSW Democrat, today is Professor Senator Doctor Peter Baume Day ... following a move by the President, Senator Sibraa, Senator Peter Baume will be Honorary President this morning.

Parliament is a microcosm of our society ... the members and senators reflect our strengths and our weaknesses. They come and go, often unnoticed by the community at large. However, every so often someone special comes along.

Peter Baume is such a person. He is admired and respected by the whole Parliament ... in fact, dare I say it ... He is much loved. He goes on to become Professor of Community Medicine at the University of NSW.

—Bruce Webster, ABC commentator[5]

---

5   Quoted by Senator Bob Collins, Senate Hansard, 21 December 1990: 6,359.

FAREWELL TO POLITICS (1991)

In early February 1991, a citizens' dinner was held in the Parliament of New South Wales in my honour. It was crowded and there were probably 350 people present from each of my four careers.

Mr President of the Legislative Council, Your Honours, Knights of the Realm, Ministers of the Crown and former Ministers, Parliamentary Colleagues, Former Parliamentary Colleagues, Mr Secretary of the Department of Defence, Auditor-General, Learned Professors, Medical Colleagues, Baume Irregulars, Liberal Colleagues, Family, Friends—

The many doctors here know the phrase *'angor animi'*[1] (which means a sense of impending doom) and everyone here will know that, at times like that, your life is said to pass before your eyes in seconds. So tonight much of my life passes before my eyes. There are so many friends here, from so many occupations, and so many who have been there in hard times, and so many who have travelled long distances to be here. Much of what is best in public life in Australia is assembled here tonight. That is the greatest compliment—for it is a compliment just to be associated with people like you. There are so many good friends not included. But how else could we have proceeded with the absolute limit on numbers here? Through Kevin Connolly thanks go to all the staff here and to the organisers of this occasion. They were [Philip] Ruddock, [Chris] Puplick, [Jim] Carlton, [Ron] Phillips, [Robyn] Young and [Ken] Wiener. Thank you, Mr President [Kerry Sibraa], for lending your presence to this function.

The groups here represent each significant phase of my life. There is family— wife, mothers, siblings, children, clan members and a godson. There are representatives here from school, from medical teaching, from the world

---

1   Available from: en.wikipedia.org/wiki/angor_animi.

of medical practice, from the Liberal Party, from the Baume Irregulars, from Parliament. There are representatives here from all sides, from the community, from the Jewish community, from academia, and there are many other dear personal and old friends. I would not want it otherwise for each group stands for some significant pleasures and times past, or, hopefully, some new occupation and activity still ahead. For each phase of my life has meant new learning and new understanding.

It would not have been possible to be in Parliament for almost 17 years without the support of a wonderful extended family. [My wife] Jenny says, and I agree, that the support and encouragement of our children, our siblings, our mothers, all our family, have made much of my time in public life possible. I thank them. The best and most fearsome drawing of a whip was that done for me by Ian Baume in 1979.

Let me look back on my time in medicine. An honourable profession. It was a good basis for public life. There are classmates from the Golden Year, and some of our teachers, here tonight. There were so many past colleagues with whom I have fought the forces of darkness—Lindsay Thompson will remember our joust with Bruce Shepherd in Canberra a few years ago. There are honourable people like Godfrey Douglas, who suffered so much in the AMA [Australian Medical Association] for being decent.

Let me look back at political life. There were [Sir John] Carrick and [Ian] Macphee and so many others. In the Liberal Party Room in 1974, party colleagues included John Gorton, Don Chipp, Bill Snedden, Neville Bonner, Ian Macphee and Bob Ellicott. All of us are now gone from that party room—to the pleasure of some of a new and harsher breed. [Paul] McLean, [Ted] Pickering, Lindley and I were all officers in the same reserve regiment at the same time and Max Willis was later commanding officer of the same regiment.

Fred Chaney and I did so many things together. I followed him in several positions and we shared some battles together in years past—Aboriginal land rights, for example.

During time of success, I was superbly served. Many staff have already been mentioned by name. Lady Violet Braddon once wrote to me and warned me not to employ Puplick—she was wrong there. There are also some superb officers, many of whom have written personally. But it is a real pleasure tonight to see Tony Ayers, John Taylor and Kevin Martin. Ayers will remember a Christmas Day when Aboriginals demonstrated at Nareen and Bill Gray will remember one late evening call by me answered by his wife, Dawn, who said, 'It must be the dunny man'.

FAREWELL TO POLITICS (1991)

It is instructive to look back on my time as an academic—first in Sydney, then in the UK and the USA, later at Cumberland CAE and the ANU. Now there is a chance to go to UNSW as a teacher to work with colleagues like Ian Webster and Fred Ehrlich. I must mention my patron, Doug Piper, and a genius—a quiet genius—named Wilson Corlis.

At the last Queen Elizabeth National Capital Seminar in Canberra, 100 wonderful year 11 students discussed their future and their wish to be involved in decisions about their future. Their passionate concern raises for us all the question, 'Why get involved at all?' That question might be put to the younger people here tonight. Why take part? Why not stay at home? The answer is that someone is going to get involved to lead and run the country. Why should it not be you? What went wrong in the 1930s, in part, was that bad people took over the task of leading in Germany and led us all to the precipice. It raises other questions about the role of people in public life at all and rests on a belief in free will—at least a certain amount. It is a belief that you and I can make a difference; Vicki [Bourne] and Paul [McLean] and Elizabeth [Kirkby] will recall an Australian Democrat election slogan that picked this up. The Liberal Party, in earlier, vibrant, less instrumental days, was built on this belief. The involvement of the young rests too on values, on confidence that you can help to express those values, that you will be heard, that people care, and on optimism about what is possible.

My values derived from the late nineteenth century and include a belief in the equality of people, in measures to empower people, in the removal of barriers that held people back. John Gorton was reported in a recent *Bulletin* as saying that, as a result of his experiences in the Great Depression:

> I then had the idea, and still have, that it is ridiculous to run a country on the basis that it doesn't matter what you do to large numbers of men as long as you keep the economy running. You can't do that. You don't make men and women the scapegoats for an economy that's not running.

His sentiments are just about right. Many of us hope that the Liberal Party listens and responds to what he has said.

Certainly, we reward people in politics—promotion, position, flattery, honour; but the pursuit of reward is not sufficient purpose to be part of it all. We should be driven by our vision of what is needed and of how we can assist in achieving that. And we should know when we enter that we will leave one day—like Carrick and Syd Einfeld and [Bob] Ellicott and Freeman and Joel and Davis and [Misha] Lajovic have done. I have left at a time and for a purpose that I have chosen.

Some ask, 'Do I leave with bitterness about the direction of politics in Australia today?' Not at all. There are cycles in Australian politics like the cycles Arthur Schlesinger describes for the USA.[2] Today's sterile and selfish environment will give way—perhaps the young here tonight are the ones who will help John Hewson and Robert Hill make it happen. Perhaps you will give successful expression to classical liberal values of individual liberty, to empowerment and to opportunity. Perhaps you will give successful expression to our belief that change is desirable and inevitable—as did Puplick and Macphee and John Maddison. Perhaps you will give successful expression to our optimism in spite of the present situation—to our hope for a more caring polity, to a more liberal and less libertarian balance of views. Perhaps you will give successful expression to views I hold.

You are my future and my hope. I do not invite you to participate. I lay it on you as an obligation. As John McRae wrote of the Great War:

> Take up our quarrel with the foe,
> To you from failing hands we throw
> The torch; be yours to hold it high.
> If ye break faith with we who die
> We shall not sleep, though poppies grow in Flanders fields.[3]

Of course we are only politically dead—but the message is clear. Go for it—for all our sakes.

I will remain the same person whatever the public persona I take on. That person will continue to value the friendship of each one of you. From Peter Baume politician, farewell. Thank you all for the honour you have done us at this dinner. Thank you all.

---

2 Schlesinger (1999).
3 MacCrae (1919: 3).

PHILOSOPHICAL LIBERALISM: PATRON'S ADDRESS TO THE YOUNG LIBERAL MOVEMENT (1994)

In August 1984, I became Patron of the Young Liberal Movement. This was a rather political statement by that political body as I was identified then as a philosophical liberal and was therefore out of step with the more conservative people running the Liberal Party of Australia. I had previously described myself as a 'political warrior'.

Tonight you have honoured not just a person but also a system of belief. To be your patron is important. You will not be tainted by association with this political warrior and your gift will not become an albatross around your collective necks.

Our liberalism is the belief that came to us from Alfred Deakin.[1] Refined by nineteenth-century philosophers, it is a system of belief that recognises our obligations to those around us and to a wider community, which accepts obligations along with rights, and which contributes to, as well as takes from, its society.

It follows that we will never reject people because of things over which they have no control, like race, or religion, or skin colour. We will give help because we recognise that some of those in society need our help, and that others in society will succeed only because of help we give, and that everyone should enjoy a fair electoral system, an independent judiciary, and protection from abuse by governments.

---

1   Available from: en.wikipedia.org/wiki/Alfred_Deakin.

We believe in fair elections.

We believe in action against racial discrimination.

We believe in a fair and adequate system of taxation.

We believe in protection against exploitation.

We believe in a vibrant and relevant public sector alongside a vibrant and honourable private sector.

It is sad that our views are not shared by all in our party or in rogue parties of protest that, alas, are popular now. That some are libertarians is a throwback to an earlier and less generous time. That some are conservatives is accepted.

But we are different. We are liberals.

We are sorry that few in mainstream Australian politics today seem to identify with our values and our needs. But that is how it seems to be. Our task is sacred and continuing. Not least it is to keep a light burning in troublesome times. We are as entitled to a view as is anyone else.

Thank you for your vote of confidence. Thank you for attending this function. Thank you for your personal support. But most of all, thank you for being liberals and for keeping the faith in this harsh and ungenerous time.

LIBERALISM AND ROBERT NESTDALE: A MEMORIAL ORATION (1994)

Robert Nestdale was a prominent Young Liberal (he was state and federal president) who later headed up the United Nations Children's Fund (UNICEF) in Australia. He was a personal friend. He died tragically in his young years. The Young Liberal Movement decided to institute an annual oration in his honour and a memorial library was established.

Two weeks before he died, Robert Nestdale came to our home for lunch. He was painfully thin, was dressed immaculately in a crisp white linen suit and was his urbane, civilised and gentle self. The other guests were shocked and unnerved by the fact of a person, obviously very ill, being at table. During lunch, my wife suggested that he lie down for a rest. So Robert had a rest, then came back to join us, and was driven home, after lunch, by another guest. We never saw him alive again.

We did attend the memorial service in St Stephen's Church where tributes were read from around the world, when a former prime minister, ministers of the Crown and close friends joined together to mourn the loss of our friend. And, in the Senate that week, Sue Knowles wept as she spoke of her friendship with Robert.

How wonderful that the Liberal Party of which Robert was a liberal member, should honour him with a library and a memorial oration. His work was substantial and significant; his endeavours for UNICEF were notable, and his loss diminished us all.

A DISSIDENT LIBERAL

To be allowed to deliver this oration is to be permitted to remember Robert, to identify with the values he always espoused, and to speak of something which is important to the orator. Thank you for the invitation. It is welcome and appreciated.

Liberalism, as practised by the Liberal Party of Australia, has meant different things to different people. To its opponents, the Liberal Party means only conservatism—they talk only of the conservatives with curling lip—but they are wrong. Some people are natural conservatives; some people are natural libertarians. Each of these strands has a coherent philosophy—but not one with which philosophical liberals like Robert Nestdale ever felt comfortable.

For the philosophical liberal, the individual is the focus, the individual is the basic unit and it is to the effects on individual people that philosophical liberals look to see the consequences of any proposal. So liberals welcomed measures, and continue to welcome measures, which empower people. Free public education empowered young people. Extension of the franchise empowered adults. Home ownership and income support empowered families. Anti-discrimination legislation empowered people otherwise powerless, consumer protection legislation gave power to consumers against corporations that are sometimes arrogant, legislation to remove gender bias empowered women, extension of Aboriginal rights and opportunity empowered the most poor and most dispossessed Aboriginal Australians, provisions of aged pensions and aged persons services empowered those who are elderly and often poor and powerless.

Each is in the liberal tradition. Each has been supported by philosophical liberals. Each has been opposed by conservatives and most have been opposed by libertarians. The opposition has sometimes been foolish, shrill, prolonged, mindless, and extreme.

The Federal Parliamentary Liberal Party has, in times past, been a natural home for philosophical liberals. In times past, it has allowed for the expression of liberal views. When, last month on television, John Gorton said that, when Prime Minister, he was a liberal and not a conservative, he was identifying the philosophy from which he came. He was—is—a wonderful man with large and generous views, with a broad vision of what our society might be. He was, arguably, the best thing the party had going for it—and it rejected him when put to the test by moralists, pragmatists and conservatives.

While ever the Federal Parliamentary Party was the party of Deakin, or contained within its parliamentary party what Patrick Weller has called 'Deakinite wets', it appealed to young women and young men. While ever the Federal Parliamentary Party believed in measures to increase individual power, it appealed to thinking men and women. While the party continued to deliver liberal outcomes—as it did during the 1980s—it remained relevant to middle Australia.

That it seems to support these things not so readily today is unwelcome. What is happening now is an undiluted conservative hegemony. It is an aberration, a denial of what the party has been about at its best and at its most successful. And there is no sign that the federal party is changing, is learning, is moving, or is adjusting to what would make liberal members of the community want to support it.

That no one in the Federal Parliamentary Party would welcome the principles behind the Mabo decision in a way that could be seen and heard is a pity. If what appeared publicly did not represent the breadth of the party views, that is still how the public saw it. That the party which abolished the White Australia Policy officially in the 1970s was unwilling in the 1980s to support a motion in Parliament decrying racially based immigration was a pity. If the party was not really a party of racists manqué, this is not how it came across publicly. That the Federal Parliamentary Party has opposed equal employment opportunity [EEO] for women and all anti-discrimination legislation is a pity. If the party is not really against EEO, the principles of EEO, and the rights of women, this is still how it comes across.

No-one should be surprised that so many young people hold their noses when they think of our once great party at federal level.

The Young Liberal Movement might be the largest youth political group in the nation, but its membership is still just a small fraction of the numbers of young people—and the majority of the young vote for other parties. Many of the young people I talk to are interested in jobs, in opportunity, in education, in the environment. They are *not* interested in economic management, in interest rates, in mortgages, and so on. If the only people speaking for the Federal Parliamentary Liberal Party of Australia continue to be those with complicated economic messages or else grim-faced harbingers of sacrifice and hard times, if we do not present the face of hope and opportunity in terms with which the young identify, then do not be surprised if young Australians continue to desert us in droves.

What is more, the way people vote in the first couple of times they get the chance tends to be the way they continue to vote thereafter. The Liberal Party federally will dispense with the vote of young people at its peril; it may lose that vote forever.

We have a proud tradition of caring about individuals. We have a record of legislative achievement. We have a proud tradition of moving to protect the environment, of overturning the White Australia Policy, of assisting women, of assisting Aborigines, of providing necessary income support and industrial reform.

We have forgotten that tradition in recent years. We have allowed a very different perception to be projected publicly. We are seen as the racist, chauvinistic, sectional interest, development at all costs, accountant-driven, heartless party.

Political parties have a life cycle. Menzies' creation—his child—had a vigorous youth, and many original members as well as some of his successors were philosophical liberals willing to join his party of hope and opportunity.

At state level, it is very different. Many of the most positive expressions of faith come from state Liberal leaders; the most eloquent testaments about liberalism come from the Greiners and Faheys. They remain vigorous and relevant. Their governments are successful. The party holds government in five states because it has identified with the people of those states.

Parties, like governments, also have an old age. You can tell when a government is old by the fact that inspiration goes and the ministers become managers, and nothing else. Parties may show different signs of ageing. In the case of the Liberal Party, ageing is manifested in several ways. First, the membership is dropping. Second, the membership is older and tireder. Third, philosophical hegemony becomes more important than the accommodation of interests with the result, in the case of the Liberal Party of Australia, that it is no longer multi-stranded. Fourth, there is little inspirational input, or input of intellectual substance. It is right in opposition to oppose and criticise—but only as one of the necessary tasks. As a woman once said, 'You have said what you are against. But what are you for?' And it is no good having vague and banal goals; they will excite no-one.

The classical liberal prescription of caring for people is still relevant. Some of the problems have changed with time, but the need to empower people has not disappeared.

We have nearly a million people wanting employment. What has the party said recently about those aspirations or about empowering those people?

We have tens of thousands turned away from tertiary education each year—and all the party promises is more cuts to be borne by students. How long is it since the empowerment of those wanting to improve themselves was part of our message?

We have tens of thousands of people waiting for elective surgery in public hospitals and how long is it since we have said anything about helping those people?

We have tens of thousands of young couples unable to obtain decent accommodation in which to raise the next generation. And how long is it since we as a party have talked about empowering them?

We have Aboriginal Australians living still in appalling circumstances and without hope for a future. What have we said about empowering them recently?

We have tens of thousands with disability sitting at home watching daytime television because there is no better alternative. What have we said lately about empowering them?

We have old Australians who cannot get aged care services or aged care accommodation or community care programs. What have we said about empowering them?

People support political movements out of self-interest or because the vision that the movement projects appeals to them for their children. This party federally has stopped appealing to the highest, the noblest instincts of voters. It has suffered the consequences and will continue to be a minority for as long as this continues.

Let us begin to speak for Australians, for all Australians. Let us become, once again, the party of hope, the party of the future. Let us articulate the dreams of people, and let us be a vehicle by which those dreams can come true.

Robert Nestdale was heartbroken at what he saw happening to a political movement which he had loved, and into which he had poured much of himself. For his sake, for his memory, if for no other reason, we must find ways of communicating again with mainstream Australia. Our elected leaders—with a few notable exceptions—have failed dismally at this task. For our party and our nation, we deserve better.

LIBERALISM DISCARDED (2004)

In 2004, I was invited to speak to a group in an inner Sydney hotel where politics was discussed regularly. I chose to talk about liberal roots and central liberal beliefs.

Three points of history are relevant and necessary. Bear with me, please.

First, my grandfather was a Liberal member of the Parliament of New Zealand. His opponents were the conservatives. He was elected as a Liberal and was opposed, in the electorate, and in the Parliament, by the conservatives. His beliefs and his traditions have come down to me—by serendipity.

Second, one of our early prime ministers was a liberal exemplar. His name was Alfred Deakin. Some of his disciples today are called, unflatteringly, by neo-Thatcherites, 'Deakinite wets'.

The third piece of history: in 1944, in Albury, Robert Menzies brought together all non-Labor parties, at a time when the non-Labor side of politics was split and in disarray. The Liberal Party of Australia was the result. The Country Party, later the National Party, refused to join. It is a more conservative party and its refusal to join was true to its traditions.

But there is no history of the Liberal Party as we know it before 1944. The Liberal Party then, because of the melding of elements, was a mixture of conservatives and liberals. In 1970 the party was still a mixture. It was possible to join it and to be a liberal and to put liberal positions publicly.

Malcolm Fraser was the prime minister who made me a minister. He was not then a conservative and is not now. Perceptions of him were wrong. He never let me down as Minister for Aboriginal Affairs. What you see of him now is how he was then.

In the 1980s, under John Howard, an avowed conservative, the Liberal Party of Australia became a conservative party, increasingly, and liberals were no longer welcome. Now, there is nothing intrinsically wrong with being conservative. Of course, there is nothing right about it either. But a conservative party is a different party. It is not my party. It is the party my grandfather opposed.

Liberals introduced, or supported, initiatives like land rights, sex discrimination legislation, equal employment opportunity for women, national parks, publicly funded education, generous social services, benefits for veterans, workers' compensation.

To be a liberal is of long tradition. Liberalism is the belief of T.H. Green, of Alfred Deakin, of so many.

Liberalism is a philosophy no longer present, or welcome, in Australia. Those who are liberals have no party today.

What exists in Canberra is a conservative party with a conservative prime minister. It is called the Liberal Party of Australia—but it is not a liberal party.

Some former liberals have become able to serve in the present government. Indeed, some of them seem to take harsh and compliant stands when previously they reacted differently.

Those few liberals who remain in the community keep the flame alive and wait. Let us note that there *are* a few liberals still in Parliament in Canberra. But preselection success is difficult for them in an increasingly conservative party, and some of them are not now taking the stands that they might have taken a couple of decades ago.

The Labor Party is too conservative for me today—it, for example, supports the present war in Iraq.

The Liberal Party of Australia is much too conservative for me. And being conservative does not entitle anyone to lie, or cheat, or not to resign when resignation is called for.

We—people like me, now disenfranchised—see a conservative polity, and wait. Our day will come again. That is our belief.

CARING FOR PEOPLE (YEAR UNKNOWN)

This is the most unusual of all the speeches in this book. The text of the speech is clear and liberal, but neither the date nor the name of the particular conference is given. The speech, however, is important as it sets out some important philosophical beliefs of mine. It becomes clear just how important medical training has been to my views and beliefs.

The title of this address is 'Caring for People'. You may find it an odd title. You may wonder what relevance it has, or could possibly have, to life at the end of the twentieth century. Well, let me explain.

I am a medical practitioner by basic training, a physician by professional training, a practitioner of the art of medicine at one time, a politician for a period, a doctor by academic training and a teacher today. As an author has written in a recent book: 'Medicine has lost the plot.' That is really what this talk is about. How medicine has lost the plot. How too many people get poorer treatment today than they need to get. How more and more people are turning to alternative medicine, to alternatives of any kind. In fact, how they are turning away from orthodox doctoring.

One could well ask why. Why is this happening? Why are people so unhappy? Why are they choosing to use net income, without subsidy or favourable tax treatment, in seeking care for themselves from more expensive alternatives in preference to subsidised care from registered medical practitioners? Why are people so ready to criticise orthodox practitioners when we deliver so much more in the way of diagnosis and treatment than we ever did before?

To answer that, and other, questions one needs to look briefly at the history of medicine and medical science.

In the beginning, many centuries ago, terrible things happened to people. They still happen—but less frequently in the rich countries. First, everyone dies. No-one has solved that problem (although some modern practitioners pretend they have). Droughts, famines and floods occurred. Children suffered and became sick. Injuries and disability occurred. Pain and suffering abounded. Life was short and brutish. Nature was 'red of tooth and claw',[1] not benign as some would have us believe.

Even today terrible things happen. Anyone here might well read the account by John Cawte of the death of an innocent child from box jellyfish stings in Arnhem Land and explain to me the justice or degree of divine intervention in that tragedy. Genocide continues to occur in our world today. There is a dreadful drought in Papua New Guinea now. North Korea has famine. The people of Rwanda are still too frightened to return home. Bosnia is still in chaos. And so on. Those permitted to enjoy a placid and serene life are a minority—and a fortunate minority too. Equally, those with access to Western medicine are a minority too; the majority of the world's people use other forms of care that probably deliver some of the benefits people enjoy here.

So people invented magic and then religion. The first explained events as the result of magical interventions, both malign and beneficial; the second sought to explain otherwise inexplicable things by reference to higher powers with special virtues, special ability to comprehend and special ability to act. Early on there was polytheism, later there was monotheism, and lately there has been monotheism with the divinity divided into three. We have eschewed the worship of idols and images—or have we? Anyhow, later still there emerged science. It seems that what makes science different is that scientific propositions are disprovable—they can be proved wrong. So the test of Einstein's great theories of relativity had to await a singular cosmological event that tested whether light rays were bent as his theories predicted. So far, those theories have not been disproved—and so they hold sway. But they will continue to be contested.

Thomas Kuhn[2] has extended the disprovability idea (which, incidentally is associated with the name of Karl Popper)[3] and developed a satisfying theory of scientific revolutions. What he has said, simply, is that evidence about a system of belief—called here a paradigm (although that word means an example)—accumulates until some inconsistent observations set people thinking. This is what happened with Newtonian physics in the nineteenth century. A period of instability ensues and eventually there is a 'revolution' in which a new

---

1   Tennyson (1849: Canto 56).
2   Kuhn (1962).
3   Available from: en.wikipedia.org/wiki/Karl_Popper.

paradigm appears, to be tested and massaged and added to until it, in turn, is overtaken. So no paradigm is final. Each is a way station along a never-ending road to truth.

Sometimes the flawed paradigms are quite useful—for example, one can rise into the air in an aeroplane and get from Perth to London using Newtonian physics and nothing else. So, even though we know that Einstein rules today, we can still go a long way with Newton.

Using Kuhn's ideas, one can understand how Galenic[4] medicine and Ptolemaic[5] cosmology were tossed aside—at the right moment and by the genius who appeared at the right time (although the story of the overthrow of Galenic belief involved several geniuses and both examples involved foolish rearguard opposition from the Church).

At this stage we have to consider René Descartes[6] briefly. Among other things, he was the originator of reductionism and of certain dualities that have pushed medicine into an imbalance. Reductionism is the movement to consider small and discrete problems sequentially and to consider them, moreover, separate from any greater whole of which they are a part. It has been a powerful tool that has allowed scientists to isolate problems and to solve many of them.

So the twentieth century has been an age of science. We have understanding of medical science that those living one hundred years ago did not dream of. Let us emphasise that: we are richer intellectually, and more comfortable, as a result of the use of reductionism in science.

But it is the other legacy of René Descartes that has led us astray even more. He proposed a duality of body and soul for philosophical reasons but that duality has dominated medical thinking ever since. It was Descartes who really introduced the concept of the body as a machine to be fixed—a machine that was potentially renewable and immortal.

The result has been that medical scientists have concentrated more and more on the body and less and less on the soul. If we want a pendulum to be centred then we have to say that the pendulum swing today between body and soul is too far in the direction of body and not far enough in the direction of soul.

So what does all this mean?

Where are we today? Why are people unhappy in a world where we can understand more, do more, help more, and intervene more effectively?

---

4   Claudius Galen. Available from: en.wikipedia.org/wiki/Galen.
5   Claudius Ptolemy. Available from: en.wikipedia.org/wiki/Ptolemy.
6   René Descartes. Available from: en.wikipedia.org/wiki/RenéDescartes.

Today, many orthodox practitioners have forgotten that people are their business. Too many concentrate on the detection and treatment of disease, instead of on the care of people. Too many concentrate on medical science when that is only relevant if it helps us to understand the people we see. If about 80 per cent of all illnesses are self-limited then surely our tasks include identifying the other 20 per cent efficiently, reassuring people effectively, and encouraging people to use what modalities of caring they wish for the 80 per cent of self-limited conditions. We should be expert at symptom relief and at the detection and treatment of distress and suffering.

One enlightened practitioner has redefined 'patients' as 'temporarily dependent people'; this alters how one thinks about another human being in need and helps one to become more relevant and more caring towards another person.

Let me tell you a story now. Recently, in a class for advanced students, an experienced counsellor was making her obligatory oral presentation. She chose to recount how her medically qualified father had suffered a stroke that left him aphasic—he could not speak—but able to hear and understand. The specialists attending him had come to the room and spoken to her—not to him. They had set out clearly the diagnosis and the poor prognosis to her in front of her father. At this point, the student wept and continued to weep during the rest of her presentation. At the end, I asked her how much she recalled about the diagnosis, taxonomy and outlook of stroke. 'Very little,' she replied. 'I am not medically qualified.' Then I asked her what she remembered about the conversation with the specialists. 'Every word,' she replied. You will probably agree that no-one should be treated like that. But they are.

Let me tell you another story. It concerns my late mother-in-law, a gracious and beloved woman who was my friend. She was dying in hospital when the specialist visited. He spoke to me about her condition and about the treatment and the prospects. The old lady was polite and she asked my wife what they were saying. Jenny, anxious to settle her mother, said: 'It's all right, Mum. They are speaking about you, not to you.' The specialist blushed and I felt sorry for him. But this was real life—this is what was happening.

The concentration of modern medicine has been on disease. Students are taught about diseases, about the detection of diseases, about the treatment of diseases. They are taught little about the care of people, about the needs of people or about how to deal with people.

The University of Tasmania has acted unusually in making an assessment task the passing on of bad news to a patient or to the relatives of a patient. This should be a basic skill of any practitioner, but it is not taught in most medical schools.

It is instructive to read a novel called *The House of God*[7] to realise that the same thing was happening in the United States (in Boston actually) 20 years ago; I am assured that things are worse, if anything, now.

Disease is tidy. It is what students want. It confers a kind of mastery over information, which students like. The descriptions of disease are exact—even if classical examples are rare. The textbooks are definite and clear—even if they are sometimes wrong. For example, a textbook published 15 years before I graduated contained a treatment for acute ulcerative colitis that would have killed my patients.

Compared with disease, people are untidy. They often have complicated and unclassifiable problems. Their needs sometimes do not match the training that practitioners have received. They sometimes use wrong words, or describe symptoms in flowery or unusual ways, or use words like 'system' or 'shock' in ways different from their medically trained interlocutors.

When we teach about people, our students become quite hostile. For them, it is disease they are on about, disease about which they wish to acquire current knowledge. It is not that they have no interest in people; it is just that the examination systems give them no marks for displaying knowledge about people. But worst of all, sometimes the problems that people bring to medical practitioners are ignored as the qualified person looks for disease as he or she has been trained to do. The patient may have little interest in any disease, except as it bears on the problems they have brought to the practitioner. It is this failure to respond to the concerns of the patient that is the cause of so much unhappiness, and resentment, and bitterness.

But it is not the only cause of unhappiness.

Another story, reported by a colleague, is instructive.

> Earlier this year I went with a friend, Marion, to see a doctor. She had been experiencing headaches and indications of a growth, possibly a brain tumour, in the centre of her brain. Friends had been called back from overseas, her son thought she might die within the week, and Marion was very frightened. She had x-ray pictures of her brain, MRI images, a radiologist's report and an appointment to see a neurologist. The pressure in Marion's head made it difficult for her to think clearly. She was too upset to be able to formulate the questions she needed to ask and wanted help to decide on the best option to follow. So she asked me to come with her to see the neurologist, to support her, and ask any questions on her behalf that she might forget. The neurologist studied the x-ray pictures of her brain, MRI images, and the radiographer's report and concluded that it was probably a non-malignant growth in the brain, a cyst, or sac of fluid

---

7   Shem (1978).

that could be drained. Only an operation would confirm the diagnosis. Yes, it was serious and the operation needed to be done within days. It would take between five and eight hours but the long-term outlook was very promising and the risks were minimal. If the diagnosis was correct, there would be a full recovery and a return to normal life.

What struck me, as an observer of this interaction between my dear friend and her highly commended medical specialist, was his aloofness. He was cold, almost robotic in his manner. Minimal in both movement and speech. He gave no indication of recognising Marion's obvious fright and fragility. The message, as I received it, was, 'This is straightforward. Marion is fortunate that there is a clear diagnosis and we have the surgical procedures that can rectify the problem.'

If it had been Marion's car, his manner would have been understandable. But this was her brain. For Marion, it was her life. Even the need to protest feels strange, as if he was from another planet and from a species with no understanding of human feeling like Dr Spock from *Star Trek*.

Yes it was good news, relative to what we knew of brain tumours and their likely fatal consequences, but the manner in which the diagnosis was given and the treatment recommended lacked common human feeling and was disturbing.

There were other complaints, too. He had not communicated some of the major consequences of the operation without being pressed. For example, he had not told Marion that she could expect intense headaches for several days after the operation, until asked. One of his responses to a question was, 'I have already answered that question.'

Maybe he had and maybe this is just an example of his cold formality. But it was also a discouragement to ask any further questions. Any textbook on communication would have told him that a distressed patient may well need to have information repeated. The message I took was, 'There is no need to worry, simply turn up for the operation and all will be well.' It was subtle, hard to identify the many ways in which open communication was restrained, yet the restraint was palpable. I am trained to ask questions both as a researcher and a lawyer, yet I felt inhibited. I imagine most people would simply acquiesce.

Is this an isolated example? A doctor on a bad day with a head cold or having had an argument with his lover? In either circumstance, I could understand, see him as human and excuse his non-caring as an occasional lapse. I suspect not, however. My suspicion is that he treats most of his patients like that.

This is an awful tale. It is a form of abuse of a patient, in my mind. It does not really matter how technically competent the practitioner was, the treatment of the person was dreadful.

So I conceive of my task differently from many of my colleagues. My business is people first, and therefore disease only secondarily and only to the extent that it serves to satisfy the needs of people. Let us be clear. Often it is the disease that brings the person to the practitioner and attention to the disease is what is asked for. In that case, both parties may share a common concern and may be satisfied. But it is not always so. Sometimes people become desperate when no-one listens to their worries but concentrates instead on some disease (or looks for some disease), which is of peripheral interest to them.

My task as a carer involves my asking early on, 'What does this person want?' Not, 'What do I want?', which is a different question. Sometimes answers can be surprising. Once, I asked a patient what she really wanted and she answered, 'I want you to help me divorce my husband.'

Mind you, if the practitioner decides to go off on another track that may be quite defensible medically but requires that the practitioner explains to the patient what is being done, why a new course is being undertaken, convincing the patient that the course being followed is reasonable and necessary. Above all, it requires that I 'hear' and 'validate' the concerns of the patient and that, whatever else I do, there is a response to those concerns that tells the patient that they have been heard, that their concerns are valid, and that I will respond to those.

Too many of our junior colleagues today do not know how to behave in the face of human sadness, of grief, of bad news, of unhappiness. Too many use denial or rejection, too many fail to hear or to validate the concerns of the patient, and too many blame the patient if anything goes awry—in spite of having control of the consultation process.

All I have to do to turn a student to jelly in an exam is to ask him or her to tell the patient some bad news.

Too many of our senior colleagues have a warped view of death and dying. If death is universal—and the mortality rate was 100 per cent last time I looked—then, whatever other expertise practitioners have, they should be particularly expert at handling dying, death, grieving people, separation and loss. Actually, each of us has to be comfortable with his or her own death—a basic requirement for anyone wishing to work in the life and death business.

What actually happens is that too many senior practitioners delegate the tasks of caring for, and speaking to, the dying or their relatives to their most junior team members. Those junior team members are often the least well equipped to deal with the tasks that are thrust upon them. The delegation sometimes says more about the senior colleague than it does about the junior. On ward rounds, senior specialists sometimes ignore the dying, either not visiting them at all or paying them perfunctory visits in which the dying are not encouraged to say anything distressing or 'real'.

In their private practices, some senior practitioners make it hard for people to communicate fears and uncertainties, because they are not sensitive to what people wish to communicate or because they have not been taught how to do this task or because they do not wish to allow any personal feelings to intrude upon the consultation.

It is said that the great majority—perhaps 80 per cent—of all communication is non-verbal and people read non-verbal signals well, including infelicitous ones. When the non-verbal signals do not accord with what is said, most people believe the non-verbal cues. We teach that 'you cannot not communicate'; it is just that what is communicated is sometimes awful and counterproductive.

So my style is to listen to people, to find what they actually want, to respond to those needs whatever else I do; to spend time with the dying and grieving, to encourage people to talk as they wish. Listening is a good medical skill but it consumes time and some practitioners hide behind time limitations as an excuse for talking rather than listening.

Without a good grasp of science, practitioners are dangerous. Without humanity, practitioners are monsters. To miss a treatable disease is a disaster; to be part of a communication failure is a disaster of a different kind.

Let us aim for a style of practice where we care for people like us, where we listen and respond to what people feel and what people say, where we accept people as themselves, and where we see disease as important but subsidiary. If we did all these things, the public would be happier—and so would we. Our work would be more satisfying, our patients would thank us, and our lives would be enriched and fuller. That medicine today has followed its great achievements into significant imbalance is sad but is retrievable. My job is to empower myself and my colleagues to follow that more appropriate and more balanced course, and it is to that task, the care of people, that I will dedicate my teaching and my practice in the years remaining.

FOUR CAREERS (2012)

In 2012, aged 77, I was invited to address the Probus Club of Roseville in Sydney, which met weekly in the Killara Bowling Club (of which I was then patron). I was invited to make a retrospective speech about my four careers.

This is a great room, in a wonderful club, and it is always a pleasure to be here. So many friends are here. Peter Wilkinson has been a good friend since Rotary days, and many in this room are good friends from lawn bowls here.

But enough of the bowls and this club. Let us consider four careers.

They represent a lack of ability to stick at any one and make it last. And retirement seems to have failed too. Each career lasted about 15 to 20 years. First, there was medicine where there were fine people. That career started at the old Royal North Shore Hospital (which was a great place in former days), continued overseas (in Birmingham, London and Nashville) and ended with a consultant medical practice.

First at Royal North Shore. That went from 1956 for almost 20 years as, progressively, medical student, intern, senior resident, medical registrar, research fellow, honorary assistant physician, clinical lecturer in medicine and lecturer in physiology at the University of Sydney.

When we passed the final exams, we had a cocktail party and the senior physician composed a verse with every name in it. What an achievement to do that on the very day the results appeared.

The examination for a specialist qualification was very frightening. The examiners decided to cut this young upstart down to size by giving him a very difficult, long case to work out. What they had not considered was that by getting the long case right, they then had to pass the upstart. But they did make the candidate do a final viva with them all in robes and floppy hats and sitting around a long table.

Overseas there was a wonderful gastroenterology in Birmingham, London and in Nashville, so it was possible to return with more specialised knowledge than before. And our time in these foreign countries coincided with momentous times.

In England, *Beyond the Fringe* was poking fun at one and all. John Cleese, Marty Feldman, Michael Palin were just emerging. It was a very cold winter night and Jenny came away from *Beyond the Fringe* laughing until she cried. And her tears froze in the cold London air. If you saw this show, you will know just how funny it was.

Richard Neville and his friends had just been put in prison for showing Paddington Bear with an erection. People were very hung up about such things at that time. We had the sight of many nude men and women in the forecourt of the Opera House just last week and nobody expressed any outrage or horror.

A young musical group called the Beatles was just emerging from Liverpool.

The Profumo affair was keeping us all agog as detail after detail was revealed in Parliament. Years later, we met one of the involved people, Koo Stark, and she was attractive and interesting and fascinating. It was easy to see how great men strayed to her.

In Tennessee we were there just after official segregation ended. There were double lavatories in the hospital—mute evidence of the segregation era. It was the year that the film *Mississippi Burning* records so vividly.

You remember: the year that three civil rights workers were buried in a dam wall after they were murdered. It was a time when African Americans did not have to travel in the back of buses any more, and when they were allowed to swim in municipal pools for the first time in some parts of the South.

At football games, people—other than the very progressive department of medicine—had their hands on their heart as the band played *Dixie*. Few of the members of the department of medicine had Southern sympathies. A midwestern friend had to tell her disbelieving Southern high school history class that the South had lost the Civil War. A professor's wife told me that 'if a nigra sits down next to me in church I will leave'. Naively, I asked 'What would Christ have done?' She answered, 'What has that got to do with it?' She won that argument.

John Kennedy had just been assassinated. We were in London when it happened and they called off the seminar put down for that evening. Our dinner companion, a coloured physician from the West Indies, said only: 'I hope it was not a black man.' Two days later at a rugby international at Cardiff Arms Park, the Welsh team wore black armbands for John Kennedy, the president of another country.

Some Southerners were happy that John Kennedy had been killed and that was hard to live with. The Kennedys helped define the generation for many like us.

You will remember that Bobby Kennedy was assassinated, too, on the West Coast while he was running for president. Later still, we saw footage of Robert Kennedy's body being brought back across the United States from California to Massachusetts, by train. Ordinary men and women, family groups, were standing along the rail line with their hats off and their heads bowed—family tributes from middle America for a dead politician.

We drove through Mississippi one time on our way to New Orleans and asked a state patrolman how long it would take to reach the state border. He answered that it depended on where we were going and why we were in Mississippi! We told him quickly that we were passing through and then he helped us.

Our very Southern 'patron' had us for a mandatory dinner before we departed. His equally Southern daughter Cornelia (a daughter of the American Revolution) said to me words like: 'Doctor Baume, do you not agree that races develop at different rates, and this is the time of the northern Europeans?' The response was along the lines of 'being Jewish, I have never subscribed to the theory of Aryan superiority'. She blushed deeply and extensively—she was wearing a strapless dress—and the evening was somewhat even more strained than it was always going to be.

There was a period in private medical practice as a consulting physician. That was a good time except that the pressure was unremitting and the busyness extraordinary. The patients were delightful.

Then into politics.

That was accidental in that the 'godfather' in New South Wales convinced me to stand. Actually, the last seat to be determined was the final Senate seat in New South Wales. It took 35 days. By the way, that length of time is not all bad—fairness of the result was improved by the slowness.

We were at a private dinner when my beloved mother-in-law phoned to tell me that the election was all over and that the final seat had been decided. The Liberal Party never told me. When we got home from dinner, Jenny insisted that we phone the hostess to tell her what the telephone call had been about. She happened to be the daughter of a senior senator and would not have forgiven me had the call not been made. Another senior senator asked me to see him before the election. He said: 'Your job is to introduce people, move votes of thanks if asked to, and otherwise be quiet. Now, how do you take your tea?'

Canberra was something else again. There are skills associated with political life and it was necessary to learn these. The then prime minister had been unwell the year before and his eventual transfer to the correct specialist had involved me. So, in Canberra, there was at least one government person known to me. But there was advantage to the system to have another tame doctor in the house. So free medical practice continued—in a fashion.

Some stories might interest some of you.

The mail was delivered every *hour* and the attendant who delivered it, hour after hour, was clearly hypothyroid. It was also clear that his own doctor had missed the diagnosis (which is very easy to happen). So the problem was: what to do? Eventually he was asked to have a blood test, which confirmed the diagnosis and a letter was then written to his local doctor (who must have hated me for that letter). No response was ever received but the attendant clearly had been treated by the local doctor.

One night the chief attendant's wife, who also worked in Parliament, saw me with a corneal ulcer. A local ophthalmologist saw her that evening, and all was well.

It was not only politicians you looked after. There are about 3,000 people in Parliament House each sitting day. Various people had various medical emergencies but mostly it was routine stuff: people forgot their medicines, girls wanted the contraceptive pill, and some politicians wanted a close watch kept on conditions that they did not want their colleagues to know about. So Labor politicians came to me. Liberal politicians went to a Labor doctor. There is an old political aphorism that states that your opponents in Parliament are the people on the other side, whereas your enemies are often those sitting behind, and around, you.

There is another story that might interest you. One night Neal Blewett, then a political opponent and minister for health, phoned and asked me around for 'a cup of tea and a talk'. He wanted to talk about the emerging epidemic of HIV/AIDS in Australia. He wanted to introduce a brave policy on this disease. Any action had to be bipartisan and free of party politics, if it was to go ahead.

He promised to deliver the Labor Party if I could deliver my parties. It was possible to deliver the Liberal and National parties—we had plenty of other things to attack the Government on—and he did deliver the Labor Party. So the

Bill went through in a bipartisan fashion and the Australian approach to HIV/AIDS became the envy of the world, and many lives were lengthened. As part of that package, we had a Parliamentary Liaison Group on AIDS, which allowed those who needed to froth at the mouth to do so. During that period there was also time as whip and as a minister for four portfolios.

But those of you who speak Latin will know the phrase: '*Sic transit gloria mundi.*'

In 1987 it was necessary to resign from the Opposition front bench on a matter of principle. The resignation was to allow me to support a Bill for equal employment opportunity for women in some Commonwealth authorities. The story is as follows: about two years earlier, with the authority of the joint opposition parties, I had called for exactly the Bill that emerged in 1987. But the balance of power in the Opposition had altered in the two years. John Howard was under attack from the 'Joh for prime minister' people and the National Party was being urged to cut its ties with the Liberals and a conservative tide was waxing. John Howard was desperate, *but* he chose support for the National Party over support for me. Resignation was honourable and inevitable and painful. That Bill for equal opportunity needed enthusiastic and vigorous support then and always. It needed my support—and it got it. Resignation was also 48 hours before my preselection was due. A colleague and friend in New South Wales was told what had happened and said simply: 'damage control starts now.' When the particular Bill came to a vote, eight Liberal senators (out of 32) crossed the floor to support that Bill.

So much for the official party position. Another story about that. Reg Withers called me in one day and asked what was going to happen with the vote. I assured him that I would speak and vote for the Bill. He said simply 'you will not be alone'. The press got wind of it all and went to see Withers, who said disingenuously, 'I would rather be stupidly consistent than consistently stupid'. That episode is not even a footnote to history now. But at the time it was very public, very painful and very significant for us.

The third career was as professor of community medicine at the University of New South Wales. That only lasted 10 years because retirement was called for at the age of 65. Teaching young medical students—they were bright as buttons. During that time there were a lot of inquiries for the Government, and all proceeds, then about a third of a million dollars, went as a gift to my school for physical improvements.

The inquiries included a reform of the drug licensing system in Australia, all of which was accepted. Interestingly, there had been seven previous inquiries with very similar recommendations, none of which had ever been implemented. So the question—a political question—became: 'why has *that* been so?' It was the correct answer to *that* question that allowed change to occur.

A former rugby international was then appointed. He explained his remit as being 'to implement Baume'. There were other inquiries—into disability employment, into veterans' compensation, and into the surgical workforce. The last inquiry almost led to lynching, and popularity was not high with other inquiries. For example, a note from Bruce Ruxton after the veterans' inquiry said words like 'you called your report "A Fair Go". How could you? I shall not forget.'

In the surgical workforce inquiry the figures used were derived from those given by the College of Surgeons to the minister for health just a year before. The college criticised me, inter alia, saying these figures were wrong! When it was pointed out to the college that not many women were applying to become surgeons, the college replied that it was not its fault that women did not want to join them.

Four former students, all surgeons, came to our home to set me right. They told me that things were awful and then told me that nothing must change. Jenny listened in covertly to that exchange and could not believe what she had heard.

During the time at the University of New South Wales, The Australian National University appointed me Chancellor. A fourth career.

The employing university was not sure how to deal with this appointment, but when it was made clear that the appointment to The Australian National University would go ahead regardless, the employing university gave way. It was the best job we ever had. And it was possible to meet some great people, like Desmond Tutu, Nelson Mandela and the Dalai Lama.

The chancellorship lasted 11 years (the longest tenure ever at that university) and came to an end in 2006 only when my hearing worsened more and more. The greatest day ever was giving an honorary degree to Nelson Mandela. There were workmen on a building next door cheering. There were crowd-control barriers. There were police and press. There were drummers playing African drums to welcome him. Everyone was smiling and happy. And Nelson Mandela was wonderful. Invictus, indeed! Did you know that when he left Robben Island, some of the guards were in tears?

Nelson Mandela's feet had been so badly beaten by bastinado that he could not process and was brought in by a short route by the pro-chancellor. Jenny sat next to your former local member who was then high commissioner to South Africa. He leaned over to Jenny and told her 'you are in the presence of greatness'. The Woden Youth Choir sang *N'kosi Sikelele Afrika* so well (in three languages) that Mandela shook every one of them by the hand after the event. He signed a wall and perspex has been placed over that signature.

Now for retirement. And family. And bowls here. But that, Mr President, is a story for another time.

PART 2: THE LIBERAL FORUM CONTRIBUTIONS

THE BIRTH AND EMERGENCE OF THE LIBERAL FORUM, 1985–1987 (1987)

The Liberal Forum was established in 1985 by a group of 'small-l' liberals to try to offset the conservative tide that was building. That the forum was unsuccessful in halting the conservative tide is a matter of history. The following account sets out some of what we did and how we proceeded.

Reflecting on the progress of the Liberal Forum in May 1987, it seems incredible that we have achieved so much in so short a time. So much! It was just over two years ago, in February 1985, that we met first and established our small, self-selected group at a time of great crisis for philosophical liberals.

Max Burr claims that he was a prime mover in the formation of the group. He acted after a conversation with Yvonne Thompson, who, after years of involvement in Liberal Party councils, was thinking of throwing it all in, and getting out of organisational politics. Alan Missen was alive then, and Peter Rae was still a senator—not yet translated to his ministerial role in Tasmanian state politics and to a closer relationship with Robin Gray, the conservative 'Liberal' premier of that state.

Things were grim then and becoming grimmer. The 'economic rationalists', 'conservative radicals', 'dries', call them what you will, were well advanced in redefining non-Labor politics in laissez-faire economic terms—and in purely economic terms. Our leaders no longer talked publicly at all, nor privately for that matter, of the liberties and primacy of individuals, and there was certainly less talk of the obligations of each of us towards all others, especially those in need. There was little talk of empowering the weak or helpless, little or no rhetoric about the role of liberalism in securing and extending our liberties, or of developing new opportunities for the less privileged in society.

On the contrary, there was a concerted campaign from within my own party, and my own side of politics, to attack and belittle the recipients of welfare as being cheats, or layabouts, anxious to prosper on the welfare handed out by their industrious brethren. The fact that few people live in luxury on welfare alone never features in their thinking or their public rhetoric. Of course those who use welfare to cheat the system are another matter.

Moves to extend power to women and to racial minorities were bitterly opposed in our party and party room, the racist regime in South Africa had committed minority party room support, and opposition to communist expansion was regarded as almost adequate defence of rotten dictatorships. Not only was it a wrong analysis, but it was a laissez-faire libertarian credo based too much on greed and self-interest.

Our political leaders were disposed to turn a blind eye to racist calls in the area of immigration, and to make calls for cuts in personal tax the cornerstone of policy. Tax cuts are admirable, provided one can identify clearly what are the consequential costs to others. The costs to others have not yet been clearly set out.

In May 1987, at the time this is written, greed and self-interest drive the tax-reduction campaign. Nothing is heard about the needy, and there has been no analysis of the social costs of proposed cuts in personal income tax. For me, the question of social costs is a prior question, to be answered in detail before cuts in revenue as a consequence of lower taxes are even contemplated.

In 1985 this dismal scenario was already well advanced, and the forces of greed and self-interest were about to organise themselves into several groupings which together became known as the 'New Right'. Not only this, but our then leader Andrew Peacock was more a prisoner of the tide of events than its helmsman. He subscribed cheerfully to the goal of a cut in the level of personal income tax, and campaigned on it. He proposed, as did his successor, John Howard, to cut the expenditures of government to fund the tax cuts. But, simultaneously, he opposed the initiatives of the Labor Government to gain alternative revenue by taxing certain lump sum taxation payments, to tax certain capital gains on investments, and to add a means test to the income test that was applied to pensions. Not only this, but there were other proposals for substantial new government expenditures in child care, family allowances, and a tendency to offer new bribes to middle Australia as part of the election manifesto of the Liberal Party.

THE BIRTH AND EMERGENCE OF THE LIBERAL FORUM, 1985–1987 (1987)

The Labor Party had a field day pointing up the internal contradictions in our policy statement. No wonder Yvonne Thompson felt like getting out. This was not the party for which she had worked for 20 years. This was no longer a party seeking sacrifice from the rich to assist those in need; rather it seemed (and seems still) to be the reverse.

The invitation to me to join the Liberal Forum, then nameless, came from my old close friend Chris Puplick. I accepted it immediately, insisting only that it should be an 'ideas' group, not a leadership destabilisation group. Named the 'Liberal Forum', the group met quietly, clandestinely in fact, for the first year or so. Partly because of this, Tom Harley nicknamed it 'the Black Hand'. The name stuck. I had joined a significant group of compatible people, people to whom I had always felt close, and to whom I was to become closer month by month. Senator Robert Hill was, and in May 1987 remains, President of the South Australian Division of the Liberal Party. Something of an expert in the area of foreign policy, he, like Chris Puplick, is a talented numbers man. He has a cool head, a liberal vision, and plenty of courage. Robert is a lawyer with an LLM degree, son of the Honourable Murray Hill MLC of South Australia, and fortunate to come from the most liberal state in Australia. His interests and parliamentary expertise lie in foreign affairs. His wife, Diana, is deputy principal of a private school in Adelaide and a liberated feminist. She and Robert have a large, rambling house with large, lolloping dogs and children, including an adopted girl from Vietnam. Robert has the problem of dealing with Bruce MacDonald, who still hopes to do to the Liberal Party in South Australia what he has already done to it in New South Wales.

Senator Christopher Puplick is probably the most formidable mind on our side of politics. He has a Sydney MA in history, and cut his political teeth working on the staff of the brilliant W.C. (Bill) Wentworth when Bill was a minister. Chris was NSW state, and later federal, president of the Young Liberal Movement of Australia. He worked on my staff in the mid 1970s until he entered the Senate as its second-youngest senator ever. Out in a bad election year, he came back a few years later, beating the awful Bronwyn Bishop decisively in a preselection. Michael Baume was selected between Chris and Bronwyn in that particular preselection. Chris is feared in the party room by stupid or ill-prepared shadow ministers. Not only does he generally know more than they do about most subjects, he is also more articulate, more persuasive, more influential, and more credible. He is not popular with those in power. I was warned on many occasions that my close friendship with Puplick was attracting adverse political comment. I was even warned that I should distance myself from him to ensure that my preselection was not put at risk. Since Chris is my friend, and has shared my apartment, and since he and I are allies in most battles, I have not acted on the advice that has flowed in. I have ignored that advice quite deliberately, and more and more openly as the Liberal Forum developed. My preselection was secured, first with a decisive win over Bronwyn Bishop for first place on a half-Senate ticket, and then for my place in the double-dissolution election of July 1987. There have even been allegations that Chris is gay. If true, this is irrelevant to questions about his capacity, and worse, if false, it is simply part of the viciousness and mutual unhappiness that characterises our current situation.

Max Burr is the least intellectual of the Liberal Forum members, but he is also one of the tough and smart survivors. He has held a difficult constituency for a long time, and has resisted both his Labor and his Liberal opponents. He is a good counter of numbers. His constituency is Lyons, which covers most of Tasmania except for the urban areas of Hobart and Launceston and the north-west of the state. Max has coped with very conservative and hostile electorate presidents and party officials. A former shearer, he gained his advanced education as an adult. He is a person with good instincts and dislikes the ideas of the 'dries' with an admirable intensity.

Ian Macphee is the best known of the philosophical liberals. He is also the most overtly ambitious. He has offered himself to the party room as deputy leader without success and will probably continue to offer himself in future party leadership elections. Originally from Sydney, Ian lived in the Mosman area and attended North Sydney Technical High School. He was a godson of Eileen Furley, who was a Liberal member of the old non-elected Legislative Council of New South Wales. Working in Melbourne as an industrial advocate and as director of the Chamber of Manufacturers, Ian came to Parliament in 1974, representing first the seat of Balaclava and, after redistribution, the renamed seat of Goldstein. He is very strongly supported locally, but has had vicious opposition from right-wing elements. These even went to the lengths of running a National Party candidate against him recently—that person lost his deposit. Ian entered the ministry early in the Fraser years and I served with him (sitting beside him) in the last Fraser Cabinet.

It is not without significance that those who complained most about leaks from the Shadow Cabinet while we three (Macphee and Peacock and me) were there had precious little to say about the same leaks when they continued after we were gone. One thing was certain: someone else was briefing the press after we had gone, and the same source or sources might well have been the source of leaks all along.

Ian alienated many in the party when he asserted in 1984 words to the effect that anyone who did not support the (then) Sex Discrimination Bill had no place in the party. He acknowledges freely that the words were inopportune and clumsy, and has not done the same since. He is impetuous, too. When sacked by Howard, his first instinct had been to go out publicly and take Howard on. Three weeks earlier, he had wanted to follow me into resignation over the issue of equal opportunity; he certainly intended to resign had the party rejected him on the issue of media ownership. Earlier, in January 1987, he was summoned to Sydney to meet Howard and Neil Brown following a statement Ian had made to the press about media ownership. Arriving in my Sydney office an hour or so before the meeting, Ian told me he had come probably 'to be sacked'. Together, we worked out a simple strategy: he would offer no opening statement but would defend himself against each accusation on the merits. He would take a 'passive defence' position and see what happened. It was an unexpected approach and worked perfectly—on that occasion.

Ian's wife, Julie, is a moderately radical feminist and they both dote on their son, Scobie. Ian is a lawyer by training and some of his language is rather convoluted and lawyer-like. But his courage is undoubted and his commitment to liberalism is strong. He differed from the rest only in his more definite personal agenda and ambition. This thumbnail sketch seems a little critical. So it should be made quite clear that Ian Macphee is a splendid, liberal, brave, and talented man, an adornment to politics, and an asset to the Liberal Party and to liberalism.

Peter Rae was a senator for Tasmania when we first met as the Liberal Forum. He was then a liberal thinker and a most interesting man. A barrister before he entered the Senate (and afterwards too to a limited extent), he maintained extraordinary hours—often working late into the night and emerging late in the morning. He liked his scotch, was very convivial and a good host, and ran an office that was a nightmare to view. Papers stood in high piles on his desk; the amazing thing was that he could find documents within the piles immediately with his excellent memory. Peter was a partisan as regards the divisions within the party. He fought with conservatives on his own state executive, within the parliamentary party, within the front bench, and in regard to leadership candidates for whom he declared his support. He was, like so many lawyers, only a moderate communicator. Like many of his profession, he found it difficult to ignore detail in the interests of greater clarity. But he was a real resource in the Liberal Forum and worked well with the group.

Alan Missen was alive in February 1985, but died at Easter 1986. He was the other parliamentarian in the Liberal Forum. I have spoken in the Senate about Alan in my contribution to the eulogies spoken after his death and will not repeat them here. It is sufficient to say that the Liberal Forum was probably more important as a symbol of support for Alan than for anyone else in the group. Always a maverick, Alan did not find it easy to be part of a consensual group, even this group. He confided to me a short time before he died that he was considering withdrawing from the Liberal Forum because the other parliamentarians had not gone to the barricades with him on some matter before the party room. Alan was always going to the barricades. He was an 'issues' man, whose underlying liberalism was expressed in relation to this or that matter currently at centre stage. He was not a gentle debater and he too presented in his speeches the extra detail that makes lawyers hard to listen to. He told me in return that he did not like my 'shrill Sydney' style of debate—so there you are, it is very much in the eye of the beholder. Alan and his wife, Mollie, lived in Melbourne. They were childless, but were a close and loving couple. After his death, Mollie confided to me that she had lost not only the man she loved, but also her best friend.

George Brandis is about 30 and lives in Brisbane, where he is a barrister. He was at Oxford when he met Tom Harley and Don Markwell and published, with them, the *Liberals Face the Future*. I recall that Kathy Sullivan (then Senator Kathy Martin) offered me the opportunity to take over her commitment to write one of the chapters for this book—but did so only 10 days before the deadline for copy. I refused her—reluctantly. Tall, balding, cadaverous, with a loud laugh, George is intellectually formidable, has good judgment, is an uncompromising liberal, and has been an initial member of the Liberal Forum. Until recently, George was a resident tutor in St John's College in the University of Queensland. He was instrumental in my receiving the invitation to deliver the oration of the college recently. He also introduced me to John Morgan, the warden of St John's College, a theologian and a liberal.

Tom Harley is about the same age as Brandis. He worked for Bill Snedden when Snedden was speaker, and spent time at Oxford with Brandis and Markwell. He is a troubleshooter for BHP. A great-grandson of Alfred Deakin, he is an elegant, very tough, very intelligent man and is probably the most important single member of the Liberal Forum. I have said more about George and Tom elsewhere.

Peter Coatman, another lawyer, was included in the group as the current president of the Young Liberal Movement of Australia. This has traditionally been the source of many of the most liberal of Liberals, but alas is so no longer. Peter contributed little to the forum and dropped out within a year.

So there we were, in the house Tom Harley shares with Rupert Myer, a scion of the Melbourne retailing family, in Vale Street, East Melbourne. This charming house with its excellent artworks is conveniently located in the same block as Andrew and Margaret Peacock; this was interesting, as Andrew knew nothing of this new grouping being established within the party he was leading.

It was obvious from the start that there were several agendas being run simultaneously, and an early task was to separate and give priority to different goals. First, there were the continuing leadership ambitions of Ian Macphee, which intruded into many of the other matters. These ambitions were valid and proper, but had to be assessed as they affected this or that decision. Second, there was the need for mutual support and a safe forum for discussion of issues. As a self-selected group, we were able to assume that our meetings were secure, or at least as secure as they needed to be. This mutual group support was a much-needed improvement on the isolation that most of us were feeling in the Federal Liberal Party Room. Third, there was the need to develop and present, as part of the intellectual debate in Australia, a formidable liberal position to counter the arguments and intellectual dominance achieved by the conservative and libertarian elements within the party. For many of us, this was almost the first opportunity to be part of a sympathetic, collegial group pursuing compatible ideological goals. It was an exciting prospect of renewal and fresh hope. Fourth, arising from the last goal, there was the need to project that intellectual argument into documentary form. We determined that one urgent priority would be the preparation and presentation of books, to complement books like the *Liberals Face the Future*, the making of liberal speeches in critical places to critical audiences, the publication of occasional papers, and so on. Fifth, the forum would give us the opportunity to create new ways to present liberal views within the party and the community. This was quickly reflected in the luncheon meetings organised by Yvonne Thompson in Melbourne, and provided a focus around which many compatible liberals rallied. Finally, the forum provided a grouping that could offer and receive mutual support in an increasingly shrill, unpleasant, illiberal party room, dominated by dries and later by a leader whose boast was that he was 'the most conservative leader the party had ever had'.

But in February 1985, Andrew Peacock was still the leader, and two members of the forum sat in his Shadow Cabinet. John Howard's agents were busy chatting to any journalist who would listen, and were setting up the conditions that allowed the events of September 1985 to result in Peacock's replacement with Howard. As with any group, we took some time to settle in, to learn to listen to each other, to respond to each person's input, to agree on collegial priorities, and to share the tasks required for completion of these priorities. We began with a degree of mutual trust and confidence, which grew rapidly as we learned that we could depend on group colleagues for loyalty and support.

The Liberal Forum met each six or eight weeks from then on. Peter Coatman quickly became irrelevant, partly due to his other professional commitments, partly due to an inability to contribute in any significant way to what we were doing. Chris Puplick and Tom Harley were the informal leaders and adjutants of the group. We met usually in Melbourne, sometimes at Vale Street, occasionally at Macphee's home at Brighton. We put in a little money each to help George Brandis to come to Melbourne; the rest of us had other ways to pay for our travel.

Melbourne was the best place to meet because it involved the least amount of travelling by the group members (with the exception of Brandis). Our first decision was to produce a book. Having considered all the options, we decided to start with a publication bringing together the published writings about what we understood to be liberalism from the time of Deakin to the present. This approach had many advantages. It would draw upon writings already in existence, and indeed, would revive some of these writings currently out of print and unavailable. It could be presented to show a continuing philosophical emphasis, associated over a hundred years, with the name 'liberal'. Further, it might be possible to find some published work by each Liberal leader that could be consistent with our theme and emphasis.

Tom, George and Yvonne were appointed as the editors. They were given complete authority to select and organise the material for the book. Each of us submitted to the editors some speeches we wished to have considered. We saw it as important to keep the politicians away from the evaluation of material, which could be their own, for publication. Not only that, but Yvonne's husband, Sid, is a printer and was to play a critical role in the publication of our book. Although it took us about 18 months to get from conception to launch of the book, events seemed to move quite smoothly during that time. Yvonne did not then have a word processor available and enlisted a team of volunteers to help with the enormous job of typing, editing and proofreading the material for the book, now titled *Australian Liberalism: The Continuing Vision*. Yvonne works for Mark Birrell, who is in the Victorian Upper House and who has been a philosophical liberal in his days as a Young Liberal leader. His wife, Jenny, worked for Alan Missen. She managed to do some of the work for us at work, while friends like Joel Martin did some of the dreary and tedious typing out of work hours.

The enormous commitment of this group to the production of our book has been too little praised or recognised. It is a splendid book. Designed to fit into a coat pocket, it is attractive and has achieved its purpose admirably. It contains some of the Menzies speeches not otherwise available any more. It moves from the early Liberals, to and through the Menzies years, to the period in and out of power, and to a final section looking to the future. This section contained contributions by some of the younger 'small-l' liberals. The book ended with a eulogy to Alan Missen—the one I had delivered in the Senate in 1985.

Continuing Vision was launched on 2 December 1986 at the National Press Club in Canberra. John Gorton attended, Chris Puplick, George Brandis and Yvonne Thompson made splendid if provocative speeches, and we all had a splendid luncheon in the private dining rooms of the Parliament.

THE BIRTH AND EMERGENCE OF THE LIBERAL FORUM, 1985–1987 (1987)

This is written as we start the 1987 double-dissolution campaign; we have two lots of occasional papers ready for reproduction and distribution, with the third group of occasional papers almost complete. We have letters ready to go to prospective contributors to our second book, to be called *Affording a Liberal Society*.

Continuing Vision received a good press and was seen for what it is: the first evidence of the 'wets' (or 'small-l' liberals, or as we call them, the philosophical liberals) fighting back. It had been financed by some generous anonymous donors and sales have been directed to replenishing our funds ready for the second book. There were later launches at state level in Victoria, South Australia and New South Wales by Liberal Forum members. Sales have been steady and, at May 1987, are continuing well. We have offered the book to schools and have offered bulk prices for colleagues in Parliament.

The Liberal Forum had to regroup after the destruction of Peacock's leadership in September 1985. It was a depressing time and Howard, though clean himself, was deeply involved via friends and agents in the destabilisation of Peacock over some months. For example, John Valder, the federal president of the party, failed to give unqualified support to Peacock at the Federal Council Meeting in Canberra in mid-1985, fuelling media rumours that a leadership challenge was imminent. In the end, Peacock could see his leadership being eroded by unseen enemies working to undermine him without ever challenging him directly. Finally, he confronted Howard and called on a challenge to Howard as Deputy Leader, a challenge Peacock lost. With it, he lost his authority and wisely resigned his leadership immediately.

The Liberal Forum was then confronted by a party leader who boasted that he was the most conservative Liberal leader ever, and who brought back into critical positions the dries and conservatives who had supported him. Jim Carlton returned from the back bench to be Shadow Treasurer, Tony Messner moved into finance, and people like Peter White and Alan Cadman were given positions as a reward for loyalty rather than ability.

Ian Macphee and I were retained in the Shadow Cabinet, though I was demoted a couple of places and given the relatively 'harmless' jobs of shadow minister for community services and status of women. Eighteen months later, sensitive to the policy imperatives of the status of women, I was forced to resign my position when the party decided to vote against an equal employment opportunity Bill. Our problems, however, were becoming more acute each month. Howard was encouraging Carlton and they were moving the policies and the rhetoric of the party to the right. What were we to do? And what could we do most effectively?

One test of our will came when there was an attempted takeover of BHP and the parliamentary party decided on a laissez-faire, hands-off approach. The call 'to leave it to the market and the shareholders' displayed scant sensitivity to the market manipulations being undertaken by powerful individuals to the detriment of shareholders. The approach reminded me of the old admonition in regard to Christians in the Coliseum: 'let's leave it to the lions.' In the event, Tom Harley and his mates at BHP beat off the challenge. BHP had precious little to thank us for as a party, but was grateful to forum members who argued against the official party position.

We realised that we had to speak more publicly of the alternative position we were offering, but the problem was how to do this so as to enrich the debate in a way that would not be seen as just destructive and divisive. First, we began to be more active in the party room, especially through Chris Puplick, who is a formidable person. He is devastating when he intrudes into a debate about which he is more knowledgeable than the hapless shadow minister. The party room has learned that it can trust his mastery of detail even if it is suspicious of his ideology. Second, we began to give more philosophical and substantial contributions in public debate and in public forums. I have made a number of substantial speeches strongly liberal in nature. They have had an excellent reception, and the liberal content has attracted strong and specific support. Third, especially after Macphee was sacked from the Shadow Cabinet (I had already resigned), we began to appear together publicly to identify a different and more liberal stream of thought and emphasis. The most celebrated of these was the appearance four of us made on the ABC *Four Corners* program with Andrew Olle in mid-May 1987. It caused a furore in the party. It incensed Howard, especially the suggestion that the party under him somehow lacked compassion and humanity. The fact that this is so, and that he and his clique talk like accountants and bankers at a convention, seemed to escape his world view. The *Four Corners* appearance was widely noticed and helped extend the feeling that a liberal group was active and defiant.

One consequence of these activities has been to stiffen the opposition to each of us. Preselection has become more difficult, and more unpleasant. I had to agree to accept the second position on the senate team for the 1987 double-dissolution election in order to protect Chris Puplick in fourth position and keep Bronwyn Bishop in number five. We have received numbers of angry and critical letters denouncing some of our more public activities, but we have received much more positive comment and commendation. My mail has run 20:1 in favour of what I have done.

Fourth, we have commenced the publication of 'Liberal Forum Occasional Papers' to feature current speeches by members of the forum and by friends. We plan to develop other structures too. There will be a 'society' with which

THE BIRTH AND EMERGENCE OF THE LIBERAL FORUM, 1985–1987 (1987)

other liberals can identify, to hold dinners, encourage discussion, produce ties and scarves, etc. Such a structure will vary from state to state; in New South Wales, we already have a group that works to control the executive election and to give support to particular candidates for preselection. It was this group that protected me at preselection two days after I had resigned publicly from the Shadow Cabinet. Finally, we are moving to enlarge the Liberal Forum. David Jull from Queensland has become a member and Bob Ellicott is considering whether he will join us.

The Liberal Forum today, after 29 months, has created a powerful alternative political force within the Liberal Party and within non-Labor politics. It is still developing. Today, in May 1987, we still do not know what its future might be. We can only dream and work. Our goal remains one related to the liberal vision of Australia. The Liberal Forum today serves that vision.

PARLIAMENTARY EULOGY ON THE DEATH OF SENATOR ALAN MISSEN (1986)

This speech occurred in 1986 when I was a senior senator. Alan Missen and I came into the Senate together 12 years earlier and sat together for a year or so. I did not know Missen before we were in the Senate. I had been a minister and was still on the Coalition front bench; Missen was not. Many senators spoke on the condolence motion in the Senate. Reading it now, it seems that I became more a 'Missen' type of senator as time went on. In that sense, what is here is prescient—it described many of my emerging views where principle became more important than political advancement or advantage. I certainly followed the 'Missen' line in my later political life: more philosophical and more issue-based and a classical liberal.

Many of us enter these debates seldom, relying on the words of our leaders to speak for us all. This will not do for Alan Missen. He was a singular person, he was a singular liberal, he was a singular senator. As a person, he was singular because of his uncompromising and quite predictable adherence to his principles. No-one else in this place, in my time here, has approached his determination in this area. More than any other, we could use about Alan Missen—in their best sense—words written by Carlyle in 1837 about Robespierre: that he was 'sea-green incorruptible'.[1]

He was not easy to deal with on issues if you were on the other side, but it was never difficult to understand the basis on which he had formed his view, or to see the principle which guided him. This was demonstrated well as early as 1951 when he risked his career and his future place in politics to attack the referendum proposal to outlaw the Communist Party. Though not yet of voting

---

1 See, for example: www.theanswerbank.co.uk/.../why-did-Carlyle-refer-to-Robespierre-as-the-sea-green-incorruptible.

age, I recall that I was appalled by the anti-liberal and anti-democratic sentiments of that referendum proposal, and was pleased that liberals as prominent and clear-thinking as Alan Missen broke ranks to oppose it successfully.

In that and in similar stands he was the continuing voice of that tradition of liberal democratic thought and practice that brought many of us to this side of politics. His personal courage was very great and his actions were taken always with complete disregard for any negative effects they would cause him.

Not surprisingly—but sadly—he was a lonely person in his public life. Some of us became even closer friends in the last year of his life and it was a privilege for us to give and to receive mutual support on political and other issues. Alan came to me for medical counsel—indeed we discussed some of his health problems by phone just three days before he died. It is sufficient to say that his health was very bad for a long time, that he had borne a heart attack privately—secretly—and that the one thing that seemed to improve his physical state most was a good stoush on an issue, whether this occurred in this chamber, or in a committee, or in the party room.

Second, he was a singular liberal—indeed he was one of the very few still around who was involved in the formation of the Liberal Party of Australia—and an examination of what Menzies was articulating then explains much about Alan Missen.

Menzies said then that 'there is no room in Australia for a party of reaction'. Alan Missen believed this. In *The Forgotten People*, Menzies said that:

> [I]ndividual enterprise must drive us forward. That does not mean that we are to return to the old and selfish notions of laissez-faire. The functions of the state will be much more than merely keeping the ring within which the Competitors will fight. Our social and industrial obligations will be increased. There will be more law, not less, more control, not less.[2]

Menzies words—but they describe Missen's view.

Menzies said too: 'We took the name liberal because we were determined to be a progressive party, willing to make experiments and in no sense reactionary.' Alan Missen was active then—in 1944—he was active in writing the early documents that defined the Liberal Party, and he was imprinted for all his life with the early Menzian vision. He was a traditional liberal—as many of us today consider ourselves to be—and Australia was the beneficiary of this commitment.

Alan Missen was—except when suspended for his stands on principle—a continuous member of the Liberal Party from its formation to his death. He was always right in his total opposition to the Communist Party dissolution

---

2   Menzies (1943: 10).

referendum in 1951, and the party was wrong, not only on the issue, but in punishing Missen for his opposition. After all, if we eschew the tyranny of the caucus rule of the Labor Party, we must accept the consequences of people acting to exercise the rights of dissent that our rules provide. He was prominent in the party councils and served it and the nation for 12 years in this place.

Third, he was a singular senator, or if not singular he was one of a small class of dedicated parliamentarians—institutional senators—who served the Parliament and its institutions first and foremost.

Perhaps it was inevitable that he gained no preferment. That was not very important, however, as he made a lasting contribution to this Senate and to the institution of parliamentary democracy with his work, especially his work on the committees of this place.

His commitment was particularly to the two legislative scrutiny standing committees—to the Committee on Regulations and Ordinances of which he had been chairman, and to the Scrutiny of Bills Committee whose establishment he promoted enthusiastically.

He was by nature an 'issues' person—perhaps quixotic on occasions but determined and passionate on a range of causes ranging from family law, freedom of information, human rights, amnesty—as chairman of the all-party group, the human rights commission in particular, south-west Tasmania, national crime authority, law and social reform, and issues affecting the environment.

He was honoured by the Young Liberal movement as its federal patron. It was a particular pleasure for me as a recent federal patron of the Young Liberal movement—one of a number of senators who have had that honour—to work and deal with Alan Missen as the long-time patron of the Victorian division of the movement.

And to the extent that any funeral can be good then Alan Missen had a splendid funeral. He would have been pleased that so many people crowded every seat in a large church, he would have been surprised that the Archbishop of Melbourne honoured him by attending and that Bishop Peter Hollingworth officiated. He would have glowed at the magnificent words spoken about him by Ian Macphee and by Peter Frankel and Peter Block. He would have enjoyed the choice of service and the tribute of Amnesty International. And he would have been pleased that Molly Missen was able to know of the real regard and respect and affection that so many people held for him.

Alan Missen was a well-qualified, well-equipped, fearless and committed servant of Australia and of this place. We shall miss him.

AUSTRALIAN LIBERALISM: THE CONTINUING VISION—PRESS RELEASE FROM THE LIBERAL FORUM (1986)

The political values central to the Australian liberal tradition are the theme of a new book to be launched in Canberra tomorrow [2 December 1986]. *Australian Liberalism: The Continuing Vision* is the first comprehensive anthology of the key speeches and writings of prominent Australian liberals, from the 19th century to the present day.

The work makes generally available for the first time the vital speeches which shaped the development of mainstream non-Labor politics. In particular, it revives a number of the long-neglected 1940s speeches of Robert Menzies, in which he outlined his vision of liberalism and laid the philosophical basis for a quarter-century of successful Liberal government.

One of the book's editors, Tom Harley, said today: 'At a time when the Deakin–Menzies tradition in non-Labor politics is under attack from interests which have never been our friends, it is important to remind ourselves of the values upon which successful mainstream non-Labor politics have been based. Those principles include a deep respect for the rights of the individual; personal freedom; equality of opportunity; acknowledgement of a positive but limited role for Government as one of the providers of those opportunities and unyielding antipathy to fanaticism.'

The book will be launched by Senator Chris Puplick at a reception at the National Press Club at 10.30 am tomorrow, Tuesday, 2 December 1986. It is edited by Yvonne Thompson, George Brandis and Tom Harley, and published by Liberal Forum.

A DISSIDENT LIBERAL

This book is the first to be published by Liberal Forum, a group established to broaden understanding of liberalism and its continuing relevance as a reformist philosophy.

QUITTING SHADOW CABINET (1987)

In 1987 there were several main events. The first was my resignation from the front bench, which is covered in detail in the following account and which was taken from contemporary diaries but written later. When I resigned from the front bench of the Opposition, many women and women's groups were supportive; the political leadership of my party and of the National Party were the ones who did not understand what I had done and why it was the proper course to take because equal employment opportunity is so important. So I came out of it as a hero and the parties came out of it as fools. However, they decided not to oppose several identical Bills not long after—so they know how to limit their losses.

During the evening of 21 March 1987, the Leader of the Victorian Opposition, Jeff Kennett, was travelling by car from central Victoria back to Melbourne. His candidate [Marie] Tehan had just held the Upper House Seat of Central Highlands against Labor and the National Party, and Kennett was pleased with himself. Using a telephone in his car, he called Andrew Peacock in Melbourne to say some harsh things about Federal Liberal Leader John Howard in robust and basic barrack-room language.

Mobile radio telephones operate as do radio transmitters, and transmissions are not secure. This conversation was recorded and released to the media almost immediately—a strangely fortuitous event not properly explained during the furore that followed. The upshot was that, far from getting the benefit of a good election victory against the tide, the Liberal Party found itself on the defensive as the more lurid details of the conversation were discussed by the media. By the time I came to Parliament House on 23 March for Shadow Cabinet, there was no other topic of conversation, with particular attention being given to those parts of the conversation critical of John Howard.

Shadow Cabinet had been scheduled for 10 am, but was put off several times. We eventually gathered at midday for what was to be my last meeting as a member of the Shadow Cabinet. Howard told us that he had sacked Andrew Peacock from the Shadow Cabinet and ministry on the basis of the intercepted conversation. He then read us the press statement he would make within 10 minutes. The only comment from the front bench came from Peter Shack, who said the sacking was, in his view, unnecessary and an error of judgment. Howard then went to his press conference and we started the agenda under the chairmanship of Ian Sinclair.

To be present during these moments of great crisis is to be impressed often with how calmly everything happens, how calmly one thinks, and how one's judgment, sharpened and alert as it is, operates nevertheless with detached calm. Within just one hour I was to face my greatest personal crisis in this room and with these colleagues of long-standing. Having endured one enormous political crisis that day, I did not imagine that another crisis of even greater personal impact was upon me.

The issue that was to cause all the trouble was some way down the agenda. It concerned the position to be taken by the Opposition in relation to a government Bill to require the application of the principle of equal employment opportunity (EEO) principles to all but four statutory authorities of the Commonwealth. The Bill had been introduced by the minister for employment and industrial relations Ralph Willis, and was brought to Shadow Cabinet by his opposite number, Neil Brown. Brown, deputy leader of the party and something of a cynical schemer, had consulted me about the submission he would make to Shadow Cabinet. We had agreed that he would recommend that we not oppose the Bill.

Quite apart from the imperative need to support the Bill on its liberal merits, support was necessary in order to keep us consistent with a position I had put publicly eight months earlier, in the Parliament, on behalf of the Opposition. I had acted then with the authority of the Shadow Cabinet, and Brown and I both agreed that support for the latest Bill was necessary. Brown recommended accordingly to the Shadow Cabinet. Realising that I might need to take part in detailed analysis of the Bill, I had used some of the time before we gathered at midday to prepare the brief, to recall details of the EEO debate of 1986, and to check my own contributions to the debate in the Senate.

It was when we began to deal with the agenda that the first warning bells began to sound. Sinclair, the embattled leader of the National Party, was in the chair in Howard's absence at the press conference at which he justified the sacking of Peacock. Ian Sinclair had his own problems that week, problems which determined his sense of priority on issues before us. Ian Sinclair faced the critical conference of his National Party at week's end, a conference which was likely to spell the end of the coalition arrangement between the Liberal and National parties. The erratic Premier of Queensland, driven by recklessness and ambition, was attacking Sinclair and his federal colleagues at every opportunity.

Sinclair believed he could deliver the numbers for several critical votes at week's end, but was desperate to avoid giving Premier Bjelke-Petersen any excuse for a 'free hit' in the few days remaining before the conference. As Sinclair saw it, the Shadow Cabinet agenda contained two difficult items, one of them the EEO Bill, and both requiring to be deferred until John Howard could be present. It was after lunch that discussion of the two difficult items commenced. Brown opened the discussion by speaking to his written analysis of the Bill and setting out his reasons for recommending that we should not oppose the Bill. He presented a good case honestly. Sinclair followed and indicated that the Bill presented a problem for his party.

At this stage, Howard emphasised what he called the 'absolute priority' of acting to maintain the Coalition and the need to act in furtherance of this strategic approach. It was only as events unfolded that I realised that his statement of 'absolute priority' was one that he really meant. Absolute—even if the alternative was the political survival of a Shadow Cabinet colleague. Sinclair then followed up by indicating that his colleagues could not support the Bill. So there we were, after having sacked Andrew Peacock four hours earlier, setting up the conditions for my resignation.

It was at this stage that I joined the discussion. In what the press later in the week, on the basis of leaked reports, called a 'passionate discussion', I pointed out the impossibility for me of any position that did not support the position I presented in 1986 on behalf of the Coalition. I warned my colleagues that this was an issue that could force my resignation if pushed too far, and that it was double jeopardy for me as I had to face my preselectors for re-endorsement at the weekend. My contribution was angry and forceful.

The Shadow Cabinet then considered (very briefly) the option of the parties voting separately on the issue, but Howard found this unacceptable. As far as Sinclair was concerned the only recommendation that met his political needs that week was total opposition to the Bill. As I realised just how serious this was for me personally, I intervened several more times. I reminded them that I had been acting on their behalf in August 1986 when I demanded that the Government extend EEO cover to statutory authorities, that they were placing me in an impossible situation in which I would have to consider resignation. Howard objected to this, saying that I could not ask Shadow Cabinet to consider the matter under threat from me; he also repeated several times his view that the overwhelming strategic consideration had to be the maintenance of the Coalition.

My friend Ian Macphee, himself to be sacked from the Shadow Cabinet within three weeks, passed several notes to me during the discussion to see what could be done. When a vote on Brown's recommendation to support the Bill was eventually taken, there were only four votes of the Shadow Cabinet in favour of the recommendation together with perhaps one of the outer shadow ministry. The four were: Brown, [Fred] Chaney, Macphee and me. The rest, including Peter Durack, Jim Carlton, Tony Messner and John Howard, deserted me and sealed my resignation—some not understanding, some understanding but not caring.

Now that the decision was made to oppose the Bill, we broke about 4.30 pm so that Brown could marshal some arguments to oppose what he had recommended we support. We reassembled as a Shadow Cabinet only at 8 pm where Brown presented a thin, miserable, incredible package. In essence, we were to demand certain amendments and, if these were unsuccessful, would oppose the Bill. We had proposed more than 30 amendments to the EEO Bill in 1986, but when these failed, had managed to support the Bill and the principle it embodied. To be told now that we would be expected to oppose the companion Bill, which I had called for, would expose me to ridicule and to criticism which I would merit.

The Shadow Cabinet settled Brown's amendment. I reserved my position, which in Liberal Party code meant that I would consider my position in relation to my place in the Shadow Cabinet and front bench. My reservation was acknowledged.

In view of the crisis, the likelihood that the Bill would be debated in the House of Representatives that week, and my preselection at the weekend, I sought out two close friends, Robert Hill and Chris Puplick, and apprised them of the problem. Their advice was that I could vote honourably for the amendment, and that there would be time to take the matter back to the Shadow Cabinet, twice if necessary, before it came before the Senate for debate.

At this stage too I let Jenny know that I had a real problem. My policy adviser Joan-Mary Hinds presented a different problem. Normally in Canberra on sitting weeks, she was in Sydney this week and would not know of the details of the developing crisis for the office. Her job would be forfeit if I resigned from the Shadow Cabinet but, as I did not trust her judgment on this matter, I did not brief her as I did not brief the other members of my Sydney office. Briefing of other people, including staff, family and friends, was on a strict 'need to know' basis. On this basis, the decision not to advise Joan-Mary was a correct one.

QUITTING SHADOW CABINET (1987)

If the Monday had been bad, the Tuesday was worse—for that matter each day that week up to Friday became progressively worse. Tuesday, 24 March was the day of our last joint meeting as a Coalition. Neil Brown, the complete legal advocate, argued for the Shadow Cabinet position (and against his own recommendation), emphasising the 'grave deficiencies' of the Bill, the 'pseudo-quotas' it allegedly contained, the 'burdens for business' and so on. Earlier I had heard him tell the backbench committee on industrial relations just what a horrendous piece of legislation this was—the effort of a real 'hired gun'. To be fair to Brown, the ability to argue passionately in public for a collegial position in which one did not believe is regarded as a virtue in political circles in Australia, and in the Liberal Party in particular. It is regarded as an essential part of the armament of any barrister, member of a cabinet or shadow cabinet.

I had never been able to do this easily. Mostly I had been spared the need to speak to some of the dreadful positions we adopted as parties. But recently I had found some of those positions morally offensive. For example, I had failed to vote on a couple of motions by conservative Tasmanian Brian Harradine designed to withhold certain benefits from people in de facto relationships and I had abstained too on a motion by Democrat David Vigor regarding the limiting of tobacco promotion.

My problem now was that the Equal Employment Opportunity (Commonwealth Authorities) Bill was considered an employment matter, not a matter affecting the status of women. So, Brown had its carriage in the House and his counterpart would deal with it in the Senate. I had no role to play, and furthermore, was required to keep silent during party room consideration of the Bill. I managed to disobey the rules and signal some of my distress to the meeting by interjecting angrily on one of the more Neanderthal of the National Party members, Michael Cobb of Parkes, when he made a more than usually outrageous statement about the legislation. Steele Hall said he would vote with the Government, Chris Puplick reserved his position. The quality of National Party concern was encapsulated by the contribution of Gary Nehl, whose total speech to the party room consisted of: 'This is another piece of socialist crap. Let's throw it out.'

The party room, inadequately briefed, and ignoring the policy imperatives implicit in the principle of EEO, endorsed the recommendation of the Shadow Cabinet. At lunch, I passed the table at which Peacock and Steele Hall were eating. Andrew asked me: 'Are you all right, mate?' Hall just looked thoughtful. I said very little but it was an interesting contact in light of what followed. My position was now extremely tenuous—but was to become impossible within a day.

That afternoon in Question Time, as I contemplated a series of awful personal alternatives, Fred Chaney came and chatted. He told me I looked awful—was I unwell? Margaret Reid then asked the same thing—it was sweet of her. During the morning of Wednesday, 25 March I visited the Law and Government Group of the Parliamentary Library Research Service and spoke to Kathryn Cole, wife of Laurie Oakes, the television commentator. He had appeared on television grossly overweight and I chatted to her about relatively painless dietary management of obesity. Quite coincidentally, about 15 minutes later, I received a phone call from Oakes himself. He wanted to ask me some questions. I agreed to hear the questions but guaranteed him no answers. The question when it came was a blockbuster. 'Did you threaten to resign at the Shadow Cabinet on Monday?' When I refused to comment, he asked no more questions.

Realising what this could mean, I went immediately to Howard and advised him of the question. Graham Morris was there. We agreed to wait and see what transpired; [it was said that] 'Martin Riordan would sniff around'. Fearing the worst, I began work on a resignation letter in the private access volume of my computer. At 4.50 pm I was summoned urgently from the Senate to Howard's office to be advised that Oakes was likely to run his story on the 6 pm news, 'in which case we would have a problem'. I understand that the leadership group met between 5 and 6 pm. I took advice from Keith Kessell in Chaney's office; we agreed that Oakes would not hold off the story and that it was not worth approaching him. I phoned Jenny to warn her to watch, and gathered Chris Crawford from my office together with Chris Wallace and Kessell from Chaney's office to watch the television.

Oakes led with the story that I had threatened to resign from Shadow Cabinet during 'an angry meeting' on 23 March 1987. We took a video of the segment. I saw Howard immediately, and from then on, at various times during the evening. In contrast to his obsessive concern with the welfare of the doomed Coalition at the Shadow Cabinet two days earlier, Howard now displayed decisive intelligence, a clear grasp of the issues, friendly and genuine concern, and distress at the course of action he now, finally, understood I would take. His office was now under siege from media heavies—the questions which could not be avoided were:

1. Will Baume resign or stay?
2. Will he or will he not support the Shadow Cabinet position on the EEO (CW Authorities) Bill?

Leaving Howard at 6.20 pm, I returned to my office and briefed Chris Crawford. The 'need to know' criterion now included him. Crawford advised resignation. I then called my wife, Jenny, again; she had a discussion group meeting at another house at 8 pm, but promised to talk to our mothers, to Sarah and to Ian.

Crawford undertook to keep the press at bay and did this magnificently during the remainder of the crisis. Puplick and Hill arrived and stayed most of the night with me. Chaney came briefly; he was late for a dinner but would return later. Robert Hill wanted me to stay but did not see how I could do so with any credibility or honour. Chris Puplick gave me two lots of advice: mindful of the weekend preselection, Senator Puplick advised me to stay, while my friend Chris Puplick advised me to resign.

I spoke again to Jenny just before she left for her discussion group. I advised her I would probably resign and would like her to be with me; she agreed to come down the next morning on the first available seat, which meant the mid-morning plane.

I saw John Howard again in his office. He begged me to stay. He pointed out, accurately, that I had been used as a pawn in an exercise directed against him. He wanted me on his front bench as a reasoned and articulate liberal voice. He indicated that a different portfolio could be arranged, that the timing of the whole thing was terrible, that it was a 'body blow', etc.

But the bottom line was always that I would be required, while I was a member of the Shadow Cabinet, to support the decision on the EEO Bill. I agreed with this appreciation, but pointed out that the requirement to support the decision was the main reason that resignation was my likely course. We agreed that a decision could not be delayed past the morning.

Back in my office at 8.30 pm, I phoned Ted Pickering to advise him of the disastrous effect in relation to preselection. He was calm and began damage control immediately. I then phoned Betty Grant, who wanted me to avoid resignation. Chris Crawford ordered some food to be sent down—I cannot remember what it was. Fred Chaney returned from his dinner and we argued on in the office, Chaney and Puplick using my whiteboard to construct decision paths, etc.

Robert Hill phoned [his wife,] Diana; she advised against resignation, as did George Brandis and Tom Harley, each of whom phoned in. Interestingly, all those who advised against resignation this night from outside the Parliament agreed later that it was the only proper course I could have taken. At some stage in the course of events, my brother Stephen phoned to see if I was all right. When I explained the problem and asked for his advice, he replied: 'It depends on how much you want the job.' That really settled it for me.

At about 10.30 pm, I found Jenny at the discussion group. She had the support of my family for anything I did. She asked did I have to support the decision of Shadow Cabinet as part of any package; if so, how could I possibly stay with any honour. I told her I was determined to go and she promised to be down as soon as possible.

At 11.15 pm, John Howard phoned again from the Commonwealth Club. When I advised him that my decision at that stage was to resign he said, 'Oh no! This is a body blow! Please sleep on it.' We then agreed to meet for breakfast at 7.15 am.

Back at my Woden Gardens unit, I found my friend and tenant Stewart McArthur busy preparing his speech for the Bill the next day in the House. I told him then what I had not been permitted to tell the party room: that his arguments were wrong and would be seen as wrong and weak by the press and public. Nevertheless, he should prepare a good and strong speech. I warned him further that I would resign from the Shadow Cabinet over the Bill in the morning. The news seemed to startle him.

I got to bed at 11.45 pm. Strangely, I had no doubt about the course I was about to take, nor about its correctness. Perhaps because of this, sleep came easily.

Arriving at Parliament House by 7.15 am, I beat the press who set up their cameras a little later. Chris Crawford was already there, hard at work; Chris Puplick arrived almost immediately. Then John Howard arranged to meet me for breakfast at 7.25 am. Arriving in the dining room, Russ Gorman, the Labor Member for Greenway, congratulated me warmly on my position, but then begged me not to resign.

Interestingly, I learned later from a Sydney Jewish journalist that he had occasion to speak to Graham Richardson during the 16 or so hours before my resignation became final. The journalist asked him what would happen. Richardson is reported to have said that there was no doubt at all that I would resign. He was right.

Breakfast was unsatisfactory as some uncomprehending MP came and sat with us. So Howard and I went to the Senate Rose Garden and walked and talked there. He repeated his offer, but with the same proviso. We continued walking to the back of Parliament House but were there confronted by television cameras, which accompanied us all the way back to the Reps side door.

Leaving John at his office, I returned to my office and settled my resignation letter. Jenny phoned Chris Crawford to check on certain press reports that I had been talked out of resignation. Unable to talk freely because of a journalist camped in with him, Chris was still able to assure Jenny that I was resigning.

QUITTING SHADOW CABINET (1987)

The office phones ran hot but Chris Crawford was able to give effect to our policy of offering no public comment at all. I finalised my resignation letter and delivered it to Howard at about 9.30 am. John showed me his response and both were released about half an hour later. My resignation letter read as follows:

26th March 1987.

It is with deep personal regret that I tender you my resignation from the Shadow Cabinet.

I have very much appreciated your support and understanding in the discussions we have held about this matter. You know from our discussions that I cannot, consistent with my principles, vote for the Shadow Cabinet and Party room decisions to oppose the Equal Employment Opportunity (Commonwealth Authorities) Bill 1987.

You will be aware that this decision is directly counter to views which I put and to amendments I proposed seven months ago on behalf of, and with the authority of, the Shadow Cabinet and the Opposition Parties.

You must be able to command full support from your Front Bench for every decision and so it is proper that I resign as a Shadow Cabinet Minister.

Thank you for your support and concern during the numerous discussions we have had in the past twenty-four hours. My object remains to ensure that the Coalition defeats Labor and to see the restoration of hope and good government under your Leadership.

I will pursue this goal and contribute towards it with vigour and determination from the backbench. You have my continuing personal support and good wishes in your great task and in the goals you pursue on behalf of all of us in the Liberal Party.

Yours Sincerely
Peter Baume

John Howard's reply was:

26th March 1987.

Senator the Hon Peter Baume
Senator for New South Wales
Parliament House
Canberra ACT 2600

I refer to your letter of today's date in which you have tended your resignation from the Shadow Cabinet. I accept your resignation with enormous regret. You are aware of the high personal regard in which I hold you. I have always appreciated your contributions to the Shadow Cabinet. They have been based on integrity.

Your deeply held views on equal opportunity are understood. However Shadow Cabinet took the view that there were differences between the Bill now before the Parliament and the amendments put seven months ago.

In the final analysis there is an absolute requirement that all Shadow Ministers fully support decisions of the Shadow Cabinet. You have quite properly acknowledged this in your letter.

With kind regards,
Yours Sincerely
John Howard

He issued an accompanying press statement as follows:

Senator the Hon. Peter Baume, L46/87

Senator the Hon Peter Baume has today resigned from the Shadow Cabinet. I attach his letter of resignation together with my response. I have appointed Senator the Hon Peter Durack QC as acting spokesman for the Opposition on Community Services and Status of Women.

Senator Baume's resignation is due to the absolute requirement that all Shadow Ministers fully support decisions of the Shadow Cabinet once taken. The Opposition is against the Equal Employment Opportunity (Commonwealth Authorities) Bill 1987 for the following reasons. First, the Government has not subjected the Bill to the examination that the Government on 9 January 1987 undertook that it would subject all new proposals for business regulation. Secondly, the Bill in effect imposes pseudo quotas on the employment of women and other groups covered by the legislation. Thirdly, the Bill applies to independent contractors in addition to employees which we regard as unacceptable.

If the Government accepts these objections and acts accordingly by amendment or otherwise, the Opposition would be willing to support the measure. As Mr Brown said last night: 'Indeed, we would have voted without any quibble for a Bill which was a genuine equal opportunity Bill based on merit and one that had been tested against the Government's own business regulation procedures and which had passed them'.

Some media reports have suggested that the Opposition's stance on this Bill is due entirely to the views of National Party members of the Coalition. Such reports are nonsense. There are widespread objections to the Bill in its present form within the Parliamentary Liberal Party as well as in the National Party. These objections have been articulated in the Shadow Cabinet, in the Joint Party Committee and in the Joint Parties Room.

The Shadow Cabinet recommendation was supported by a clear majority of those who participated in the Party room debate. The arguments in the press release were those that had been developed by Neil Brown after his original recommendation to support the Bill had been lost in Shadow Cabinet. They were either minor matters requiring amendment, or they were wrong, or they were contrived. I answered the merits of the arguments when I spoke to the Bill in the Senate a month later.

Friends continued to phone frantically urging me to stay. They missed the point that to stay would be to lose all credibility and potency—to become just another compromising time server. George Brandis phoned again to say that he had now reversed his opinion and believed 'this is the most noble resignation in Australian political history'. Maybe. Maybe not.

I phoned and advised everyone in the Sydney office. Joan-Mary was shocked as she lost her job with the decision. She was appalled that I had not asked her to come to Canberra to share the crisis and the decision making, but the strategy of leaving her in Sydney was correct in view of her personality and persona. I talked to all the heavies in Sydney again and offered Frank Hooke the chance to take the hotel room at preselection alone without me. Jenny arrived before midday and it was good to be together.

Once it was all over I felt right: the Shadow Cabinet had turned its back on me when it should have given loyalty to the position I had taken on its behalf. My leader had placed his Coalition priorities ahead of those of a Liberal colleague and the primacy of that Howard priority made my resignation inevitable. I felt clean. And I felt free. Above all, I had not failed myself or those I love. When the crunch came I had been able to resign my position and seniority, built up over 13 years, and had been able to do so with calm detachment and no regrets for myself. My regrets had been for my colleagues and party, and for Frank Hooke, whose chances of beating the dreaded Bronwyn Bishop for a Senate nomination in New South Wales were now reduced.

Later in the morning I was called to Hill's office where, with Puplick, we talked Ian Macphee out of resigning with me. Little did we know he would be sacked within a few weeks. He was genuinely ill with an abscessed tooth so we sent him back to Melbourne, still in the Shadow Cabinet, for urgent dental care.

Now for the future! For the Liberal Forum; for publishing, writing, lecturing, thinking, and for saying what I thought necessary for Australia. After more than nine years as an office holder, minister, or shadow minister, the back bench would offer some real opportunities and possibilities. Just how many I did not know then.

Epilogue to my Resignation from Shadow Cabinet

The Federal Coalition ended after the Parliamentary National Party repudiated one of the elements of an agreement between Howard and Sinclair. This occurred on 28 April. On the next day, I asked the party—the Liberal Party alone now—to reconsider its handling of the EEO (Commonwealth Authorities) Bill. I pointed out to the party that our task was to find a way to handle the matter with least damage, that we were now no longer subject to National Party veto or pressure, that to adhere to our position would inevitably lead to mass defections in the Senate, and that in all the circumstances the best course might be to allow a free vote in the Senate. This would have involved least direct challenge to John Howard.

The party was not interested. The conservatives led by [Shirley] Walters, by Carrick et al., argued that there was no need to alter our position. John Watson made an interesting contribution to the debate. He mentioned that he had been unable to demonstrate to his daughter the gross defects allegedly present in the Bill. He offered the view that the party room had been misled in March and that we deserved better. The decision nevertheless was to stand with the March decision.

On 30 April the Bill was debated at the second reading in the Senate, and early the following week a division was called in the Senate to oppose the third reading of the Bill. Seven senators crossed the floor: Puplick, Hill, [Baden] Teague, [Mike] Townley, [Reg] Withers, [David] Macgibbon, as well as me. [Don] Jessop did not cross the floor but abstained. [David] Hamer, in craven style, said nothing and had himself paired. He sat in the gallery and some may have concluded, incorrectly, that he too was abstaining.

The effect was damaging for Howard and for the party. The damage could have been avoided either by taking up Neil Brown's original recommendation to Shadow Cabinet or by granting senators a free vote. The leadership, through arrogance or foolishness, adopted neither course. The party was so shaken by the size of the defection (25 per cent of the Liberal Party voted for the Bill and one other abstained) that in the very next week, when the same EEO provisions appeared in another Bill (The Wool Industry Bill) the party decided to support the Bill, and the provisions, rather than face another mass defection. So we won on the issue. But at enormous cost.

When the Parliament was dissolved and a double-dissolution election called just one month later, each of us suffered in the preselection that followed. Robert Hill was demoted from first to third, and Baden Teague was placed fifth in South Australia. Don Jessop was dropped entirely. Mike Townley withdrew from preselection when it was made clear that he would not be re-endorsed. Reg Withers retired. I was relegated to second on the New South Wales ticket and Chris Puplick went down to fourth. The only saving grace was that the dreaded Bronwyn Bishop failed in an attempt to have us demoted further in her favour.

My speech in the Senate on the Equal Employment Opportunities (Commonwealth Authorities) Bill was the best and most important speech I have ever given. It is reproduced in this book, together with the remarks made about it by Senator Peter Cook of the Australian Labor Party.

EASTER AT POINT LONSDALE (1987)

The second main event of 1987 was our Easter at Ballara (the old Deakin house) south of Geelong. This is described in the following words. The holiday brought together members of the Liberal Forum and some of our wives in a congenial atmosphere.

Jenny and I spent the latter half of Easter 1987 at Point Lonsdale on the western side of Port Phillip Bay. The invitation had come from Tom Harley, our colleague and collaborator in the Liberal Forum. This body had been established in February 1985 to advance liberal thought, and had enjoyed greater success than we could ever have imagined.

Tom Harley is the great-grandson of Alfred Deakin. Tall, dark, slim, handsome, intelligent and very tough, he is indispensable to the forum and its operation. Educated at Oxford, he had already helped George Brandis and Don Markwell to edit one liberal book—*Liberals Face the Future*—before joining George and Yvonne Thompson in producing *Australian Liberalism: The Continuing Vision* at the end of 1986.

Someone told us that they once phoned a restaurant seeking Tom Harley. The waiter did not know him by name, but recognised him immediately when the caller described him as being tall and handsome, and right out of Brideshead. Tom is a good strategic thinker. He had worked with Snedden when Bill was Speaker of the House of Representatives during the Fraser years, and worked now as troubleshooter for BHP. He had played a big part in BHP's successful defence against a series of takeover bids in 1986.

It was Tom who invited us to join his family at their beach home at Point Lonsdale. This house had been built by Alfred Deakin and named 'Ballara' after his then constituency of Ballarat. It is a splendid old wooden, rambling, basic, comfortable, relaxed place with a large garden containing ample ti-tree for the open fires we needed in the late autumn cold.

On Sunday, 19 April, Jenny and I flew to Melbourne using Jenny's one annual free interstate trip. We had visited our oldest friends, the O'Malleys, in Wollongong and stayed with them the previous night. We were driven from Tullamarine to Geelong where we met Tom and George in the car park of the rather unpleasant looking (and sounding) Dinosaur Hotel on the Bellarine Highway. The arrangements worked perfectly. They arrived just a couple of minutes ahead of us and no-one had to wait for the other.

Harley had spent the previous two days showing Brandis some of western Victoria. George had hired a car, which had come to grief in a ditch some hours before we met them. But there they were, laughing hugely at it all, with various pieces of Mr Avis's vehicle lying loose in the boot among the luggage, and speeding us from Geelong to Point Lonsdale.

That weekend at Ballara there was a full house. Geoff and Judith Harley, Tom [Harley], George Brandis, David Harley and three of his friends, Jenny and me, and Sid and Yvonne Thompson. There was room for us all, the whole being tremendously evocative of my own childhood when we had similar weekend gatherings at my Collaroy home.

Geoff Harley was an ophthalmic surgeon and was then chairman of the medical staff of the Royal Melbourne Children's Hospital. He was calm and unruffled, and very liberal. Judith, his wife, was artistic and sensitive, intelligent and fey. She was an excellent hostess precisely because she did not worry about anything, and enjoyed events as they developed around her.

Liberal Forum ('Black Hand' to its members) was thus, as to the majority of its membership, together for several days. Tom, George, Yvonne and I were in one spot. We had phone contact with Ian Macphee, Robert Hill and Chris Puplick at various times as the great events of the weekend developed.

Three weeks earlier I had resigned from the Shadow Cabinet and had spoken against party policy in relation to the Human Rights and Equal Opportunity Commission in the Senate a few days later. John Howard had sacked Andrew Peacock from the Shadow Cabinet two days before I resigned. The National Party Conference on 28 March had given Ian Sinclair only qualified support for the continued Coalition of the Liberal and National parties in opposition, and the future of the Coalition would depend on the next meeting of the parties when the Parliament resumed on 28 April. Two Queensland shadow ministers, Ray Braithwaite and Stan Collard, had already resigned in accordance with the orders of their state organisation.

Howard had negotiated the elements of a possible continuing coalition with Sinclair earlier in the week before Easter. It required the National Party to distinguish between the treatment of its 'coalitionist' and 'separatist' groups—something we doubted that party would accept.

History was to prove us correct and the National Party repudiated one key element of the package at its meeting on 28 April. But during the weekend at Ballara we could not foresee that with certainty. What we could foresee was that John Howard would reshuffle his shadow ministry that weekend to fill the four vacancies (Peacock, Baume, Braithwaite, Collard) that had emerged over the preceding month.

The press had been suggesting that Ian Macphee, 'small-l' liberal, shadow minister for communications, and member of the 'Black Hand', might be dropped completely in the reshuffle.

Ian and Howard detested each other heartily. This had begun probably in government, but had become marked when John Howard interfered with the policy areas within Macphee's responsibility during the leadership of Andrew Peacock. Peacock's leadership had been fatally destabilised by the actions of friends and agents of John Howard's over a year or more. Many of us had been uncertain of Peacock's leadership and of his commitment to any particular policy direction, but his superlative performance in the 1984 general election had convinced most of us that he deserved another go.

As leader, John Howard had moved Ian Macphee 'sideways' into the communications area, only to see some of the most delicate and politically sensitive issues involve that area in the year that followed. Howard and Macphee had clashed repeatedly over the desirable direction of communications policy, reaching a crisis in January when Howard returned from holidays to carpet Macphee for a particular public statement likely to offend powerful media owners.

On that occasion Macphee had chatted to me before he met Howard and I had advised him to hold his comments and to reply only to the charges as they were levelled against him. It was my judgment that, handled in this way, he could easily respond to any criticism. That advice proved correct, but many people harboured the belief that, given any excuse, John Howard would sack Ian Macphee altogether.

The papers that weekend were full of anticipation about the reshuffle, including the possibility of a Macphee sacking. There was also increasing recognition of the emerging power and influence of the 'wets' or small-l liberals, now finally in the open and in the field challenging some of the worst nonsense of the economic rationalists.

We at Ballara, and the other Liberal Forum colleagues in phone contact, had provided the focus for that small-l revival by providing a visible and strong point about which friends could gather. As events were to unfold, our influence and power were to increase dramatically and to become even more unwelcome than they were that weekend. But it was to be the power and influence of a large minority excluded from decision making—a certain recipe for destabilisation and disaster.

Ian Macphee had taken his wife, Julie, and son, Scobie, to Canberra for Easter, and they were combining the role of family tourist with that of waiting for news. We were in frequent contact from Ballara, as the hours and days ticked by.

On the Monday morning the group considered my immediate future and my needs. It determined what should be the content of the speech I would make on the Equal Opportunity Bill that had caused my resignation, and advised me on a medium term course within the party, which could be useful and constructive.

Later that day we walked in a cold autumn breeze to the ocean beach with headlands stretching away to the south and west as far as Barwon Heads, while a few happy, hardy souls walked happily through the sand towards the lighthouse that dominates the point. Later still we went across to a local restaurant for a superb meal, which took us through to midnight. There was still no news of the details of the reshuffle although inspired leaks from the Parliament House gave us no comfort.

On the morning of Tuesday, 21 April George Brandis returned to his practice at the Brisbane Bar, taking Mr Avis's injured vehicle back with him to drop it off at the airport to a startled company. Sid Thompson went up to Melbourne with Geoff Harley, who had to start work again and we were left to wait.

Quite early, soon after 9.30 or so, Ian Macphee phoned from Canberra to tell us that Howard had called him in and sacked him completely from the Shadow Ministry. He had indicated that the reasons did not relate to Ian's technical competence, a thinly veiled reference to Howard's belief that Ian had been a main source of Shadow Cabinet leaks. It appeared that some astounding appointments had been made to fill what were now five vacancies, although these remained unconfirmed for the present.

EASTER AT POINT LONSDALE (1987)

Ian was proposing to hold a press conference to attack John Howard frontally. We advised strongly against this, recommending instead the 'more in sorrow than anger' approach. Ian Macphee eventually adopted this suggestion—for the first few hours anyway—and one crisis was averted.

Tom advised Creighton Burns and Peter Cole-Adams of *The Age* of what had happened and the phone then ran hot as Michelle Grattan and others phoned in for confirmation.

Gradually the other new frontbenchers were identified. Alexander Downer, my cousin Michael Baume, Jim Short, Peter Reith and Wal Fife resurrected from the dead and moved into the Shadow Cabinet. John Moore and John Spender moved to the front table as well. The new five were a pretty motley lot. But one thing they all had in common was that they were Howard loyalists. It became crystal clear that this was the most ideological reshuffle we had ever seen with one wing of the party picking up all the positions, with the other wing gaining nothing and losing Macphee by sacking.

We were able to brief the press accordingly, and this was the line taken by everyone. The reshuffle got a panning from the moment its details became known. Our line that 'the party now had more talent on the back than on the front bench' was run widely. And Ian Macphee, having taken the high ground in his initial response to the news of his sacking, was able to go on to the attack with spectacular success later in the day.

After lunch we drove up to Melbourne with Yvonne and Tom, listening to news bulletins and comment as we drove. We left our gear at the Walsh Street house of the Harleys and then left with Tom to eat dinner in East Melbourne. On this occasion Bill Snedden came in with his friend Rowena and we all sat together and ate a long and alcoholic dinner. During this meal, Bill explained solemnly that it was all nonsense to worry about liberal and conservative philosophies. The difference was between a belief in socialism on the one hand, and capitalism on the other! He assured us that this simple difference would explain all—sadly it does not seem to fit the phenomena I met daily in Canberra and in the Parliament.

After dinner we returned briefly to Vale Street, to the house Tom shares with Rupert Myer. Rupert had made a video of a sensational *Carleton–Walsh Report* in which Ian had confronted and got the better of John Howard. So we returned to Walsh Street and to bed.

The reshuffle was known. Ian Macphee had been sacked in an act of hairy-chested machismo and five undistinguished people had been paid off for loyalty. It meant that Howard had decided on a path of confrontation, a kind of 'crash or crash through' in the Whitlam tradition. It meant that he was now doomed to function as a factional rather than as a party leader, and doomed to destruction in the longer term.[1]

It meant that he had rejected any kind of *rapprochement* with the more liberal elements in his party at the very time he should have been talking and presenting himself as the healer and unifying force. In short it signalled the end of John Howard, at least in the medium term, sooner if the Coalition fails.

Everyone, including John Howard, realised in time that the Easter reshuffle had been a disaster. After he had led us to our third successive election loss, he discarded several of the Easter appointees, and added Chris Puplick from the Liberal Forum to his Shadow Cabinet.

But as Easter 1987 ended these events lay in the future. The press reaction to the reshuffle was uniformly hostile, as it should have been. It was a devastating demonstration of the judgment of John Howard and of the ineptitude of those advising him. It put the final nail in any hopes we might have had of an election victory in the mid-year.

The drama of the weekend made it unique; the decisions made it sad. But withal, the beauty and atmosphere of Ballara and Point Lonsdale made it pleasurable—and quite unforgettable.

The next morning we analysed the uniformly hostile press, spent an hour or two in the Municipal Art Library where Jenny did some research on her great Aunt Ada Whiting, then back to Sydney, to a meeting of our 'Black Ankle' group to discuss the state preselections. And so to bed.

---

1   I was quite wrong.

REFLECTIONS ON A TRIP TO QUEENSLAND (1987)

These are reflections on a trip to the annual conference of the Queensland Division of the Liberal Party, in which a blunt and difficult discussion took place between liberal wets and the parliamentary party leadership.

John Howard had just started his address to the Queensland conference of the Liberal Party when I reached the ballroom area of the Hilton Hotel in central Brisbane. I slipped into the back of the room, ignoring the other federal parliamentarians sitting in the front row, and stood behind the last row of seats to listen to the speech. Standing with others in the same area, behind the last row of seats, were Tom Harley and George Brandis. Greeting them briefly, I then stood on my own and attended to the familiar messages of the leader. He spoke from a lectern to the right of the top table as I looked at it. The lighting was poor so that he was inadequately highlighted; never a tall man, he appeared as an insignificant talking head and shoulders above a standard hotel lectern.

Sitting closest to Howard was federal president John Valder, then successively were Queensland president John Moore, state director Gary Neat, federal deputy leader Neil Brown, and Senate Liberal leader Fred Chaney. Each of the politicians noticed me with surprise, and in Chaney's case, with some alarm too. Uninvited and unexpected, I had come to Brisbane at the suggestion of Liberal Forum colleagues Brandis and Harley, and stood now, like Banquo's ghost at the back of the room.

The speech was flat and uninspiring. It emphasised the themes of industrial relations and reduced government expenditure as the main elements of a Howard strategy for election. Not only does he sound like a boring accountant, not only does he now sound like a beaten man, but I doubt that the message will enthuse or attract the average Australian.

If that is what our election strategy is, we are going to get a bath—and perhaps the sooner the better. What is more, if this is his message and inspiration for Australia, he does not deserve to succeed. Not only that, but were he to become prime minister he would do the task without inspiration—a pedestrian, plodding, decent politician promoted beyond his capacity.

After the speech I joined Brandis, Harley and Hill for coffee. Trish Worth also joined us and we got from Hill and Worth an account of the unhappy federal executive meeting of the previous day. It appears that Hill and Chaney had a blunt talk on the plane on the way up and agreed that they should extend the talk at the Queensland state conference. Chaney joined the table briefly and suggested that arrangements be made for me to join the discussion with Howard and Robert Hill. Chaney then left the group. Howard supporter (Colonel) Peter White MC MP, the new shadow minister for defence, saw us at the table, approached, greeted us briefly, then left rapidly. He has been promoted to the front bench solely as a reward for loyalty, and wanted nothing to do with oddballs like us.

We determined what should be the elements of the conversation later in the morning, deciding to make the leaders explain to us their concerns, outline what they wanted from us, refusing to allow them to define all the party's problems as arising from us, and confronting them with the failures of leadership that have made the problems inevitable. Then we went down to set up a table and sell a few copies of *Australian Liberalism: The Continuing Vision*, into the meeting to hear from successful and sleek middle-class lawyers some ugly debate on limiting the unemployment benefit for those unable to find work within six months. To the credit of the party, the motion which they were supporting was lost resoundingly. Neil Brown came and chatted, clearly trying to make conversation and win friends. He does not allude to his awful gaffe after the coup in Fiji a week earlier. That coup by the Royal Fiji Military Forces had overthrown the government elected three weeks earlier, mainly because it was supported by and contained a large number of Indian Fijians. Brown had met the press, had been extensively reported and quoted, but had failed to mount any unequivocal condemnation of the coup. There is no doubt that he is a third-rate deputy leader.

John Moore came and said a friendly hullo. Don Cameron was there along with Kathy and Bob Sullivan, and also Jane and Ian (and George) Prentice—she very pregnant. Then Fred Chaney delivered a strong and vibrant speech to the convention, showing Howard up in the process. During the speech, he rejected attacks on middle-class welfare, angrily, identifying the difficulties faced by intact families with dependent children. Chaney extrapolated from this to declare that a Liberal government should direct extra cash assistance to intact families. This is simply bad logic—a simple non sequitur. In times of financial hardship resources must be directed to the neediest, not necessarily to those in the 'tightest' period of their life cycle. Chaney was angry as he made these arguments, looking at me, and speaking to me particularly, though he is addressing a large audience. John Moore recognised me from the chair as I left the hall—there was a note of surprised interest in his voice that I was there at all.

The Queensland Liberals are flat, disheartened, discouraged and uncertain of how to proceed. No wonder. The leadership is discredited publicly, the Government is leading in the polls, and the course on which they have determined to take us is not only being contested by we liberals, it is a course that will repel rather than attract voters.

At midday, with Chaney and Hill, I went to Howard's suite on the twenty-fifth floor. It was 'palatial impersonal' but quiet and adequate for our purpose. Howard joined us a little after we had begun and we continued the discussion until just after 1 pm when I had to depart for the plane—never having explained to anyone how I have come to be in Brisbane at all. The conversation is direct and brutal, albeit still unsatisfactory. Chaney had the audacity to assert that our difficulties with the EEO Bill were due in part to the attempts of my colleagues to accommodate my difficulties; really it is hard to deal with people so blinkered in their comprehension of events that have involved them. My difficulties with the EEO Bill were created by the Shadow Cabinet of which I was a member, and by the party room to which I belonged. My contribution to the crisis was limited to a stubborn and determined refusal on my part to support any dishonourable decision, and in fact to force the matter to public attention by resigning. That is what they really have against me.

But, apart from that matter, it was the *Four Corners* program that has them most exercised. They are astounded at the direct challenge to their own authority in taking arguments and issues directly to the public, rather than containing them within a system that they control. The *Four Corners* appearance in mid-April had been an interview between Andrew Olle and four of us, Macphee, Hill, Puplick and me. In that television interview we had asserted and discussed an alternative and liberal agenda to balance the arguments of the 'dries' and 'economic rationalists'. We had taken part in the program in the belief that alternative, and more compassionate, views needed to be presented as part of the wider spectrum of liberal belief and tradition. It arose as a natural extension of the work and priorities of the Liberal Forum agenda, and was resented by the leadership of the party precisely because of this.

Hill explained, directly and very quietly, that the situation now existing is largely of their own making. He outlined the new ideological directions, the corruption of the party room, which is now an unpleasant and confrontational place, the inadequacies of the recent frontbench reshuffle, and the responsibilities that the leadership must bear for many of these failures. Chaney wants to argue and reject the criticisms; Howard is more ready to take the criticisms on board—he is an essentially decent, even if dull and dreary, man. As time runs out, I suggest that we reconvene the meeting in Canberra at a convenient time.

EXECUTIVE GOVERNMENT AND THE FUNDING OF PARLIAMENT: THREATS, CRISES AND CONSTITUTIONAL CONFRONTATION (1989)

> It was the Revolution of 1688 that gave to Great Britain freedom and efficiency together, because it tipped the balance of power permanently on the side of Parliament.
>
> — Trevelyan, *A Shortened History of England*[1]

Recent events in Australia suggest that Trevelyan was wrong. The balance of power is not on the side of Parliament.

On 17 October the Senate debated a motion to establish a new select committee to examine issues related to in-vitro fertilisation and human embryo experimentation. During that debate, Senator Peter Walsh,[2] speaking on behalf of the Executive Government, questioned the justification for another select committee and said:

> I do not accept the proposition, which was accepted by the previous Government, that the amount of money appropriated for the Parliament is a matter for the Parliament to determine. It is a matter for the Executive to determine.[3]

---

1   Trevelyan (1942).
2   Senator for Western Australia.
3   Walsh, P., Speech on proposed senate select committee on human embryo experimentation, Senate Hansard, vol. 11, 1985: 1,425.

In relation to the proposed select committee, he made his threat more explicit, and linked the Government with it, by saying:

> That is my position and that is the policy of the Government … to the extent that this adds to the demands for funds for the Senate and for Senate committees, I certainly give no guarantee that that demand will be met.[4]

Senator Walsh raised clearly the issue of the funding of the Parliament by the Executive Government in Australia. He raised for examination a delicate relationship that has existed for 85 years between the Executive (representing the Crown) and the Parliament elected by the people, a relationship complicated by the fact that members of the Executive are also members of the Legislature.

He focused attention on the Parliament's need to be strengthened against attack by the Executive. Professor Gordon Reid, then deputy vice-chancellor and professor of politics at the University of Western Australia, now Governor of Western Australia, observed in a submission to the Jessop Committee in 1981:

> In the context of the vast scale of government we now practise in Australia, with the extensive accumulation of enacted legislation and the widespread delegation of authority to officials, the elected Senate needs to maintain, even strengthen, its procedures for scrutiny and enquiry into the affairs of the Executive Government. That is becoming increasingly important to the people of Australia.[5]

The relationship between the Crown and the Parliament in England was settled after the turbulent years of Stuart rule and formalised in the settlement reached after the 'Glorious Revolution' of 1688. This settlement established that the Crown had to come to the Parliament for its monies and no ruler or government since then in a Westminster system has been able to depart from that practice.

What has never been settled is an arrangement for the financial support of the Parliament itself. The question has assumed more importance as the cost of legislatures has risen and the roles of legislators have increased.

What emerged in the seventeenth century as the sole power of the legislature to authorise supply for the Crown has been eroded gradually as disciplined parties emerged and the Executive came to dominate the Legislature. In a sense, the Executive has replaced the seventeenth-century Crown in its domination of the Parliament. Further, although the Parliament won important controls over the Crown's resources, it failed to distinguish its own resources from those of the Crown and allowed its own requirements to be met by Treasury.

---

4   Walsh, Senate Hansard, vol. 11, 1985: 1,425.
5   Walsh, Senate Hansard, vol. 11, 1985: 1,425.

There is at least a 'creative tension' between Parliament and Executive, and clearly any move to 'starve' a Parliament would precipitate a major constitutional crisis.

The Executive sometimes argues, as did Senator Walsh, that it has sole financial responsibility, including responsibility for the Budget and for the revenue. Such an assertion is incorrect. The Executive prepares and presents the Budget, other appropriations and revenue proposals—but it is the Parliament that approves or disapproves them. It is the Parliament that bears ultimate constitutional responsibility for them all.

Between Parliament and the Executive two extreme positions could be envisaged. On one hand, a reckless and spendthrift Parliament could indulge itself unreasonably, and demand that the Executive fund and bear responsibility for those indulgences. Such a course would scarcely accord with notions of accountability and reasonableness. But on the other hand, the situation could arise where an Executive, in pursuit of total dominance of the political institutions of the nation, determined to starve a Parliament into submissive obedience by withdrawing from it the funds it requires to discharge its democratic functions and duties.

In between is a whole series of more reasonable positions that could be negotiated between the Executive and the Parliament to ensure that the legislature received adequate funding for its task within spending guidelines acceptable to the Executive. Between parties of goodwill and good sense, a middle course will always be found. What could be dangerous and difficult is the possibility of a confrontation should views like those of Senator Walsh be pushed to their extreme.

The Senate recognised this problem several years ago. As a result of a landmark committee report brought in by Senator Don Jessop, an agreement was reached with the Fraser Government that the appropriations for the Parliament would be presented in a separate Appropriation Bill, and that the size of the appropriation would be settled by negotiation between the two parties.

But the issue itself remains unresolved, and it is the issue that has re-emerged. If one looks to find some constitutional principle or convention that requires that the Legislature control its own finances, one is in difficulty. In Australia the Executive's dominance is reinforced by Section 56 of the Constitution, which provides that no monies may be raised by Parliament unless the purpose of the appropriation has been recommended in the same session by a message from the Governor-General. Since it is widely accepted that the Governor-General will act on the advice of ministers, no message authorising expenditure can come to the Parliament except with the concurrence of the Executive. Further, it seems that the Parliament itself cannot increase the amount to be appropriated over that specified in the Governor-General's message without a further enabling message. Finally, it is possible that the courts would refuse to rule on these matters and might refer any challenge back to the Parliament for resolution.

Parliaments in other democracies have faced the same problem, and have devised a variety of solutions. The British House of Commons is now funded by a House of Commons Commission established under its own statute. In France, funding is determined by a conference of the presiding officers and magistrates of the Court of Accounts. In Israel, the budget for the Legislature is the sole prerogative of the Knesset itself. And so on.

Following Senator Walsh's outburst, Senate Estimate Committee A saw fit to discuss the issue in its *Report to the Senate* of 11 October 1985 and to recommend that the Senate agree to a resolution calling for negotiation and agreement to resolve any disagreement. On 2 December the Senate adopted this recommendation. While the immediate threat of crisis was averted, the issue behind it remains unresolved. There is still no right of the Parliament to a penny of funds, and the Parliament is still exposed to the threats posed by the Peter Walshes of the world.

So back we come to Senator Walsh. Just in case his point was missed, the Honourable Senator finished his 17 October speech by saying:

> Finally, I explicitly do not accept the proposition that the Parliament determines how much money the Parliament will get. The Executive Government has the financial responsibility, and in the end the Executive Government will determine the question.[6]

If this view of the Hawke Government (or of any other government) was to be pressed we would be in for a major constitutional confrontation. It would be 1688 all over again. Meanwhile, reason and good sense—not any constitutional safeguards—are what avoid such a crisis.

---

6   Walsh, Senate Hansard, vol. 11, 1985: 1,425.

PART 3: POLICY CONCERNS

EQUAL EMPLOYMENT OPPORTUNITY (1987)

I lost my political career over the Equal Employment Opportunity (Commonwealth Authorities) Bill 1987 when I resigned from the Shadow Cabinet of John Howard in March 1987 and voted to support the Bill soon after. I faced Senate preselection within two days of resigning and was 'sent into Coventry'[1] by some of my colleagues. I was not punished officially by my party for my stand, but was put off the front bench (and was never put back on it—although, to be fair to the party, I was once invited to a junior position) and my ideas were not popular. There were motions put forward within the party to discipline anyone who departed from the official party position. I believed the provisions of the legislation were consistent with my liberalism and with the positions the party had traditionally taken. This speech, given in the Senate, outlines my position.

The Equal Employment Opportunity (Commonwealth Authorities) Bill 1987 will have my support. As a philosophical liberal, I can do nothing else but support the Bill. Liberalism is not and has never been just some economic doctrine. Liberalism cannot be presented as such to an informed electorate. Philosophical liberals believe passionately in equality of opportunity and in removing barriers, wherever they may be, which prevent people from exercising that equality. The greatest achievements of philosophical liberalism have been to remove such barriers. The ending of slavery, the emancipation of Jews and Catholics in Protestant England, public education, reform of the electoral system, the vote for women—these are just some of them. This Bill continues that tradition of extending equal opportunity and liberty.

---

1   This is a British phrase that means to treat someone as if they are not there—no speech, no contact, and so on. Available from: en.wikipedia.org/wiki/send+into+Coventry.

There are 30 Commonwealth authorities, employing 213,847 people, not otherwise covered by equal employment legislation, which will come under provisions of this Bill. To put the need for the legislation into some context, let us consider just two Commonwealth authorities. Of almost 90,000 staff employed permanently by the Australian Telecommunications Commission in 1986, fewer than 18,000 were women. In the Australian Postal Commission, while all typists and all word processing operators were women, there were no women among 53 divisional managers, there were just three women among 105 executives and there were no women among 274 persons classified as storemen.

I turn now to the specifics of the legislation. Consideration of this Bill resolves itself easily into several matters that can be taken *seriatim*. The first concerns the genesis of this Bill. This Bill emerged as a direct consequence of action taken by the Opposition in the Senate in August 1986 and of undertakings given by the Minister for Education and Minister Assisting the Prime Minister on the Status of Women, Senator [Susan] Ryan, during that debate. Honourable senators will recall that the Opposition sought then to extend the cover of equal employment opportunity [EEO] legislation to women employed by Commonwealth statutory authorities. Not only did we seek the extension of EEO to those quarter of a million or so employees; we moved an amendment to secure it and we pressed that amendment to a division.

Despite Opposition support for the amendment it was defeated by the combined votes of the Government and the Australian Democrats. Senator Ryan declined to accept the amendment but she had this to say in the debate:

> The other statutory authorities about which Senator Baume and Senator Haines have both expressed concern will be covered by specific legislation. The Bill is being drafted and will be introduced as soon as Government business permits.

With this Bill, the Minister for Employment and Industrial Relations, Mr [Ralph] Willis, on behalf of Senator Ryan, has responded to our demand that a considerable number of women be covered by equal employment opportunity legislation. With this Bill, therefore, Senator Ryan has discharged the promise she made last August.

Not only did we demand the introduction of this Bill; we also made some other demands that are now embodied in the legislation before us. We sought a title different from the title of the Bill before the Senate in August. We expressed that demand in an amendment. We pressed that amendment to a division. This Bill that we are debating tonight is named the Equal Opportunity (Commonwealth Authorities) Bill 1987. That is to say, the Government has now given expression in the title of this Bill to the sentiments of the amendment we proposed in August.

Senator Teague: It is a tribute to what you urged.

Senator Peter Baume: I thank Senator Teague.

Senator Haines: Senator, it was May. You said August when you meant May.

Senator Peter Baume: The Committee stages of the Bill took place in the Budget session, I believe. I have the Journals of the Senate for 22nd August.

But that is not all. We also sought a different definition of discrimination for the purposes of the Bill debated in August. We moved an amendment to that effect, too, and we pressed that amendment to a vote. This Bill contains a definition of discrimination consistent with what we asked for in August.

Another matter that has concerned some of my colleagues is the number of classes of persons whose interests are to be considered in this Bill. Honourable senators certainly have not forgotten that this Bill complements not only the affirmative action legislation of 1986, which dealt specifically with the needs of women for employment equity, but also the *Public Service Reform Act* of 1984, which concerned itself with the interests of wider groups of people.

The *Public Service Reform Act* makes specific references to women and to designated groups, which include Aboriginals and Torres Strait Islanders, certain classes of migrants and people with physical or mental disability. The opposition parties did not object to that provision in 1984. There is no objection in substance in the fact that this Bill contains reference to several classes of persons whose rights to equal opportunity should be considered. It does not constitute a ground for opposing the legislation. On the contrary, we should welcome the chance to secure equal opportunity too for those classes of persons, if it is needed.

Some concern has been expressed about the power of the minister, pursuant to Clause 12, to give directions to a relevant authority with respect to the performance of its obligations under the Act, when it is passed. It has been suggested that this power is new and sinister and that it could lead to the giving of inappropriate directions in relation to employment matters. We have heard reference to that tonight. Such concern is ill founded. Clause 12 is a standard type of clause found in most Acts constituting statutory authorities. The clause is very similar to Section 7 of the *Telecommunications Act*, Section 20 of the *Trade Practices Act*, Section 9 of the *Parliament House Construction Authority Act*, Section 7 of the *Australian Broadcasting Corporation Act* and Section 18 of the *National Crime Authority Act*, which allow ministerial directions to be given to Telecom Australia, the Trade Practices Commission, the Parliament House Construction Authority, the Australian Broadcasting Authority and the National Crime Authority, respectively.

The next matter to be discussed in considering this Bill is whether it contains fatal defects. Let us first consider some minor matters. Later let us look at the major question of whether this Bill leads us down the road to quotas. Clearly the Bill has a number of deficiencies. For example, it contains the same objectionable definition of employee as did the Bill which we considered in 1986—a definition which includes independent contractors as employees. We opposed such a definition then and we will oppose it now. It is as objectionable now as it was then. It is as unnecessary, as inappropriate and as unwanted.

Second, it has been claimed by those opposing the Bill that the Government has failed to submit this Bill, as it promised recently it would do with all legislation, to the scrutiny of its Business Regulation Review Unit before submitting the matter to the Parliament. We now know that the Government did make the Bill available to that unit. The Minister for Industry, Technology and Commerce, Senator [John] Button, told the Senate on 28th April, just a day or two ago:

> The Business Regulation Review Unit was given the opportunity to comment on the new regulations involved in the Government's equal opportunity reforms as drafted in the Equal Employment Opportunity (Commonwealth Authorities) Bill 1987. I understand that the Business Regulation Review Unit was also given the opportunity to be involved in discussions on this and other policies the Government has introduced in the equal opportunity policy area.

So, it seems that that objection too, raised by the Opposition in another place, is without major substance. I will have no difficulty voting for amendments related to technical deficiencies in the Bill before us. But these technical deficiencies are not fatal now, just as other deficiencies were not fatal back in August. The Liberal Party of Australia and the National Party of Australia were unsuccessful with some 30 or more amendments in August 1986, but we still found it possible to support both the second and the third readings of the legislation.

This now leaves the question of quotas. It has been variously alleged that this Bill contains quotas, that it contains quotas manqué, that it contains de facto quotas, that it implies quotas, that it gets Australia on the road to quotas, that it opens the door to quotas or that it goes further than other legislation which we have supported. If valid, these are serious concerns that could provide justifiable grounds for opposing the passage of the Bill. Many of my colleagues believe the Bill does introduce quotas; I do not. We must determine the substance of those claims in this debate. This is best started by reading the legislation—reading the document and seeking from it the plain meaning of the words it uses. The concerns of many of my colleagues are focused on words in Clause 6 (g) (ii). Those words have been read to the Senate several times, and doubtless will be read to it several times more. But applying to those words their plain meaning, their normal English meaning, it is not possible to assert that they introduce quotas, impose quotas for employment in Commonwealth

EQUAL EMPLOYMENT OPPORTUNITY (1987)

statutory authorities, or open the door to quotas. The words themselves have been copied, with a one-word change, from Paragraph (c) of the definition of 'program' contained in Section 22b (1) of the *Public Service Act*. That definition was inserted by the *Public Service Reform Act 1984*—another Act of Parliament to which we on this side raised no objection just three years ago. The difference in the words transferred from the *Public Service Reform Act* to this Bill is that the word 'or' in the 1984 Act has become the word 'and' in this Bill. That is the only difference. We made no suggestion in 1984 that these words represented quotas in employment, because they did not. Yet it is now being asserted, and many of my colleagues believe, that a change of the single word from 'or' to 'and' alters the effect of the Bill to such an extent that one can adduce the imposition, partial imposition or potential imposition of quotas in public service employment. Really, such a proposition is unsustainable.

Honourable senators will realise that to understand the Bill before us, we are comparing its text with two Acts from which certain words have been taken. To make that comparison, we need to look at all three documents. The second Act from which words have been taken, the *Affirmative Action (Equal Employment Opportunity for Women) Act 1986*, states in Section 8(g)(i):

> a requirement to set objectives, and

I emphasise the word 'and' as this is the argument on which the quota argument is based:

> set quantitative forward estimates against which the program can be assessed.

The words in the Bill that are alleged to imply employment quotas actually reflect the sentiment of that provision from the 1986 Act. We supported that Bill containing those words just eight months ago. They did not suggest quotas then, and words almost identical did not suggest quotas in the 1984 legislation. Even with the single drafting difference, they do not suggest quotas now. Unless those who claim there are quotas in the Bill can make a compelling case out of a single word 'and' the difference is insignificant. Certainly it is not of itself sufficient to give or sustain a ground for voting against the Bill. More than that, any words contained in that part of the Bill—the part about which all the argument has been—are contained in the interpretation section. Clause 3 (4) contains the words critical to resolving the argument that this Bill imposes or suggests quotas in employment. These words have been quoted before and I shall quote them again:

> Nothing in this Act shall be taken to require any action incompatible with the principle that employment matters should be dealt with on the basis of merit.

Put precisely, this provision puts into legislation the assurance that no-one can be required to act other than on merit—for example, by setting any quotas.

My advice from lawyers to whom I have spoken is that the words in Clause 3 (4) would, in fact, enshrine the merit principle, no matter what interpretation, however extreme and unreal, one decides to place on the words in Clause 6 (g) (ii). Pearce, a leading authority in statutory interpretation, argues that each Act of Parliament must be read as a whole, so that no section is divorced from its context and so each section is considered as part of the whole instrument. Therefore, every part of this Bill will be construed subject to the overriding merit principle enshrined in Clause 3 (4).

Further, honourable senators will be aware that Section 15ab (2) (f) of the *Acts Interpretation Act*—well known to honourable Senators, I am sure—provides clearly that a court called on determine a matter covered by this legislation is now able to go to the Hansard and read the second reading speech to be clear about the intention of the minister who introduced the Bill. That second reading speech, given by the Minister for Employment and Industrial Relations (Mr Willis) in another place, made it clear that the Government's intention is that there should be no quotas imposed by the Bill and, indeed, that the merit principle should continue to have overriding precedence. He said:

> I wish to emphasise the programs are not intended to, and will not lead to, positive discrimination. The Bill expressly confirms that employment matters are to be dealt with on the basis of merit, and the whole thrust of the legislation will strengthen the merit principle, by ensuring the review of any existing discriminatory personnel or employment procedures.

Not only is that a statement of government intent, but it is a statement that could be put before a court should the need arise. So it is not possible to argue convincingly that this Bill has anything at all to do with quotas in employment— and, on that test, the major objection to supporting the legislation fails.

It is clear that valid objections to this legislation are minor in nature. There are no valid major objections. In particular, the claim that this Bill has something to do with quotas in employment is contrived and quite unsustainable. It rests with those who would continue to press such a claim to establish a more compelling and credible case than they have done so far if they expect anyone from the middle ground of Australian politics to believe them.

However, that still leaves unanswered the question of why I have found it necessary to resign my position and, for the first time in 13 years, cross the floor and oppose my party. After all, everyone is on the losing side of a Cabinet or Shadow Cabinet argument from time to time. One does not resign easily from a position of responsibility. But one should never resign from one's principles or integrity. One should never resign from one's wider duty to the Liberal Party or to its traditional commitment to issues such as this.

It was just over eight months ago that I argued in this Senate, as shadow minister and on behalf of the Opposition, for the precise measure that we are considering today. I spoke then with the authority of John Howard, and on behalf of the leader, and of the entire Shadow Cabinet and the Opposition parties, to demand that women employed by Commonwealth authorities should enjoy no less right to equal opportunity in employment than women in the Commonwealth Public Service or in the private sector. We are asked now, just eight short months later, to reverse that stand, to abandon the collegial position we took then, to deny what I then demanded on behalf of the Opposition and to vote against what is fair, and just, and reasonable. Equal opportunity is fair and just and reasonable. It is also thoroughly Liberal. It empowers citizens to compete on an equal basis. It removes barriers that prevent them from so doing. It is my party that has moved in that eight months from a civilised stance to a position which I find discreditable and which made my position impossible.

We have heard a lot in the last week or so about loyalty and teamwork. They are important requirements of any shadow minister and of any shadow ministry. Implicit in the relationship that a minister or shadow minister has with his colleagues is the bond of loyalty, the collective spirit that sees the individual support the decisions of the team and the team support the individual is his advocacy of their joint cause. Loyalty and teamwork involve obligations, too, upon the group towards its individual members. Loyalty requires, for instance, that those who go out with the message on behalf of the party, a message endorsed by their party, and who sell that message, are not then abandoned for the advantage of the moment in the absence of compelling and credible new argument. Where a team member finds himself or herself in such a circumstance, resignation becomes the only appropriate course.

I will fight still for a continuing liberal vision of a society of free and powerful individuals, each able to control her or his own life. Equal employment opportunity based on merit is such an issue and this is such a Bill. In pursuit of that goal, I would oppose measures to give unmerited preference to women or to take any action in employment and employment matters other than on merit. But this is not such a measure.

This Bill is supported widely by women within the Liberal Party of Australia. It is supported by most of the significant women's groups within the party, including the Federal Women's Committee, certain state women's committees, Liberal feminist and network branches and Liberal business and professional women's groups. This Bill is supported by every branch of the Women's Electoral

Lobby across Australia, by many associations of women employees, by at least one state branch of the Young Women's Christian Association, by groups representing women in professions, by the feminist legal action group, by state women's advisory councils, by branches of the business and professional women's organisation and by the Federation of Ethnic Community Councils of Australia. It has support, all right!

Every measure to empower women has been opposed bitterly by conservative elements in Australia since Federation. This Bill is no exception. The objections raised to this measure now before us are in the tradition of that resistance and those objections. They are based on a false construction of the Bill and they have no merit.

I will remain loyal to a vision of individuals and of the society they can create together, loyal to measures to empower individual people to participate. I will remain loyal to the collegial view I made of this Government on behalf of all my colleagues here in the Senate eight short months ago—which I made with their authority. I will remain loyal to the history and traditions of the party.

In summary, this is a measure that I demanded on behalf of the Opposition, containing amendments that I also demanded. Yes, it has some objectionable features requiring amendment, and I will vote for the amendments. But it contains no elements at all that warrant opposition to the Bill as a whole. This Bill is the logical and necessary accompaniment to the Bill that we supported in 1986 and it follows that I will vote for the Bill.

Responses to the speech

> It is perhaps my unfortunate duty to speak in support of the Equal Employment Opportunity (Commonwealth Authorities) Bill 1987 after such an eloquent speech by a member of the Opposition who has delivered a tough, logical, researched, and may I say, courageous address in support of his principles, principles which I think are eternal, which reach across this Chamber and which should invite the common support of all parties here. During that address a number of my colleagues asked me to say that they, as well as I, admire the stand Senator Peter Baume has taken and which I understand a number of his colleagues will take in defence of those principles.
>
> —Senator the Hon. Peter Cook

EQUAL EMPLOYMENT OPPORTUNITY (1987)

30/4/1987

Peter

I was about to have a quiet cup of tea in the lobby when you commenced speaking—naturally, I felt compelled to come back in and listen to your very fine speech.

Quite apart from the particular issue, the explanation of liberalism was such as to explain why it is so attractive—I intend to raise your advocacy in my speeches (with attribution as appropriate).

Regards

Michael
(Hon. Michael Tate
Labor Senator for Tasmania
Minister for Justice)

[Handwritten note]

Brilliantissimo!

—Christine Wallace
Staff Officer, Sen. Hon. F.M. Chaney
Later a journalist and author

I must write and congratulate and thank you for the stand that you took.

—Daphne Kok
Deputy Chancellor
University of Sydney

It was a superb speech—measured, courageous, passionate. Australia very much stands in your debt. Venceremos.

—John Funder
Deputy Director
Baker Medical Research Institute

Your resignation—as I said—was a great sadness for me too, as a friend and as a female. Keep up the good work—we need you.

—Margaret Peacock (3MP)
(then wife of Hon. Andrew Peacock)

I wish I could toss a vote in the direction of Senator Peter Baume who was prepared to sink all chances of promotion in his party because he believed in a principle.

—Keith Dunstan[2]

For many it was his finest hour.

—Marian Sawer[3]

Senator Peter Baume and Ian Macphee are men of principle.

—*Sydney Morning Herald*[4]

---

2   *Sydney Morning Herald*, 23 June 1987.
3   Sawer (2003: 175).
4   Editorial, 27 March 1987.

SOCIAL POLICY AND DISADVANTAGE (1995)

I was invited to deliver the second Betty Pettit Oration at the St George Hospital on 6 October 1995 and chose to talk about social policy and disadvantage—a liberal conjunction that is often ignored by those of a more conservative bent.

The essence of the theme you have chosen for this conference concerns the people with whom we interact, their disadvantage, and the possibilities of their empowerment.

Such a theme is what traditional philosophical liberalism has always been about— the empowering of people and the taking of steps to make such empowerment possible. So philosophical liberals supported universal education, supported the extension of the franchise, supported the vote for women, supported income support for the elderly and for those in other need, supported decent industrial legislation, and supported equal employment opportunity for women. Philosophical liberals support anti-discrimination legislation and support the thrust of native title legislation.

I believe in those things still. That belief helped spell the end of my career in politics.

Social workers operate in that tradition. They care about people. They care about people independently of the diseases or problems with which those people present. They see the intrinsic value in people. They believe that the power and vitality of a society come from individual people. They work to empower many people to do things that will make their lives more satisfying. They do this either by helping people to develop latent skills and powers or they do it by placing people and community services in contact.

Almost 25 years ago I had a social worker working in my then private consulting practice. She took her own referrals and helped offer a range of continuing services and support that transformed that practice.

Betty Pettit was social worker in charge at this hospital until 1994. She was at St George Hospital as a social worker for 22 years, for most of that time as director of social work services. She was only the second person to hold this position—and her predecessor did not stay long. At the time of her retirement, she was also head of the division of allied health at St George Hospital. She saw the department move from one typical of a small district hospital to its current position as an important part of a major teaching hospital. During her time she also saw the move in social work from the old almoner to the modern social worker we know today.

She is described warmly by an associate as 'a fantastic boss', as a motivator and as someone remembered with affection as an inspirational colleague.

Though it may seem a digression, the training of our medical students in ethics today is based on many of the same principles. In my day, we were taught about relationships between care providers—how a letter was written, who preceded whom into a room, and how the expected courtesies and civilities between colleagues were carried out. But my profession was then quite paternalistic and authoritarian—as other professionals tell us now.

Today we teach a quite different kind of ethics. We teach young women and men about the ethical principles that should govern behaviour between care providers and care recipients. The relationships between care providers might be covered as a minor part in a more satisfying and more relevant course.

It is interesting that practitioners aged under about 45 take the newer view of ethics—that it is about relationships between people—while those over 60 are almost all 'old fashioned' and most are incapable of re-education. Older practitioners are likely to be more authoritarian, and more paternalistic. So those of you trying to get democratic messages across to care providers can be more persistent with younger people and with older people might just wait for them to fade away.

Today we believe in patient sovereignty and autonomy. So modern ethicists and teachers see experts as advisers—not as decision makers. Many older or more dogmatic colleagues do not wish to share decisions with their patients—well, maybe the development of case law will help solve that if nothing else does. Just yesterday my nephew phoned about whether or not he needed surgery. While I gave him advice, it was combined with the insistence that he owned the decisions, that he was 'in the driving seat'. It seems clear to me that every major treatment decision is owned by the person affected and that we specialists are advisers to whom they may turn for accurate analysis of the problem and for expert advice about the options for treatment.

But the decisions are, and remain, theirs.

Some colleagues do not agree. A cautionary tale was told to me by a friend recently. She told of a person who was found to have glaucoma. That person returned to her specialist with some questions she had written down following a visit to the glaucoma association. 'I ask the questions around here', answered the specialist. Today she has a new eye doctor who does answer her questions.

A surgeon told a group of our students two years ago that no woman with a lump in the breast was in a fit state to make a decision for herself. So some practitioners still do not accept patients as equal human beings—and they should.

We also teach about confidentiality—something that was observed more in the breach in my young days. It comes as a shock to some colleagues to be told that no one, no-one at all, should know private details about anyone else, except with explicit permission or for purposes of direct treatment. To test this, I asked recently why a colleague was absent. Actually I did not care why he was away—this was just an exercise to test the system. It will not surprise you to learn that I was told his diagnosis—and all the gory details—when it had absolutely nothing to do with me.

We teach about fairness, about beneficence, about non-maleficence and about duty of care.

And we are aware that sometimes difficulties can arise when ethical principles come into opposition. So I have some sympathy with those trying to balance confidentiality with duty of care in the rare instances of a practitioner having as patients two sexual partners one of whom has a sexually transmitted disease. Does the practitioner observe confidentiality in which case a duty of care to the unaffected partner might be breached, or does the practitioner tell the diagnosis in which case the principle of confidentiality has been breached?

But we teach some other interesting things too. We teach that mortality is universal, that life is a fatal sexually transmitted disease, that our task is to add quality to whatever life people have, that death is part of life, that death does not equal therapeutic failure, and that a lot of treatment should be directed to situations in which cure is not an option. Our task is not made any easier by the way large hospitals are structured or by the way they conceptualise themselves. Hospitals today, especially large hospitals, are dedicated to diagnosis and cure—and activities not directed to either of these aims are likely to be devalued in large hospitals. They work to power and economic agendas that take too little account of the needs for care of the large populations of people in which they are located.

We emphasise the roles of care, symptom-relief, compassion, tenderness— especially where cure is not an option. We have to convince young men and women that these are important things when the young do not want to hear about physical imperfection or about mortality in general or about the inevitability of death and particularly about their own mortality and their own inevitable deaths. Any of you who have seen the reluctance of professionals even to talk to the dying will know what I mean.

Actually, the best students for this kind of teaching are those who are in their thirties and have some experience of life. Sadly, bright and attractive young 20-year-olds sometimes find our messages disturbing or irrelevant. And five years later these same people are running the hospitals and making critical decisions about care.

It follows that much of what we say and teach is not understood or appreciated by some in our faculty. But it is clearly important to do well what we do. The Australian Medical Council is demanding more of our kind of teaching, and in our groups dealing with communication skills, with general practice and with aged and extended care we have areas of medicine which are often consonant with our own views.

Social workers understand what we are saying, what we teach, and what we do. Our goals seem similar, our comprehension of human life and death is similar, we are both able to face our own mortality, our appreciation of human frailty is similar and our concept of what is possible is similar.

Incidentally, I teach students to be relaxed about alternative therapies. While public subsidy is a separate question—let us not deal with it today—the use of alternative therapy sometimes gives relief which has been denied with more conventional approaches. So it is that hypnotherapy is fine, chiropractic is fine, naturopathy is fine, megavitamin therapy is fine, and so on—provided that we have done what we do well, that we have excluded treatable disease, and that we have some arrangements for future review of the situation. Often patients need a telephone contact number as well. But back to the disadvantaged.

Dr Bob Gregory from the ANU has shown recently that the gap in Australia between haves and have-nots is widening. The rich are getting richer and the poor are getting poorer. More of the wealth of the nation is controlled by fewer people.

SOCIAL POLICY AND DISADVANTAGE (1995)

This means a lot for our clients—or customers—or patients. It seems beyond doubt that to be old in Australia is generally to be poor, to be powerless, and to be a non-person. To be an Aboriginal in Australia is to be poor, powerless, educationally disadvantaged, unemployed, and to have worse health and worse experience with police and the legal systems. To be a migrant in Australia is to be isolated by differences in language and culture, often to be ghettoised, to be foreign in a somewhat xenophobic country and to have to struggle for economic parity. Let us add another group—those with some disability. As a group (and actually there are many groups) they often are poor, powerless, 'non-persons', and in danger of being isolated from the rest of society.

The word power has come up several times in the paragraph above. Power over one's own life, power over resources, power over where one lives, power over how one eats, power over recreation, these are the things that divide our society into two—those who have such power and those who lack it.

Is this the kind of society we want? Are these the features that we find desirable or acceptable? Is this the way we think things ought to be? Do we believe that poverty, or powerlessness, or lack of education, or unemployment, are in some way good for people? Is there a place for social Darwinism—does it serve some social good and should we be supporting it when we find it? Or might we say that it represents the message of a bygone era, that it is unfair, that it is not consonant with today's beliefs and values, and that it should be rejected? Do we wish to have a society in which the only valid measure of success is economic? Or do we think that the costs of going down such a road are too high to bear?

It is my belief that values and attitudes are what we need to examine and the values and attitudes are what need to change if some of the groups with disadvantage are to receive a fair go.

One particularly bad thing about the 1980s in Australia was that selfishness was a dominant value. People actually admired those who became uselessly and excessively rich, admired those who paid too little tax, and responded to promises from politicians to reduce personal income tax.

There are costs as well as benefits to almost every action. So, the acquisition of great wealth may occur at the expense of others who become poor, the avoidance of income tax diminishes the public revenue that maintains services, and any reductions in income tax will diminish our capacity to meet our obligations to our fellows. In the same way there are costs to everything that hospitals do—shortened lengths of stay have costs as well as benefits, the failure to admit, or to delay admission has costs, the inability to offer care has costs, the closure of theatres over Christmas has costs, and so on. To argue that these things are cost-free is a convenient misrepresentation of fact.

Let us propose instead a different system of values. Let us espouse the value of mutuality, of caring for others, of being responsible for others, for paying our share of tax, and of rejecting as foolish any moves, by anyone, to reduce the tax base. Every person we treat, or with whom we consult, or whom we direct towards some service, could be us. It could be us from childhood if our parents had been unfortunate. It could be us from young adult life if we were black, or if we had an injury or incapacity, or if we could not speak the language or understand the culture. And it could be any of us tomorrow when we too are aged, demented and dependent.

We today have the capacity to influence those who represent us in the parliaments of the nation. What they need to hear from us are messages about values, about what we do support, about what we expect, and about what we reject as crass, crude, or unfair. Will you, remembering the service given by Betty Pettit, remembering her service, and her inspiration and her leadership, and determined now to do what you can, make known to all politicians the values that you hold to be important? They will listen, perhaps only over time, but they will listen.

Not only will I do this but as a philosophical liberal, will do all I can to empower more people and to prepare young professionals—doctors and social workers—who will work to empower people too. This may mean altering the dynamics of many interviews in the helping professions where we have presently a great disparity of power in favour of the provider. It will involve making people more aware of their rights and of their own capacity to have a role in all matters that involve them.

If we can succeed—even partially—then every caring professional will find new enrichment and new worth in what they do. They will feel better about their work and they will be better practitioners to know and to attend. It is a noble crusade. Will you be part of it with me?

WELFARE AND TAXATION (1987)

This paper to the Liberal Forum concentrates on cash transfer and income redistribution. It does not deal specifically with provision of services. Three main questions arise.

- *What are the issues that are important to us as liberals?*
- *To what extent do our social goals happen to coincide with conservative policy outcomes?*
- *To what value positions and what policy lines should we be giving priority?*

The Present Tax/Welfare System

1.

Two systems of cash transfer operate in Australian welfare. Welfare is also provided by systems of service provision, by the welfare effects of other taxation measures (such as the reduced living standards from the imposition of indirect taxes), and by the provision of universal benefits such as health and education allowances. The traditional cash-transfer system operates through the social security apparatus. The other, the tax expenditure system, operates through the taxation apparatus. Some features of the two systems are compared in the table below.

Social Welfare System	Tax Expenditure System
Mainly the poor	Mainly the well-off
Visible/stigmatising	Hidden/no stigma
Costs known	Costs unknown

Social Welfare System	Tax Expenditure System
Beneficiaries known	Beneficiaries unknown
Majority women	Majority men
Beneficiaries	Beneficiaries
Subsistence support	Affluence enhancing
Means/income tested	Often universal
Often criticised	Seldom criticised

In 1981 women received 67 per cent of age pensions, 95 per cent of the Supporting Parent Benefit, all widows pensions, 31 per cent of invalid pensions, 30 per cent of unemployment benefits and 24 per cent of sickness benefits. Tax expenditures also have an important impact on tax revenue and, through this, on the capacity for provision of other social welfare expenditure. It was estimated that in 1973–74 in the UK, the effective tax base was more than halved by tax expenditures. Asprey estimated that in 1971–72 in Australia, deductions and rebates reduced the tax base by nearly 20 per cent and involved a loss of revenue of more than one-third of the sums actually raised.[1]

2.

At present there are more than six million taxpayers and three million people dependent on welfare. In addition, most Australians receive welfare through universal benefits for substantial periods of their lives. Identifiable needs and possible beneficial interventions far exceed the ability of a society to pay. This requires a priority-setting process between competing demands. Priorities do not always demonstrate consistency with any coherent set of principles or with the pursuit of clearly articulated and accepted goals. So cover is incomplete, many in need receive no benefits, and many not in need do receive benefits.

3.

Issues important to Liberals. There are liberal issues of equity, opportunity and responsiveness to need set out already in the sections above. Liberal values include:

- the empowering of individuals
- responding to need
- minimum unmet need
- maximum independence and dignity
- maximum incentive for self-provision.

---

1   CCH Australia Limited (1975).

4.

In addition, liberals need to examine the tensions between ideals of 'needs-based' and 'universal' systems of provision. Each has advantages and costs as set out below.

Needs-Based Beneficiaries are:	Universal Beneficiaries are:
Poor	Poor and middle class
Inarticulate	Often articulate
Unorganised	Often organised
Powerless	Often powerful

Systems are:	Systems are:
Complex	Simple
Fairer	Less fair
Penalise self-provision	Reward self-provision
Cheaper	More expensive

Whenever one group of taxpayers receives an allowance, another group must pay for this with higher marginal tax rates. High marginal tax rates may influence decisions to undertake paid employment, especially for women.

Liberals believe that a welfare system should display:

- efficiency
- neutrality
- simplicity
- fairness
- acceptability.

All these features were identified by John Stone [former departmental head of Treasury] as desirable for any 'good' tax system.

5.

Coincidences of liberal and conservative positions. Both groups recognise the requirement to gather sufficient revenue to fund welfare expenditures. Liberals would gather sufficient revenue to meet genuine needs while conservatives seem to argue that the revenue base should be contracted and welfare outgoings reduced.

6.

Both groups emphasise wealth creation—but for different reasons.

7.

Both groups believe in the encouragement of incentive and self-provision—but for different reasons.

8.

Both groups acknowledge the vulnerability of poorer groups to changes in indirect taxation; liberals believe that those dependent on welfare should be fully compensated for any such changes.

9.

Both agree that poverty traps should be eliminated, perhaps by trading off the income test and making all cash payments taxable. The key is to reduce the effective marginal tax rates that are the essence of any poverty trap.

Liberal Priorities

1. Remove poverty traps. This might be done by removing income tests while making cash transfers taxable or by maintaining income tests and reducing effective marginal tax rates by other combinations of adjustments.
2. Separate consideration for retirement income policy in view of its 'superannuation' function. We should seek universal 'basic' super cover, including a contributory universal taxable benefit for those not in private schemes, and still provide a supplementary benefit for those who qualify on need.
3. Needs-based benefits for those whose need is potentially temporary, ensuring that poverty traps are dealt with.
4. Consider Commonwealth withdrawal from certain service provision functions that are more properly the area of state sovereignty and responsibility.

Prime Tasks

We need to determine:

- whether we seek some 'needs-based' or some 'universal' system of welfare, or whether some mixture of the two is inevitable, and what mechanism is best suited to give effect to the desired goal
- the proper responsibilities of different levels of government, the proper policy responses to the federal system of government and to the Constitution
- the desirable balance of cash provision or the provision of services in or benefits in kind.

Priority Areas

Priority areas include:

Retirement income policy. This is especially difficult in view of the stands taken on assets testing and on capital gains tax. There are three basic elements to any income support scheme not based on insurance principles nor related to earning:

- the maximum level of entitlement
- the withdrawal rate as extra income is earned
- the cut-off point at which entitlement ceases.

Any two of these elements determines the third. Because of the interrelationship of the elements there are inherent conflicts between:

- providing adequate income support for those with no private income
- ensuring reasonable levels of incentive for self-help
- maintaining costs of any scheme within reasonable limits.

Taxation and wealth creation. In addition to the welfare interactions identified below, we believe as liberals in the interdependence of the tax system and the creation and encouragement of the incentive to create wealth by the population. In that sense the tax/welfare interactions need to be seen as part of an integrated package that recognises also the central importance of wealth creation as a prerequisite to any system of welfare.

Tax/welfare problems. The tax system enters the welfare field when it provides tax concessions or rebates for certain social expenditures. Such favoured taxation treatment is an expression of certain value positions which have found favour with governments—e.g. value placed on education, on home ownership, on 'family'. Additionally, certain new initiatives in the tax area, for example BBIT [Babcock & Brown Infrastructure Trust], will cause real income losses for poorer people and for welfare beneficiaries. So any scheme will need an extensive system of compensatory payments included. Taxation of welfare benefits is one way to achieve fairness because it will reduce the net benefit of payments to those with significant other income. On the other hand, taxation of welfare benefits is one factor, along with high withdrawal rates of benefits, of the emergence and extent of 'poverty traps' in welfare. John Stone has identified certain criteria which are desirable in a 'good' taxation system. These include: certain characteristics are mutually antagonistic, for example, considerations of horizontal and vertical equity often do not sit well together.

Welfare-tax problems. Welfare affects the tax system because of the size of the welfare subventions and the revenue requirements that they generate. Taxation of welfare payments is required to satisfy certain equity requirements. Yet the taxation of benefits is one of the prime causes of the emergence of poverty traps. Liberals need to resolve the dilemma of different values which suggest different approaches to the taxation of benefits and to the acceptance of 'need' or 'universalism' as a basis for welfare provision.

What is clear is that it is not possible to design a new tax system without

- clarification of the values that should underlie it
- recognition of the mutual interdependence of taxation and welfare considerations in the final tax/welfare systems that emerge.[2]

We do not have a system that has done these things. Therefore the threshold tasks identified above are the first and most important jobs lying before us. Their achievement must precede any detailed consideration of this or that benefit or tax measure.

---

2   See Podger et al. (1980).

A SEPARATE POLICY FOR ABORIGINAL AUSTRALIANS: A PAPER TO THE LIBERAL FORUM (1987)

On 13 December 1985, Alan Missen wrote reminding me that he and I were to produce a paper on controversial aspects of policy directed towards Aborigines. No action was taken and, with his death, the opportunity for a joint paper was behind us. Nevertheless, I offered these thoughts to colleagues.

Why a Separate Policy?

One of the arguments being advanced increasingly frequently is that there is no justification for a separate policy for Aborigines and that we should make one set of arrangements for one homogeneous nation. Apart from this being a thin veil over a racist approach, it is inconsistent with our approach to other areas of policy where special programs and policies have been judged to be necessary. The most obvious example is in the area of veterans' affairs. Anyone propounding the 'abolish Aboriginal affairs' argument should be asked whether, in the name of consistency, they are willing to abolish veterans' affairs programs too? Generally those who are against Aborigines are not against veterans and their argument falls down.

But the main justification for separate programs rests on the demonstrated special needs and on the desperate social condition of Aboriginal Australians. In an attached paper from 1981, I set out some of the dimensions of Aboriginal disadvantage. The extent of Aboriginal disadvantage provides complete and sufficient argument for special responses and initiatives on behalf of government.

The Emerging Racist Backlash

Even at the time that Malcolm Fraser introduced the *Aboriginal Land Rights (NT) Act* in 1976, the coalition of interests sympathetic to the cause was only just strong enough to carry the day. Thinly veiled racist sentiment was always present in the joint party room and was certainly present in the public. It was fed by recognised extremist groups like the League of Rights and other 'white Australia' groups. Lately it has been exacerbated as an incidental spin-off from the campaign by mining interests to gut the *ALR (NT) Act* and to prevent any new legislation to secure Aboriginal land tenure. To the extent that the miners' campaign continues, so the racist backlash is likely to continue to gain strength.

Faulty Conceptualisation

But part of our problem rests with faulty (or absent) conceptualisation of the relationships between Aboriginal and non-Aboriginal Australia. Part of this problem is a product of history. We have passed through several policy stages in our two centuries here. The phase of conquest and dispossession was bloody and lasted for much of the first century. The phase of paternal protectionism lasted for another half to three-quarters of a century. It meant that Aborigines were guaranteed food, shelter, schooling, jobs at part-pay, but in return for this, they surrendered much decision-making to those providing for their needs, they surrendered their rights to equal treatment as citizens, and they surrendered control of their own lives.

There were some benefits in this model—Aborigines were not drunk (they were forbidden access to alcohol), they did not cause trouble (they were denied access to power), they were cleaner, etc. This philosophy merged closely with the concept of assimilation—the idea that the 'successful' Aboriginal was the one who most successfully adopted white standards and who succeeded in our terms.

Some people are fixed in the protectionist/assimilationist philosophical mould even today. The Queensland Government, for instance, and its Director, Mr Killoran, act as though they can do best by taking certain classes of decision from Aborigines and making decisions for them. People forget that Joh Bjelke-Petersen really was the chairman of the board of Hope Vale Mission for 15 years and that he did an enormous amount for (not with) Aborigines. People forget that Charles Court really did go annually to the Kimberley and visit each community in the heat of mid-summer for decades. It is just that they are fixed in the wrong game—and that they still want to play by yesterday's rules.

The later developments were in a theoretical framework that identified first, integration instead of assimilation, and later, self-determination as models for Aboriginal advancement. As liberals, we would of course wish to be associated with a philosophy that liberates and empowers people. For this reason we would support self-determination and would reject any proposal that sought to remove from Aboriginals power over those vital matters that affect their lives.

Lord Hailsham once said that giving freedom only has value if it includes the freedom to do things of which we do not approve. So we liberals have to accept that freedom for Aboriginals carries with it our acceptance of decisions that we consider wrong or inappropriate. It does not mean that we do not insist that power over decisions should be divorced from responsibility for them—and as minister I insisted that the two went together.

Controversies

With this conceptual appreciation, and with the contextual factors of special need and deprivation set out in the attached paper, all the controversies fall into place.

Some are racist—overt, naked and ugly. Some are racist manqué. Some relate to bad judgements by Aborigines in the use of their new power over their own lives—for example, the decision to become and remain an alcoholic (I am aware of the dual role of victim and autonomous decision maker here but offered the example anyway). Some relate to bad administrative decisions by government.

Some relate to interface problems—for example, the Aboriginal Secondary Grants Scheme (ABSEG) does help keep Aboriginal children in secondary school. The interface problem arises because equally needy white children cannot draw the same benefit. Some relate to faults in legislation—for example, the need to get amendments to the *ALR (NT) Act*.

Some relate to non-racist value differences, for example, between a paternalist/protectionist and a self-determinator. Many are aggravated by concurrent agendas and games, for example, between a state Labor premier and Labor prime minister and many are aggravated by the ignorant, banal, or mischievous treatment which the press gives to the issues.

Party Policy

Within our Coalition (both within the Liberal Party of Australia and between that party and the National Party) many of these factors operate today. They are added to by a sizeable dose of ignorance and ill-will.

At a minimum we must insist on full personal autonomy for Aboriginals, we must insist on special programs to respond to demonstrated need among Aboriginals, and we must insist on special arrangements, including adequate arrangements for land tenure, for Aboriginals in special circumstances.

We should be careful about the rights to royalties to mining available under the *ALR (NT) Act* at present. These are not, a priori, essential and could be replaced with other adequate government arrangements to provide an economic base to Aboriginal communities. In particular, while we oppose uniform national land rights for proper federalist reasons, we must not allow the parties to abandon all commitment to secure tenure of land under circumstances appropriate to need and location.

IMMIGRATION MOTION IN DEFENCE OF NON-RACIAL SELECTION (1988)

In mid-1988, some senior Coalition figures made equivocal statements about racial matters as they affected immigration—an issue that still raises its head today. Sadly, other senior Coalition figures then widened these comments with more specific and more racist statements. In the midst of all this, the press came to me and I told them, 'John Howard could fix this with a single sentence'—meaning that if the leader made a robust anti-racist rebuttal, the matter would die. The Labor Party took political advantage of the situation, introducing a motion that stated that immigration policy should never be based on racial grounds. The Opposition decided to move some amendments and to oppose the main motion if the amendments were unsuccessful. In the Senate address below, I indicated that I would support the amendments but also Labor's motion as its intention was consistent with liberal principles. My speaking slot was at 1 am.

Senator PETER BAUME—It gives me no pleasure to take part in this debate. It gives me even less pleasure to know that I will be out of line with my colleagues when the vote is taken. We are debating a Government notice of motion on immigration and an amendment moved thereto by my Leader, Senator [Fred] Chaney. My colleagues have chosen generally to speak to the amendment. That is quite proper. It is provided for within the Standing Orders. They have set out reasons why I will want to support that amendment. I will address the motion itself. I will not discuss the Liberal Party policy that has been well set out and well-defended today. I will not talk about our past or our record; only the motion and the position that I intend to take. It is of course a mischievous and malicious motion. Its purpose is blatantly political. It is designed to advantage the Australian Labor Party (ALP). It is designed for fishing in troubled waters. Earlier someone said that this is a political chamber—that is fair play in this chamber. I wish to participate in the debate not in any sense of anger or petulance and hopefully with no bitterness but I do need to participate. I point out to colleagues that I have now been here for more than fourteen years. Only two senators…

Senator Chaney—It sometimes seems longer.

Senator PETER BAUME—Senator Chaney and I came in together. Only two senators have served longer. They are Senator [Arthur] Gietzelt and Senator [Peter] Durack. Recently we had to count the number of divisions I had voted in. It was for my lawyers for a defamation action that I am involved in. We have voted in divisions about 1,300 times. I have voted with my colleagues and the Australian Labor Party together against the Australian Democrats many times, as my colleagues have voted with Labor in those lopsided votes. I guess we will do so again. I have voted with the Australian Labor Party against my colleagues once only in 1,300 divisions. Today it looks as if I will be voting with the Australian Labor Party against my colleagues for the second time. I guess it is my duty to explain to my colleagues and to the party that preselected me why I am doing so.

Senator [Brian] Archer—You don't have such a duty.

Senator PETER BAUME—I thank my colleague for the interjection but I would like to do so. I start by setting out for colleagues the position of a Liberal Party parliamentarian. This is laid down in the Valder Report of the Liberal Party Committee of Review 'Facing the Facts'.[1] I notice it was produced in 1983 by a very distinguished group of people. They are all friends. In fact, my former research officer, now Senator [Chris] Puplick, was a member, as was another former research officer, Mr Chris Crawford, as was my present helper, Mrs Elizabeth Grant. So we have quite a proprietorial interest.

Senator [Chris] Schacht—You certainly had the numbers.

Senator PETER BAUME—We almost had the numbers. This Committee actually laid down in black and white the fact that the Liberal Party does not have a caucus rule, that it does not bind its members but gives them freedom within certain defined boundaries to cast their votes. I will read the paragraph and a half that is important:

> In Parliament, a high degree of discipline is necessary if the Party is to be really effective. The Liberal Party does not require of its Parliamentary candidates a pledge to always vote with the Party in Parliament. The Party's belief in the

---

1 Valder (1983).

importance of the individual conscience means that it accepts that there are occasions when a Liberal Member of Parliament may vote against his colleagues without incurring sanctions from the Party (or expulsion, as in the Labor Party). The Committee believes that it is important for the conditions under which this right is exercised to be clearly understood if the Party is not to be damaged by its Members crossing the floor.[2]

The next few words are emphasised in the report:

In particular, it is important that it be recognised by all Liberal Parliamentarians that the general expectation is one of loyalty and support for the Party in the Parliament, and that crossing the floor is to be regarded as an exceptional act. It is a right which should be exercised only under the following two conditions—

Where the issue is one of personal conscience, and not merely a difference of policy or political judgment; and

Where the Member informs his Parliamentary Leader and his Party colleagues beforehand of his intention.[3]

This will be the second time in 1,300 divisions—so I have not made a frequent practice of that. I will make the case that it is a matter of conscience and principle and I can advise the Senate that I satisfied the second condition, under quite difficult circumstances, by advising my Leader and colleagues.

For many years the Liberal Party that I joined would have proposed a motion such as the one before us. It would never have allowed a statement like one by Senator Stone, which I will mention later, to have gone unrepudiated or unchallenged. I was proud of the Liberal initiatives of the Liberal Prime Minister I served.

But why take this course? Why decide that it is important to take part in this debate and vote on the motion? I will set out very briefly some of the events of the last few weeks. They have been set out in this debate.

The immigration policy debate was initiated from our side, as has been said, by my Leader on his return from overseas. It was set out not in racist terms, but in terms that were ambiguous and capable of misinterpretation, particularly malicious interpretation. I have to say that my Leader has not made racist statements, but he has made ambiguous statements. The trouble is that the statements were then made explicit—not by John Howard but by Senator John Stone, in colourful phrases which were referred to earlier:

Asian immigration has to be slowed. It is no good dancing around the bushes.

---

2 Valder (1983: 102).
3 Valder (1983: 102).

I do not question the right of any of my political colleagues or members of the National Party to make such statements. They represent a view they hold. That is fine: I have no objection to that. If I have any objections I will express them in the party room. However, it is a pity that the statement was not repudiated immediately. When it was not repudiated immediately, I felt that I had a duty. All the people I respected and might have expected to respond were out of the country. Not one of them, including [Ian] Macphee, [Michael] MacKellar and [Philip] Ruddock, was in Australia. I think that Robert Hill was out of Australia at the same time.

Senator Hill—Rare.

Senator PETER BAUME—He was on one of his rare absences from Australia. It was at that stage that I made a public statement. I want to read that statement because it relates to the motion before us tonight. My public statement was only five sentences and read:

> There is no place in Australia for any revival of a white Australia policy, overtly or secretly. No tests of racial origin should be applied to any applicant for migration to Australia. I expect that the assurances of my Leader that he is not moving to a racial immigration policy should resolve that matter. Since we have become a multicultural society, we have been enriched beyond measure. I hope we will continue to use the strength of that multicultural heritage in pursuit of a unified Australian community.

I add that the reason I issued such a short statement was that I had the pleasure, I thought, of being at the third national conference on AIDS. However, that is another story. My position has been quite simple. That is the message. Having issued the press statement, I then repeated that message on television, radio and in the press and made it quite clear that if there were any suggestion of a racist element in an immigration policy, I would want to be part of repudiating such a suggestion.

I find in the motion before us—in the important last part of it—exactly the sentiment that I was advocating publicly in that press statement and in other statements that I made to the press. I understand that many Australians are concerned with social cohesion. I understand, too, that many Australians are racist and that many Australians actually want less Asian migration. In fact, to say so might be a very popular thing. However, as [NSW] Liberal Premier Nick Greiner said when asked for a comment, there had probably never been a time when popular opinion had supported more migration. He said that it had always been unpopular. I wonder why it is that people do not want Asian migration. Perhaps it is based on the many faces of Asians in the streets. The Asians we see in Australia at present do represent migrants. However, they also represent second and third generation Australians. They also represent the tourists that we need—the tourists who are bringing in foreign currency as part of our booming tourist trade.

Senator [Bob] Collins—They are our guests.

Senator PETER BAUME—Yes, they are our guests. They represent students, both secondary and tertiary students, and people in Australia for short-term language study. Most of the time they represent welcome guests to Australia. According to the 1986 census, only 2.6 per cent of the Australian population is Asian born. It has already been pointed out that even if the present trend of migration is continued for another 25 or 30 years the percentage will not exceed 7 per cent of the population. I believe that the position I have advocated, and the position contained in the motion, is essentially a Liberal position. That is not only my view. If it is essentially a Liberal position, then I would want to support it. I would like to quote in support of that from a book called *Liberal Thinking* written by two eminent liberals, C.J. Puplick and R.J. Southey.[4] In several parts of that book they make reference to the fact that race is not an adequate basis for policy. On page 28 of the book, in talking about differences among groups, they say:

> Some categories (race, religion, political affiliation) are generally accepted to be improper grounds for legal and social discrimination.

They go on to talk about other categories. Further on they say:

> Discrimination against a person on grounds of race, in order to secure higher status to those who are of a different race, is not an acceptable objective.

So we have good Liberal reasons for saying that any suggestion of racial discrimination is unacceptable. I am attracted to some of the aphorisms at the back of the book that help enrich the book, may I say to one of the authors. One of them attributed to Daniel O'Connell says:

> Nothing is politically right which is morally wrong.

I believe that any kind of policy that even admits of the possibility of taking into account the race of a potential migrant is unacceptable. I reject it, as some of my colleagues have, as a logical impossibility to claim that a policy aimed at slowing down immigration from Asia can also be termed a non-discriminatory policy. I am indebted to a colleague for pointing out that to me.

---

4   Puplick and Southey (1980).

I have been told this week in words of one syllable that politics is about compromise. Well, yes, it is. We have all compromised. If I have voted in 1,300 divisions and managed to stay with my colleagues 1,299 times there must have been a fair amount of compromise in that time. But in the end, as Senator [Baden] Teague has said, there is a moral element to politics, or there should be.

It is different for every person. I do not ask anyone else to accept my judgment of where the point is. Principle sometimes has to come before compromise. The question, of course, is when.

It is different for every person; I accept this. But for each of us there are some bottom line issues on which we say we will not accept this and we will not go further. I found one last year and I found my way onto the backbench at the same time. Racism, overt or covert, open or implied, is another such bottom line issue for me, so much so that I welcome any declaratory statement that rejects even the possibility of racism in any of our policies. The words in the policy do that. The words that have been objected to—I quote from the motion—are 'race or ethnic origin shall never, explicitly or implicitly, be among them.' That is the criterion that might be applied.

I note, as has my colleague, that former Liberal Immigration Minister, Michael MacKellar, refused to oppose this motion in another place tonight. I also know that my Leader here, Senator Chaney, and my colleagues, have argued for an amendment that sets out and defends the alternative policy which our parties have put forward. I will have no difficulty supporting that amendment. But if it fails, and if we are then faced with a government motions impliciter, as of course we shall be, I am also aware that another former Liberal Immigration Minister, my friend, Ian Macphee, a former Liberal Shadow Minister for Immigration, Phillip Ruddock, and a former Liberal State Premier, Steele Hall, all found it necessary to vote for the proposition in the other place tonight and, like them, I will support it because it makes explicit and clear what needs to be made explicit and clear to Australians at this time.

Response to Immigration Speech

> Your speeches on the War Crimes and in the immigration debate in the last session are still the two best speeches I have heard in the Parliament in my short time here.
> —Senator Chris Schacht[5]

---

5   Labor Senator for South Australia. Senate Hansard, 21 December 1990: 6,372.

WAR CRIMES AMENDMENT BILL (1988)

I rate this speech, given in the Senate in 1988, as one of my most significant.

This is historic legislation. It is an attempt by Australia, through its Parliament, to come to grips with one of the most murderous episodes of this century, to bring to justice, even 45 years after the event, any Australian citizens among the remaining perpetrators of the World War II Holocaust of the minorities—the Jews, the gypsies, Russian prisoners of war, handicapped, Germans, and children. It was not just a Jewish holocaust and it should not be remembered as just a Jewish catastrophe. We must not deal with it today as if it were just a Jewish catastrophe. But it was for the Jewish people a catastrophe that wiped out six million among a dispersed world population perhaps less than twice that number. In some areas of central Europe the Jewish population has disappeared totally and permanently. It was all done deliberately by humans to humans, in planned fashion—to round up, to isolate, to torture, to starve and to kill.

It is the perpetrators of those events—those inhuman humans who slaughtered innocent women and children by shooting them, naked, into open pits or gassed them, and enjoyed it, who actively participated in mass execution of defenceless minorities and who openly violated the Geneva Conventions and the morality of mankind—that we cannot ever forgive. They have been sought and pursued across the world, from country to country, from hiding place to hiding place, unceasingly, for more than 40 years. This legislation seeks to ensure that we pursue here any war criminal who may have sought to make of this gentle country a haven and a refuge. For major war criminals there is no haven and there is no refuge. For minor Nazis, for collaborators, on the other hand, let us leave them now. But the major war criminals we will pursue unceasingly.

The issue is justice—not revenge. For me, justice will be done if we expose any war criminals, any genocidists; if we tear away their masks of respectability and let people know what is in their pasts. I do not expect that we will send old men to prison. I certainly do not wish to see them put to death, even where in the past they put many to death. What I do want is for those people to be exposed for what they were in those dark past days.

As is always the case here, the debate on the second reading of the War Crimes Amendment Bill is about the purpose and principles of the legislation. Important matters of detail, particularly matters relating to the drafting of the legislation—and there are quite a few—will be addressed during the debate in the committee stage.

What are the principles and purposes of the proposed legislation? The issue before the Senate is so simple and so clear, even if some of the means by which the Government seeks to implement the principles are troubling to some of my colleagues of good will. We are proceeding from the likelihood that we have in Australia some persons who played a significant role in the criminal events in the Nazi Holocaust in the Second World War in Europe and that our duty now requires that we do something about it. We know that many of the perpetrators of serious war crimes did escape. We know that many escaped punishment. Some did this by escaping from Europe to South America, Canada, the United States, or possibly to Australia. It does not matter for the purposes of the debate today how they escaped or how they managed to reach their various havens. That may be a subject for another debate. In almost all cases they assumed a new identity as part of their escape. What does matter is that some of the perpetrators of the Holocaust may have come here. We think that is so. Our searches of archives—documents available only after the passage of 30 years, only available in the last decade—suggest it. Mr Andrew Menzies, to whom reference has already been made today—he is a former senior officer in the Attorney-General's Department—in his Review of Material Relating to the Entry of Suspected War Criminals into Australia told us that it was likely that some of those people had come to Australia. In November 1986 he said:

> It is more likely than not that a significant number of persons who committed serious war crimes in World War II have entered Australia and some of these are now resident in Australia; certainly the likelihood of this is such that some action needs to be taken now.

What we are considering today flows from his statement. We are considering the action taken by the Government flowing from his statement. These people would most likely have come to Australia after the war as migrants when Australia, to its credit, was opening its gates to the displaced and dispossessed of Europe and in the process being enriched and changed forever by the welcome influx of the millions who have made this continent their home to the benefit of us all. I repeat that the circumstances that would have allowed people to escape post-war justice in Europe are not strictly matters for consideration today. We have all read about the establishment of rat lines down which some of these people were run. We have heard from other senators some of the details, so I do not intend to repeat them. Some outlines of the ways in which this might have been done have been canvassed publicly.

Someone referred to the Australian Broadcasting Corporation radio program. I do not intend to do so now. What I will say about the program is that it matters only that what was revealed was correct. It does not matter who revealed it. We will do a lot better if we concentrate on the worth of the message rather than on the background of the messenger. In the same vein, may I observe that those who see in this Bill the operation of some malign international Jewish conspiracy, and who write to the newspapers in those terms, demean themselves and detract from the quite substantial matters of substance which can be offered as criticisms of some parts of this Bill and to which I hope the Government will respond.

The alleged association between Jews and Communists—a common theme of some of those who have entered this debate—has been a common cry of Nazi propagandists. It is echoed today in this country by groups such as the League of Rights. I am ashamed to say it has been given credence by the public statements of some who should know better. There is no doubt that the great majority of those who helped make up the new Australia were the victims of persecution and war. They came here because they were victims, seeking only to make new lives for themselves and their families. We have no quarrel with them.

On 24 April each year the Armenian community commemorates the Armenian holocaust. This year on 24 April the Armenian community in Sydney commemorated the seventy-third anniversary of the start of the Armenian genocide of 1915. Honourable senators may recall that this was the first major genocide of the twentieth century, in which two-thirds of the population of Turkish Armenia perished in awful circumstances. The grief of the Armenians today in 1988 for the lost generation of grandparents is continuing and deep. It is made worse by the continual refusal of successive Turkish governments even to acknowledge that the events occurred and by the refusal ever of Turkey to bring to justice the perpetrators of that genocide. Honourable senators will recall that Hitler, in his planning, is said to have asked rhetorically, 'Who remembers the Armenians?' Time has not healed the scars of the Armenians, and neither should it.

Today in Australia we have to consider and deal with the possibility that people who were part of the cause and execution of the horror of World War II, willing partners in the atrocity, may be in Australia—perhaps someone who worked with Adolf Eichmann, perhaps someone who murdered or who caused the murder of thousands of innocents. We have the capacity to do something to bring such people to justice. I suppose I should say that we have the possibility of bringing such persons to justice. That would be a much more accurate term. After all, the course proposed in this Bill presents formidable difficulties. It would require—and properly require—the presentation and testing of evidence in Australian courts to Australian standards of proof and in circumstances which would allow an Australian jury, properly directed and properly instructed, to return a verdict.

Right now we have Konrad Kalejs, a Latvian-born Australian citizen who has been branded as a war criminal by a United States court and who, subject to appeals, is about to be returned from that country to us. That is the situation we face now. Are we to ignore his past or the evidence adduced about that past by American investigators? Is that what we are to do? I remind honourable senators of the speech given by Sir Robert Menzies on the *Genocide Convention Act 1949*. That Act gave effect to the International Convention on the Prevention and Punishment of the Crime of Genocide. Speaking in the House of Representatives as leader of the Liberal Opposition, Mr Menzies said:

> I do not desire to debate this Bill ... The contracting parties under the convention undertook to enact the necessary legislation to give effect to the provisions of the convention, and in particular to provide effective penalties for the persons guilty of genocide, or of any of the other acts enumerated in Article III of the convention ... All I wish to say about the present bill is that in the last ten years, abominations have been practiced in this world, and in no place more terribly than in Germany under the Nazi regime. Every member of this Parliament must view with equal abhorrence the practice of mass killing, and of persecution of people to the death, for reasons of race or religion, or for other reasons of the kind referred to in the Convention. Not only everybody in this Parliament, but also anybody in this country detests the kind of thing which is referred to in this Bill.

He went on to say:

> This is not a measure upon which there is any party division of opinion. This is not a party matter.

I end the quote from Robert Menzies. Our duty is to grasp the moment. The task has fallen unasked to us. We did not ask to be here at the time these matters became known. We did not ask to be here to have to deal with the report of Mr Andrew Menzies or with the situation that faces us. But it is our duty and no-one else's. We have the possibility, we have the capacity and we have the responsibility to investigate the facts that seem to be emerging and to take the steps that will allow the outcome—wherever it leads us—to occur. As far as I am concerned, that is really the only question to be answered in the second reading debate. It might be argued—indeed it has been argued by some—that time has lessened the crimes and made void the right to pursue and punish those who committed them. There is no statute of limitations on war crimes. I cannot believe that people would put that argument seriously. That argument is of no weight.

I go back to Mr Andrew Menzies who reported to the Government in the following way:

> It must be said that a new generation has come forward, one at first dimly aware of the atrocities committed in the war period, but, in recent years, increasingly conscious of the depravity and scale of these crimes.

Some of the offences the subject of allegations recorded by the review are of such seriousness that, if confirmed by a full investigation, justice, however long delayed, should be, and be seen to be, administered.

It might be argued that the search is selective—that we ignore Soviet war crimes while pursuing Nazi war crimes or that we ignore Japanese war criminals. I believe one of these matters may be dealt with by amendment to the Bill later. But what the critics overlook is that our postwar migrants came predominantly from those parts of eastern Europe in which the unhappy events of the Holocaust occurred. That is why we must deal with those crimes, with that theatre, with that time and with those people.

Consideration of this Bill by the Senate requires that we balance the demands of history, the need for exposure and the giving of information to our young— as Senator [Terrence] Aulich said, if we forget the messages we are doomed to repeat them—with the requirements of justice and of due process as we know and practise them. That is our dilemma today. It really will not do for any honourable senator to deny the complexities, the contradictions or the valid arguments for and against what we are being asked to determine here today. Nor will it serve us well to attribute to those who come down with a different conclusion any element of malice, disinterest or lack of concern. I would not do so.

But for me the demands of history are supreme. Our right is to know our past. Our right is to know whether any war criminals are here in Australia. We might have been better served by a different proposal—perhaps by a commission of the kind proposed by His Honour Mr Justice Einfeld. But we do not have that option; we have this Bill. If we defeat this Bill, there will be nothing—no examination and no disclosure of any war criminal. So let us support the Bill at the second reading stage. Important matters will be discussed in the committee stage of the debate. I beg of the Minister for Justice (Senator [Michael] Tate) to err, if he has to during this debate, on the side of generosity and to allow this Parliament to work towards a united view and a single voice when it finally determines this Bill at the third reading stage.

It may assist honourable senators to recall the following words written in *Time* magazine by Lance Morrow on 20 May 1985:

> There were many voices muttering, 'Must we hear about the Holocaust again?' There have, after all, been other great tragedies in history—the Turkish slaughter of the Armenians, Stalin's liquidation of millions of Kulaks and the enforced famine in the Ukraine in 1932–3, the destruction of perhaps 2 million Kampucheans by their own Khmer Rouge countrymen.
>
> One cannot engage in a contest of comparative horrors. Yet there is about the Holocaust a primal and satanic mystery. And no cheap grace can redeem it. The Third Reich was the greatest failure of civilisation on the planet ... Germany represented one of the furthest advances of the culture, yet the Third Reich profoundly perverted the entire heritage of Western achievement. It was as if Goethe had taken to eating human flesh. The scientific method, perfected over centuries, fell into the hands of Dr Mengele and the engineers of the ovens. Hitler was not alone responsible. More than a few Germans enthusiastically followed him, saluted him, and died for him. They seized the accumulated trust of 3000 years and distilled it into unimaginable evil. They sought to extinguish not only Jews and gypsies and the rest, but the lights of civilisation. That is not easy to forgive.

It is only if we do our duty, unpalatable though it may be, with care, courage, generosity and attention to detail and to all the difficult questions of legal process that have been raised already, that we can help those who suffered or died to sleep in peace.

LEGALISATION OF DRUGS (1994)

This is an emotional subject and one on which I have held strong views and on which I have spoken often with passion. This speech is typical of many of my speeches about drugs and was given on Wednesday, 23 November 1994 to the Medico-Legal Society of New South Wales.

Because this is an emotional subject, an attempt will be made to put some simple propositions and to develop what seems to be a 'least worst' policy position.

First, we might ask why was it that we prohibited the use of some drugs—totally in some cases, recreationally in others? After all, heroin is just a white powder. It has no value and no addictive properties except as humans use it. The demonology of drug use is enormous with people who should know better, presenting accounts that are simply at variance with the truth.

We probably prohibited narcotics early in this century for two reasons. First, because the Americans told us to do so. Second, our own racist tendencies—specifically our anti-Chinese racist tendencies—also played a part. When the Americans asked us to prohibit the use of cannabis two decades on, we complied. When, later, the Americans leaned on us to become party to some treaties about use of prohibited drugs, we agreed. And lately we have undertaken even more treaty obligations—even as the game has changed and such obligations have become more ridiculous and inappropriate.

Some people support the prohibition of certain drugs because they believe that prohibition is good policy. This is a view consistent with acculturation that emphasises law, rules, sanctions, punishment. After all, there was a majority of Americans who supported the introduction of prohibition of alcohol in 1920—but that majority evaporated when the entrenchment of criminality and corruption as a direct result of the policy of prohibition became public knowledge in the decade that followed.

For other people there is the desire to protect children from evil people and from evil events. But children meet these things anyway. Prohibition does not prevent exposure to evil—it may actually make property and personal crime more frequent. Still others see society in an idealised way. They view society as being drug-free (or at least a society free of drugs that they themselves do not use) and frame laws and rules accordingly. That this seems not to accord with reality worries them not at all.

What has happened as a result of our prohibition approach has been sad indeed. Many people have been convicted of drug-related crime and some estimates have up to 60 per cent of the prison population being there for drug-related convictions. But young people know only too well that while many of the drugs they want to use are illegal, those used by their parents are legal. They know that arrest and conviction rates are related systematically to socioeconomic status. They call us hypocrites—and with some justice!

Perhaps the greatest indictment of current drug policies is that they have not worked as even their most fervent advocates had hoped they might. While the overall numbers using some substances might be reduced by current approaches (a not-inconsiderable benefit), this is not the whole story. Importation of illegal drugs occurs contrary to the law. Production of illegal drugs occurs contrary to the law. Distribution of illegal drugs occurs contrary to the law. Sale of illegal drugs occurs contrary to the law. Use of illegal drugs occurs contrary to the law.

There has been corruption of customs services, of police, of the magistracy, of prison officers. We were told once of a time when there was so much heroin inside Pentridge Gaol (where it was forbidden) that the excess was being exported back to the streets of St Kilda for sale.

The amount of current use is staggering. Cannabis has been used by about five million Australians and is used currently by a significant minority of that number. Some people use opiates at weekends and not all opiate users are addicts.

Criminal syndicates have become wealthy. It is a classic market situation with high demand and criminal sellers willing to supply that market. Their business is lucrative, they pay no taxes, they obey no rules, they dilute drugs with toxic or infected substances, they corrupt and subvert the forces arrayed against them, they provide whatever legal services are needed for operatives who are arrested.

Add to that the alterations in fashion for drugs—some drugs are used only by particular generations, some are in fashion one year and out the next (LSD is a good example). So it is that we have recently seen an increase in deaths from opiates—from a tiny number to a larger but still tiny number. But it remains a fact that almost all drug-related deaths (97 per cent) are due to legal drugs, not to those we have declared illegal.

Future options are few. We could opt for more of the same. After all, it has meant that few deaths are due to proscribed drugs. But the current system does not produce what its proponents hold out as the goal, it forces our young to have contact with criminals and it is associated with widespread corruption. Those who do use illegal drugs pay exorbitant prices for products that may be toxic, and run risks that they will contract hepatitis C or HIV.

We could opt for more severe laws, for a more draconian system of control. We could call for longer sentences, for deeper dungeons, we could throw away the keys, we could reintroduce capital punishment, we could fill the gaols, we could introduce phone taps. The trouble is, that such a system would work no better than the present system. After all, Malaysia, which has the death penalty, has more opiate users than we do.

We could, on the other hand, go more towards harm minimisation. We could accept that drug use is here permanently, that our choice is limited, that people will use psychoactive substances, and that we may have a role in helping people to remain within society. We could aim to identify and respond to dysfunctional drug use rather than just punishing people—this is the basis of methadone maintenance programs, which allow so many opiate addicts to eschew property crime and return to work.

Might we not accept now that we are a drug-using society and will be forever? Should we not follow the lead of the ACT and SA and alter the sanctions for personal possession of cannabis—so-called 'prohibition with civil penalties'—forthwith? Should we not move to discover what education messages might work and then introduce them—remembering that many drug users (for example, cigarette smokers) do have a good knowledge base about some of the adverse effects of the drugs they use? And finally, should we not at least consider legalisation—not the libertarian position, but availability without advertising and through government.

It seems a 'least worst' option which would, in one move, eliminate much of the protected preferential position of criminal syndicates. It would provide users with cheap, pure substances and reduce the risks of coincidental infection. The downside to legalisation might be increased numbers of users but a balance would have to be struck carefully between the costs and benefits of any policy change. The costs of our current policy are high. Above all, let us improve the debate about drugs in Australia. Let us end what has been called 'the drug problem problem'.

This has been a personal view. No-one else is to blame for any of the contents of the message. Those who have a different view might care to begin any rebuttal of this argument by explaining how much evidence of policy failure they require before (as with current policy) they are willing to admit a policy is not working.

TAKING ON TOBACCO (1997)

Michael Kirby is a celebrated Australian judge. He was a Justice of the High Court of Australia. On 30 October 1997, I was invited to deliver the second Kirby Lecture by the Australian Institute of Health Law and Ethics at The Australian National University. In my speech, I elected to highlight the antisocial behaviour of tobacco companies, which were pursuing markets for products they knew were harming health.

Your invitation is very welcome. By conducting this session, you honour the singular and special Michael Kirby, and in your choice of speaker you make another choice that is very much appreciated by that person.

Michael Kirby is an old friend. He was president of the Sydney University Union one year when I was a director and our paths have crossed often since then, usually to my benefit and edification.

He is one of the finest of all Australians living today. He holds two bachelor degrees and a Master's degree, has two senior communal honours, is a Justice of the High Court, has been chancellor of a university, holds honorary degrees and has played a prominent and important role in issues related to the rights of people within this society and its legal system as well as in other societies around the world. He is an outstanding person. It has been a privilege to know him as a friend and the naming of this lecture by the Australian Institute of Health Law and Ethics is a proper tribute to him.

The theme of your conference this year is 'Public Health and Private Risk'. No doubt many of your contributors will want to approach this in their own way, just as this contribution will do. Consider just for one moment, and as an example of the awkward interface between public and private health, the question of smoking and health. The tobacco companies have shown that they are bad corporate citizens. They have behaved outrageously over a long time.

They denied the obvious in asserting over many years that smoking caused no diseases and that nicotine was not addictive—when for a long time they knew differently. The first papers linking smoking and fatal illness appeared in about 1948—almost 50 years ago—and for the decades after 1948 the companies put their commercial position ahead of intellectual honesty and ahead of their responsibility to the societies in which they live and operate and from which they drew their profits.

Now, knowing what they know, they are knowingly and deliberately promoting death and disease in compliant emerging nations, again pursuing commercial advantage and ignoring the health consequences of what they do.

What has become clear is that tobacco companies will do, in relation to smoking, whatever is permitted under the law, irrespective of the consequences that their actions may have for the society. In quality what they do is equivalent to those who allowed, knowingly, blood contaminated with the HIV to be transfused into people when that action could have been avoided. Those who allowed infected blood to be transfused were spreading sickness and disease—so are the tobacco companies. So it is war. We have to respond by making the laws do what we want, for it is only the law and regulations made under the law that will force the companies to change their disgraceful behaviour.

That they argue a right to injure people in the name of 'freedom of choice' is bizarre—but it illustrates the extent to which value questions determine how people regard these various issues. It is especially poignant in view of the efforts of tobacco companies to minimise or neutralise the information going to the members of the public to allow people then to make their own decisions.

On the other hand, I recognise the right of people to make their own decision about whether or not to smoke, asking only that they have an adequate basis of information on which to base any decision. Later, I will present arguments about individual rights versus communal rights that might be relevant here.

But let me digress for a moment. A late colleague was a surgeon and refused to carry out certain surgical procedures on smokers. He demanded that they became ex-smokers before he would act. His actions seemed wrong—he was an agent trained to give a specific service and appointed by society with monopoly rights to render that service; he was not a moral watch-dog appointed to look after the morals or actions of his patients.

In approaching public health generally we have a dilemma presented by underlying questions of philosophy. Most clinicians are trained to respond to one patient at a time—to the person who is seeking their assistance rather than to the society of which that person is a part. In ethical terms we call most clinicians deontologists—they respond in terms of the ethics of duty of care and ignore the needs or rights of the wider society. It is not that they do not care about the society in which they live—it is rather that they see themselves as champions for the patient rather than for the society.

Public health practitioners are different. They tend to consider the society first and the individual second. In a philosophical sense they are more akin to utilitarians who look to the good of the whole society before the needs of any individual within that society. Of course, their utilitarian tendencies disappear when they or a member of their family falls ill.

Epidemiologists, who are one brand of public health practitioner, are dazzled by the figures they gather and are liable sometimes to abridge individual rights in the pursuit of data. An example is the testing of pregnant woman for infection with the HIV. This is an important and a valid pursuit of public health. The information is necessary and important for obstetricians as well as epidemiologists. But, unless there is specific informed consent, and unless there is pre-test counselling, the general conditions for performance of HIV testing of individuals are compromised. So far, the public health practitioners have not done well in this area and few women, if any, have received pre-test counselling before HIV tests were carried out on them.

And many public health interventions do limit individual choice. The prohibition on driving under the influence of alcohol limits the right of people to drink to excess and drive motorcars. The reasoning is that the freedom that is gained by drinking and driving is more than offset by the costs to society as a whole and by the collateral injury to innocent third parties who might chance to get in the way. Not only that, but the doctrine espoused by John Stuart Mill says that damage to innocent third parties is sufficient reason (he actually says the sole valid reason) for society to limit the freedom of action of any individual person.

We do not allow people to drive without a seatbelt for the same reasons. We restrict permissible speeds for the same reasons. In each case we restrict individual freedom and in each case the benefits to society outweigh the costs to individual freedom and in each case the consequences of greater individual freedom include increased costs to all citizens through higher hospital costs or to 'bumping' of some people out of accident and emergency departments to make way for the victims of avoidable road crashes.

Not that public health is insignificant. Most of the advances in general communal health up to 1950 were brought about by advances in the public health system. Those improvements were due to things like improved housing, improved nutrition, waste removal, provision of clean water, adequate birth control and so on. In almost every case, some restriction of individual rights was involved, but in every case the gains to the society as a whole far outweighed these costs to individuals. The rights limited were often rights to exploit or be exploited or the limitation in individual rights associated with the payment of rates and taxes.

Since 1950, advances in longevity have been due partly to improved public health, and partly to improved methods of treating people with disease. Interestingly, the correlations of health are most obvious with income and with the shallowness of income gradients—by which I mean that the more economically egalitarian a society, the better seems to be its overall health.

So with tobacco we have moved now to restrict the right to advertise, to sell and to use tobacco products. The companies and their allies argue that these restrictions curtail their rights. But, we could ask, their rights to do what. To injure? To kill? To maim? To cause addiction? To mislead? To obfuscate? In developing economies of course, tobacco companies appeal to the cupidity of governing elites, offering jobs and taxation revenue in return for avoidable death, sickness and addiction—and the elites accept the money.

We can go from the example of tobacco to the issue of fluoridation of water. My children grew up with just one cavity among them whereas I, who grew up before Sydney water supplies were treated, had what is called 'the great Australian mouth' full of amalgam from dental caries. The considered opinion of public health practitioners is that fluoride in water is the difference and we now add fluoride to the drinking water of many conurbations.

But the decision to fluoridate a water supply affects the water that is drunk by all the citizens using that water. Unless someone can get an alternative supply, or unless they remove all additives, there is no way of avoiding the fluoride. And some citizens, whether or not you think they are muddle-headed, are opposed to fluoridation and to fluoride. They stand up for their freedom to damage themselves if they so wish. As legal guardians, they assert their rights to injure their children—and, much as I disagree with them, think they must be heard. Using Mill's doctrine, they injure only themselves, and we have little right to interfere.

We have to determine when we will introduce things across the whole society against the wishes of a minority. It seems proper that it only be done when the benefits are great, when the case is well proven, when failure to act affects innocent third parties and when we can justify the loss of individual freedom. Being Jewish, I would have this view. Coming from a minority that has had its share of oppression and maltreatment it is easy to understand that minorities do have rights to be heard and respected—our challenge is to balance those rights properly against the rights of the whole society.

Not all public health practitioners really accept that there is often a loss of autonomy or personal liberty in the decisions they favour. They have their own ideological blinkers of which we need to be aware. Their decisions might make good public health sense but frequently involve losses to other people. Our challenge is to balance one right against another, and to make wise and fair choices in the process. It follows that, rather than answers which are absolute, we are often involved in making subjective assessments as one usually does with value questions.

As a digression, it might be mentioned that in Cabinet, a large number of decisions involved no controversy and were made quickly, and a small number involved the balancing of competing values, one with the other, and took a very long time to determine.

So it is easy to see why gun control is needed in the interests of communal health and the protection of vulnerable groups; it is less easy but it is still possible to see how some people conscientiously believe that gun control should not be imposed. It is most difficult to make policy with the interests of both groups in mind. But it is necessary to try, unless one turns to Mill *simpliciter* and rolls over the top of the gun owners.

Another example we might consider is the level of ambient lead. Lead does affect intelligence adversely and those taking in the lead often have no say in the level of environmental contamination with that metal in the areas they live or work. So public health legislation is needed to alter the ways that motor vehicles operate, to control vehicle emissions, to alter the costs of lead-free petrol, and to reward companies that reduce the levels of lead in petrol for those motor vehicles still requiring leaded petrol.

The final example is the case of immunisation. Put briefly, it is possible to eliminate some diseases by making the whole population resistant to them. Smallpox has been eliminated from the world. Researchers are working today to apply this goal of eradication to malaria and to HIV and we have the examples of the elimination of poliomyelitis. I remember a teenage friend dying of bulbar poliomyelitis—almost the last death from that disease. We now have no polio in this country because enough people are immune to have communal resistance high. We talk of 'herd immunity', which comes into play only when the susceptible minority is small. The unpalatable fact is that while we can prevent many illnesses now—smallpox, diphtheria, pertussis, poliomyelitis, measles, rubella, hepatitis B—we do not do so for many of them. One of my staff has been off most of this year with pertussis and its sequelae; a medical colleague had measles in his child; most of my staff are not immunised against hepatitis B, and so on.

Let us look at malaria vaccines for one moment. It is possible to attack the plasmodium at several points in its life cycle. But so far, researchers have had trouble developing a safe and reliable vaccine.

Some years ago a vaccine was developed, was slated for trial in the Gambia where many people had malaria. The trial was knocked back by the MRC [Medical Research Council]—the British body controlling such trials. The problem then became an ethical one: does one do the trial and thereby carry out in the Gambia a trial which was rejected in Britain—you know, not good enough for Britain but good enough for the Gambia—or, does one not carry out the trial and have many people die, perhaps unnecessarily, of malaria. Most difficulties arise where two perfectly proper principles come into conflict.

With immunisation generally we face the classic ethical dilemma. We face John Stuart Mill head-on. On the one hand we understand the benefits to be gained from widespread immunisation. We know that some of the benefits come from raising general herd immunity and that this in turn comes from high levels of community practise of immunisation. On the other hand, we know that some parents and some practitioners actually disapprove of immunisation, and that some children, for technical reasons, cannot have immunisation carried out.

The response of the Minister for Health has been to offer a bribe to parents to encourage immunisation practice and the response of some school authorities has been to link entry into kindergarten to possession of a certificate of immunisation, or a certificate of exemption, or a certificate of conscientious objection. So public health legislation is being considered with attempts to balance a public interest against private interests. If we stick with Mill, we can determine simply enough that action by party A is likely to affect party B—and that is the trigger that Mill demanded for communal action.

In summary, I resolve this matter in favour of the public health and against the individual objectors and look forward to some stronger action to force people to consider immunisation of children, in a wider as well as in an individual interest. But one word of warning—there is a small risk of serious reactions to immunisations, irrelevant for the society but devastating for the individual. And should a reaction occur in a child immunised against the will of parents, there will be hell to pay.

All these examples have shown how difficult it is sometimes to resolve issues that pit public and private interests, the interests of society against the interests of individuals. I have suggested that using Mill's principles will resolve most of the conflicts and show us the way to move, the way that is fair as well as effective.

One feature of the life of Michael Kirby has been the eclectic nature of his interests—in the breadth of activities with which he has been associated. While his role as a Justice of the High Court may impose some new limitations on his life, I do not expect that he will change his life-long commitment to justice or to issues within society. I certainly hope not. Michael Kirby has enriched the life of his community in many ways. This conference itself holds the promise of significant community enrichment. Let us hope that Justice Kirby continues to give to all Australians the continuing benefit of his wisdom and humanity. We can only be the better for it.

MADNESS AND HYPOCRISY: DRUG POLICY IN AUSTRALIA (2000)

In December 2000 a conference on 'Building a Better Today' was held at the University of Sydney and I was invited to speak on drugs and policy in Australia.

Some people have strange logic. We should act on evidence. That is, we should do things, then look at what happens, and then act on the results. This is what happens when we play bowls. If a bowl goes way off course, theoretically one adjusts the next delivery to correct for the error. Hopefully the next time we will do better. You might think we would do the same in public policy. But we seem not to do so.

Let us consider the example of our attitude to drugs. We might observe first that we are schizophrenic about drugs, accepting some and rejecting others. The ones we accept we say too little about. So we tend to under-report the ravages of alcohol and tobacco, in the process happening to expose coming generations to trouble they might otherwise avoid.

Actually, it is easier to worry about the ravages of any drugs than it is to address the circumstances behind drug use—for example, poverty, hopelessness, unemployment, physical or sexual abuse, and so on. And more than 90 per cent of all drug-related deaths and by far the largest amount of the misery and ill health that come from drugs are the result of legal drug use. Those drug-related problems are both medical and social—for example, all the way from emphysema and chronic bronchitis to domestic violence and motor vehicle crashes.

Yet the same people who are somewhat reluctant to get concerned about legal drugs get hysterical whenever the talk turns to illegal substances. There was a caricature cartoon that appeared 20 years ago. It showed two red-nosed gentlemen in the bar at a cricket ground, whiskey and cigars in hand, saying: 'Isn't it awful about Botham. He uses drugs.' And people lie much of the time.

It appears that some tobacco companies *knew* that nicotine was addictive 70 years ago. And they kept that information to themselves and promoted their nicotine-containing products vigorously. It appears that they *knew* their products were dangerous to health 50 years ago. Certainly, the first paper linking health and smoking appeared in something like 1948. The tobacco companies kept that information to themselves and denied, wherever they could, the horrors that were being recorded, and measured, and presented. And they are still trying to sell ever more of their rotten products—now to third world nations. Death and disease for a handful of silver. Some sense of social responsibility there.

But this is not a talk about legal drugs; it is about illegal substances. And anyway, we need to get back to my belief that we are schizophrenic anyway—in different areas.

We have rules about illegal drugs. First, they are illegal. Now this is a matter of definition and changes from country to country and from decade to decade. What is legal, and what is illegal, at any instant is an accident of legislation and history. So what is illegal in one country at one time might be legal at another time or in another country. For example, did you know that opiate narcotics were not only legal, but were widely prescribed, both in this country and in the United States during most of the nineteenth century and that cannabis was a legal substance here until about halfway through the twentieth century? This is not intended to suggest that such widespread use was good or that the addiction to those substances was desirable. No addiction is desirable. The presentation of that history is only to bring home that the issues of legality and illegality change over time.

Second, the use of illegal substances is increasing. We have the unprincipled and aggressive marketing of narcotics and amphetamines in this country now. We have increasing numbers of deaths and of people with problems. We have the mass use of cannabis in our community.

Third, there are enormous profits being made. They are leading to corruption of our police and indeed of all the organs we establish to administer our law and social arrangements. The marketers of illegal drugs pay no tax and have a market which they expand all the time. A demand exists and markets will arise or have arisen to satisfy that demand. The marketers also have plenty of money to pay lawyers and to pay for the corruption for which they are responsible.

Which all leads me back to schizophrenia once again. The statistics seem to make clear that we are not winning in our attempts to control use of illegal drugs. You might be prepared to say, after hearing the evidence, that our arrangements are not working well enough, or indeed that they are not working at all.

The Americans, who are mad, think they are doing well—they are wrong. Their society will suffer because of their madness, just as they have managed to have 60 per cent of IV drug users in New York City HIV positive—a signal achievement and one result of the social arrangements there. But here we know we are not doing well.

We have more people importing illegal substances (although importation is illegal). We have more people producing illegal substances (although production is illegal). We have more people selling illegal substances (although sale is illegal). We have more people using illegal drugs (although use is illegal). We have personal and property crime occurring as a result of drug use. We have more deaths from illicit drug use and more overdoses from narcotics. We have more gang wars related to drug use.

Any examination of figures would tell us that all these things, which we do not like, are increasing. They are increasing in spite of arrangements we have had in place now for many decades to prevent them. The evidence screams out that we are not doing well, that our arrangements are not working, that we are failing. It is not a question of how much we detect, or how many people we arrest. In spite of those acts our figures are worsening.

Yet when did you last hear a mainstream leader say that things are not working well enough? They cannot even think such things. They tell us how effective our arrangements are and how well they work. The evidence seems to show that we are not winning, that, on the contrary, we are losing, that use of illegal substances is increasing, that corruption is increasing, that medical and social problems are increasing, that gang violence is increasing, that money is being lost to public revenue, and so on.

Making things stricter—Brian Watters and the prime minister notwithstanding—does not seem to work either. Malaysia has had the death penalty in place for certain offences—this does not stop people doing the bad things associated with addictive drugs. If people become sufficiently desperate, if they are addicted (say), and if the chance of detection is (say) 10 per cent, then people often will try to get away with things. This is the same as the line of thinking in elite sport as regards drug use and it is the line of thinking that drives some drug couriers too.

We should be prepared to say that the emperor has no clothes; that our policy approach is not delivering what we desire; that it is time to work out some alternative arrangements. But what does a zealot do in such circumstances? A former colleague, Don Chipp, used to quote Santayana and say that in such a circumstance a zealot says 'Let us redouble our efforts'. This is what the Americans are saying now. They want us to become party to more and tougher international agreements, to have more interdiction, more punishment, harsher minimum sentences. There are millions in gaol in America at present. The Americans say that they are succeeding—figures seem thin and their assertions are self-justificatory rather than accurate.

We need now to work out what we might wish to achieve as a society. There are things we might want for society more than preventing other people using addictive drugs. It might be to limit corruption of our magistracy and our police, for example. Our present arrangements are not the best way to achieve this goal. We may wish to limit the social disruption which drug addiction brings—if so, we would support more methadone maintenance programs, which give social stability at the cost of methadone addiction. We might wish to limit the spread of blood-borne viruses, in which case we would support more needle exchanges. And so on.

What we should not be about is punishment. Not while we have such an unequal society, one in which the inequalities are getting worse and in which the rich are getting richer and the poor getting poorer. Not while there is deprivation, or hopelessness, or structural unemployment.

You may care to ask yourselves who would oppose any change in drug laws? First, there would be those who want to punish people. They would punish people who are different, and people who are deviant—that is, deviant from values they hold. Sadly, many of these people are religious—and their punitive views seem to an outsider to be inconsistent with the expressed views of great religious icons. Others who hold this view are a certain kind of politician who follows rather than leads or contributes to the formation of public opinion.

But second, there would be those who stand to do so well from present arrangements—you should expect that drug traffickers, drug manufacturers, drug distributors, drug sellers would be as opposed to change as the tobacco companies were—and for much the same reason.

Third, there would be those who really believe in the hard line, which has failed so spectacularly in Australia so far. You should be aware that the likelihood of an arrest for drugs is greater if one is young, if one is male, if one wears jeans, if one looks 'alternative'—whatever that means.

We might do better to address some of the underlying social problems to which I referred earlier. But to address those problems is difficult and it is easier to focus attention on the drugs as if they are *the* problem—they are probably manifestations of deeper despair, alienation and deeper problems.

This is not a plea for a particular solution. It is a plea that we look at the evidence we have today, that we realise when things have not worked, and that we exhibit some wish to do better than we have. Drug use is dumb. Addictive drug use is dumb and tragic. It is not enough just to pick up the pieces efficiently—although such activity is necessary. In addition, let us work to make general conditions better so that fewer of our brothers and sisters will have to turn to drugs. Let us exhort, certainly, but let us realise that this is not sufficient. And let us do something different; otherwise it is certain that corruption and drug use will continue to spread and to destroy the society we are trying to preserve.

THE AUSTRALIAN DRUG REVIEW OF 1991 (1992)

In 1991, I did a review for the Government, produced a book and reformed the drug pharmaceutical licensing system in Australia.[1] It was a major and successful exercise. In September 1992, I was invited to a meeting of the International Pharmaceutical Manufacturers' Association in Singapore and set out what I had done in the previous year.

In 1991, Australia began a major reform of its drug licensing system and is implementing the outcomes now. This course of action follows a report done for the Government during the first half of 1991 and accepted by the Australian Government. A public service task force has been established to implement all the recommendations.

Australia's drug licensing system evolved, like that of other Western industrialised countries, during the 1960s in response to disasters like the thalidomide tragedy. That particular event had impacted heavily on Australia. Indeed, many of the early reports about the adverse effects of thalidomide came from Australian sources. Outsiders—that is, people not trained in pharmacology—understood little about therapeutic drugs generally but could comprehend the adverse effects of thalidomide; it was the dramatic simplicity of the thalidomide disaster that led to action.

In responding to that tragedy an Australian system of drug licensing and evaluation was put in place. It stressed safety and, to a lesser extent, efficacy. It did not stress efficiency or timeliness. It evolved over years, becoming progressively more complex, more bureaucratic, more technical, more idiosyncratic and more difficult.

---

1 Baume (1991).

One result was that Australia became an unsatisfactory market, one to which companies were loath to go. Companies figured that they could market products with less difficulty in other places, that anyway Australia represented only 1 per cent of the world market, that Australian prices for therapeutic drugs were too low, and that there was just too much trouble involved in jumping through the hoops required in Australia, as Australian regulators controlled the licensing process. Although the minister took advice from a committee of experts, that advice went through a delegate who happened to be the senior regulator. The same officer happened to be the person who serviced the expert committee. Certainly he could control the agenda of the committee and the flow of advice to the minister. What happened was that if the regulator was overruled in the expert committee on any matter he could then veto the committee recommendation later in his capacity as ministerial delegate.

Officers developed over time a unique Australian format for new drug applications (NDAs), and built so many steps into the process that it was painfully slow. Further, most therapeutic drugs are supplied to the Australian public on a national formulary for which the Government pays only about half the current world price. So the low price was another disincentive to companies.

Not only that, but the officers were determined to keep the system as it was. They believed fervently that other systems were deficient in not examining the individual data of every patient, and they managed to prevent any action on no less than seven previous inquiries into the licensing system. That there were seven inquiries was itself a measure of industry and political dissatisfaction with the performance of our regulators. Officers managed even to prevent full use being made of opportunities presented by a memorandum of understanding with Sweden.

One main element of the problem, by the time of the 1991 review, was major confrontation between the pharmaceutical manufacturing companies and the industry organisation on one side, and the regulators on the other. The degree of mutual dislike and mistrust became marked. In itself it became one extra Australian problem.

Finally, it got through to very senior officers, and to ministers, that we had a serious problem. It was in light of this that the 1991 inquiry was conducted, culminating in a report that was made public in July 1991. The Government set up the inquiry, funded it and gave it good resources. Consultations were held with most affected parties—regulators, officers, professionals, manufacturers, unions, consumers. One innovative event was a 'confrontation meeting' at which various parties were presented with the different things they had asserted—

often about each other—and invited to fight it out there and then. It was a most productive encounter. Another technique was to gather many interested parties together for relatively unstructured public meetings of some hours' duration.

That report made 164 recommendations for change, all of which were accepted immediately by the Government. Officers had stated confidently during the inquiry that they had beaten the other seven inquiries, and they would beat this one too. They had a formula for beating inquiries but it was possible to short-circuit their process and to prevent their well-tried formula from operating. Each recommendation had a time frame attached and officers are attempting to meet the times laid down. Some rearguard action continues and will result probably in some subversion of some recommendations and reforms.

The outcome of the review was a printed report known to some of you. The process itself, even before any report appeared, started some change, the Government decision to accept the recommendations helped further, officers then dug in to resist what they could, and the implementation team has worked to give effect to much of the report.

Significant recommendations were

- to accept NDAs in European Community (EC) format
- to pursue international harmonisation in relation to requirements for NDAs and for sharing results
- to end the requirement for routine provision of individual patient data
- shortened target times for evaluations
- increased fees, payable in part on performance
- the engagement of a top administrator to run the agency
- an obligation for the agency to achieve the outcomes identified
- simplified arrangements for the very ill
- an end to confrontation between companies and the agency
- an acceptance of the balance between safety and timeliness
- mechanisms to allow recruitment of more academic evaluators.

It is the hope of all concerned that international companies will see again that Australia can be a sensible place in which to seek to market drugs. We hope to re-establish a viable pharmaceutical manufacturing industry in Australia and to allow safe and effective drugs to be available for our community. We hope that effective drugs will be available more rapidly with benefits to ill people— we want to avoid ever having a repeat of the situation in which long-acting oral morphia came on to the United Kingdom market in 1981, but was not available in Australia for another 10 years.

If the licensing system is reformed there will emerge new problems associated with the national formulary. Issues such as which products are listed and what prices are paid remain to be settled. They will occupy more of the attention of industry leaders as questions relating to licensing become less critical.

One gains from an exercise of this kind a certain amount of incremental progress. What varies is the amount of the increment. On the old analogy of the archer who fires an arrow successively halfway to the castle wall, we may never reach a goal of perfect drug evaluation procedures. But while we make progress, things are on the right track. It may be that the Australian reforms of 1991 are no more than one step on the way. But at least we have made a start.

NSW PARLIAMENT: VOLUNTARY EUTHANASIA (1996)

In 1996 the Parliament of New South Wales (the Legislative Assembly of that Parliament) decided to have a non-party debate on euthanasia. It was decided two 'strangers' (that is, people who were not members of the Legislative Assembly) would be invited to open the debate. I was one of them.

> Mr Speaker: Order! I wish to remind honourable members of the historic nature of today's proceedings. Professor Baume of the Voluntary Euthanasia Society and Mr Tony Burke of Euthanasia–No! have been invited on to the floor to address the House prior the House discussing the issue of euthanasia.

Professor BAUME [10.02]: Mr Speaker, first, six brief stories. The first concerns Motte Gur, an Israeli commander, who captured the holiest place in Jerusalem in 1967. In 1994, faced with a painful terminal cancer, General Gur took his own life.

The second story concerns Jacqueline Onassis, who left hospital one day and died the next at home surrounded by family and friends. At the very least, she dealt with her painful terminal condition by choosing the place of her dying.

The third brief story concerns a British medical practitioner who was found guilty of murder a few years ago for having performed voluntary euthanasia. The British court gave him a derisory sentence and the registration authority in the United Kingdom declined to take any action against him.

The fourth brief story: last year in this state a Mr Hoddy was found guilty of assisting in the suicide of a lover. Again the sentence was derisory.

The fifth story is well known to you all. A brave and determined man named Bob Dent ended his own life just a few weeks ago, in accordance with the law, at a time and a place, and in a manner of his own choosing.

The final story concerns the famous British author Professor Richard Dawkins, who on the day Bob Dent's death became public said, 'On the subject of euthanasia, today, if I was an Australian, I would be proud to be an Australian.' He was, Mr Speaker, echoing the sentiments of 78 per cent of Australians on this matter.

Death comes to us all. Being dead does not matter. It is a consequence of being born. It is a final universal experience. But getting there, how we die, does matter, and many of us do not find the gentle or sudden death for which we hope. Many of us here will find only wild deaths at the end of the road. We may wish that it was otherwise, but it is not.

Voluntary euthanasia is an expression of the right of people to take decisions about themselves for themselves. It gives expression to the value of autonomy and to the concept of sovereignty, a concept which has been upheld recently in courts in this country. It is opposed by those who, whether or not they will recognise it, wish to tell other people how they must behave in a matter concerning them alone. The Wolfenden Committee in the United Kingdom addressed this very point when it asserted that, unless there is a desire to mix sin with legality, there are some things that are no business of the law to forbid.

Let us look a little more at this question of autonomy. Autonomy is a philosophical ideal which has been supported by people like Kant, Aquinas, Cardinal Newman, and which was supported publicly and recently by the last governor-general in this country.

Yes, we know that power is unequal between medical practitioner and patient; yes, we know that many medical consultations are the meeting of two unequal people; and yes, we know that medical concepts are complicated, but we assert that it does not have to be a case of 'doctor knows best'. We assert that change is necessary and that taking decisions for other people is no longer appropriate. We assert, too, that one task of the modern practitioner is to make each patient sufficiently knowledgeable and powerful about his or her own condition that he or she can take vital decisions himself or herself.

Some of our opponents—those who make car stickers for example—extol the sanctity of life. Such an argument would be easier to accept if there was not so much evidence of the same people having killed, of having burned people at the stake, of having tortured people, of having sponsored wars across Europe, of having stood silent while there was genocide. Such assertions would be easier to accept if there were not moves by some of the same people to reintroduce capital punishment, or people extolling the need to have religious persons in armies whose purpose is to kill people, or if we did not see so much wanton disregard for life around the world today—too much of it based on different ways of worshipping one god.

But let us turn to palliative care, that is, care whose aim is the control of symptoms. Palliative care is valuable and its recent development has been substantial. But there are perhaps 5 per cent of people for whom even the best palliative care does not relieve symptoms, and there are some symptoms from which relief can be obtained only at the cost of loss of consciousness or loss of individuality.

Let us be clear here. It looks as if good quality palliative care, best quality palliative care, will relieve symptoms for about 95 per cent of people. But, Mr Speaker, the moral problem for the remaining 5 per cent is a real one for you. It is real if even one person is unrelieved. It is as real if one person is left without relief as it would be if a thousand people were left without relief. Let us be clear, too, that there is no reason in New South Wales to consider anything except voluntary euthanasia, that is, an act performed as the result of a sustained request by a competent person.

Euthanasia goes on now in New South Wales contrary to the law. In fact, about 2,500 medical practitioners in New South Wales today say they have actively hastened the death of patients. Sometimes this occurs by not treating illnesses—especially intercurrent infections—sometimes by increasing doses of narcotics to fatal levels, and sometimes by more actively and directly ending life.

So do not imagine that it does not occur, for it does—every day. It occurred yesterday; it will occur today and it will occur tomorrow. Our present laws mean that when it occurs now it is outside the law, it is unregulated, it is without limits, it is without supervision and it occurs without rules. You control what laws we pass in New South Wales, and many of us believe that we, as a community, can do better than we do now with voluntary euthanasia.

A final point that you may wish to consider: about 15 per cent of us will become incompetent in the legal sense before we die. That means that we will no longer be able to make binding, vital decisions about ourselves for ourselves. Only if you complete an advance directive and/or appoint an enduring attorney, both in legally binding terms—as I have done already—while you are well and competent can any practitioner know for certain in the future what your wishes might be. So in summary, Mr Speaker, first, let us agree that the question is one of how we are to die. Second, let us state quite firmly that palliative care should be available in this state for all who need it. Its practitioners are doing more clever things, and they will continue to improve what they do year-by-year. There is no argument from supporters of voluntary euthanasia about this.

But even the best palliative care will not relieve all problems. Third, let us regulate and control voluntary euthanasia rather than leaving it illegal and uncontrolled as it is now. It is at present an activity totally unregulated. One disturbing effect of current arrangements is that the powerful and wealthy are more able to get access today to palliative care and to euthanasia than are the powerless and poor.

In the process of bringing voluntary euthanasia within your control many people might benefit.

But fourth, and most importantly, let us recognise the rights of people to make victimless decisions about themselves for themselves, and then let us ensure that only those considered views are acted on under the laws of New South Wales.

No-one saves lives. Everyone dies. Death is not the problem. It never has been. Sometimes dying takes months of suffering; sometimes death creeps up on people, visible and inexorable. What is being sought in this debate about voluntary euthanasia is to empower more people to have control of their own deaths. Our goal is to help ease their way, to recognise the right which people have to sovereignty over themselves, to make the completion of their lives less unpleasant than it is today. Nothing more.

AIDS AND DISCRIMINATION (1999)

In August 1999 I gave this speech on AIDS. The subject was then very topical and socially divisive. My conservative contacts took a punitive view of the HIV infection generally; I did not.

A metaphor came up in a film called *Il Postino*. It was a magic film in which, inter alia, the man pursued the woman with metaphors taught to him by a poet. So what is a metaphor? It is defined in the dictionary as:

> Application of name or descriptive term or phrase to an object or action to which it is not literally applicable.

HIV/AIDS has been a metaphor.

Now what do I mean by that? Well, the infection has exemplified some issues and problems. Face HIV/AIDS and we were facing those issues and problems. We had no choice. The infection has forced us to address some old issues in new ways to the benefit of a wider group than just those with the particular virus infection.

One example has been in the area of discrimination. You have not had a session devoted particularly to this matter. Discrimination is as old as humankind and has appeared throughout history. But in 1992 I sat on the Anti-Discrimination Board and we found that discrimination against men infected with HIV was so great that we wrote a book about it and formulated some rules about discrimination that have now been accepted widely.

By examining discrimination in HIV/AIDS, we learned something new about the extent of discrimination in society. We learned about it as a general problem—and learned how to do something about the general problem by learning how to address discrimination against people infected with the virus. So today I will take the analogy of the metaphor a little further.

Let us digress a little. Randomised clinical trials were the rage over a quarter century ago. They were the way to determine if something worked. They were referred to often as 'the gold standard'. The way they operated was simple. One divided a sample into two by some random method and if possible one had a random sample of the population under study. One gave the treatment being tested to half the group and did not give it to the second half. One then compared the results in the two groups and showed whether the group receiving treatment did better than the control group. Louis Pasteur used the randomised trial with devastating results to prove that he could prevent anthrax in sheep.

When HIV/AIDS appeared, scientists had the problems of treating the infection and of preventing the infection. They thought it would be business as usual, that randomised clinical trials would allow a simple determination of whether or not a treatment worked and whether or not a prevention program was effective.

But HIV/AIDS was *sui generis and* it occurred in a special population. There has seldom been an infection like it. It is a slow virus and the infected people remain well for many years. Not only that, but antibody testing allows people to know that they are infected and that they will die eventually. The infection is serious and almost uniformly fatal. And they know this fact for many years. It tells you a lot about the courage of people just to realise that. Mind you, life is fatal too. It has been described as a fatal sexually transmitted condition—but more of that later.

Not only that but the infection occurred in a special population. The people in Australia who became infected in the 1980s were gay men—younger, articulate, educated men who knew how to use the media. They were not prepared to sit quietly and do nothing, to die with stoic indifference while society pretended that they did not exist.

Let me tell you just how much denial the community is capable of. First, the community dislikes having to face and consider deviance, sex and death. HIV/AIDS actually involves all three. President Reagan managed not to allow the name of the disease HIV/AIDS to pass his lips in five years—quite an achievement in a nation where infection is widespread and where the epidemic was raging even while he was refusing to utter the name of the disease. If any of you is interested in HIV/AIDS you may care to read the book *And the Band Played On*,[1] which gives a graphic history of the epidemic.

But back to denial. Denial is a human coping mechanism—just pretending something does not exist when it does. We all use it. We teach little children to use it. Many of you deny that the old men and women you see are you with

---

1   Shilts (1987).

50 years added. Many of you deny (or ignore) the fact that each of you will die. You laughed about life being a fatal sexually transmitted disease, but you probably felt it did not apply to you. If so, you were using denial. It is not that you are bad—it is simply that it is easier to leave those matters to another day and to pretend that they do not exist now.

Now let me come back to the randomised clinical trial and tell you about a famous trial in the 1960s. Up to this time we did not really know whether treating high blood pressure made a difference. In that famous trial some investigators divided a group of people with high blood pressure into two groups. One group had treatment for hypertension; the other group did not. The results were dramatic. Deaths from heart attack and stroke were high in the control group and low in the treatment group. So, for ever more, from the day that the trial was published, we knew that treating elevated blood pressure was worthwhile.

Now you help me. I will assert that the trial was ethically disgraceful. You tell me why.

When HIV/AIDS appeared, gay men, articulate and educated, examined the randomised clinical trial and did not like what they saw. They understood that if a treatment was ineffective, then no-one would be better off or worse off. But if a treatment was effective, then half of them would benefit and half of them would die as usual. They reasoned that the investigators would use death, or the complications of the infection, as the ways of assessing effectiveness. And they realised that they would be helping, not themselves, but some future generation of people, to get more effective treatments.

They denounced randomised clinical trials. They demanded a different kind of trial. They demanded trials with proper informed consent. They questioned the levels of evidence which medical scientists required. They demanded that everyone got effective treatment immediately. They got together in groups and pooled tablets—so that no-one got dummy tablets and everyone got a half dose of the active drug. They substituted a new equity for old benefits. They emphasised individual needs and rights against group needs and rights. They preferred present rights over future rights. They also demanded in Australia that public subsidy be made available to pay for their drugs. They used HIV/AIDS as a metaphor for understanding clinical trials.

Clinical trials have changed as a result. Not just for HIV/AIDS, but for everything. Today, a control group will receive the best standard treatment. Today, a running statistical assessment will be made so that people can stop a trial early—as soon as a watertight result has been obtained. Today, proper written informed consent is mandatory and enforced by law. Gay men forced us to see, almost for the first time, that the 'gold standard' we were using was unfair to people being tested today, even if the system helped future cohorts of sufferers.

Perhaps it was just time, but perhaps it was this group that led us towards the use of meta-analysis in which we combine many small trials to allow the detection of results which were 'hidden' in some smaller trials. And thanks to the HIV/AIDS lobby, we now have a better understanding of ethics, of the need for ethics committees, of the need for investigators to listen to those committees, and so on. So clinical trials were altered by the virus, and our understanding of the issues raised by trials was advanced.

Now let us turn to vaccine trials. Early in HIV infection the virus is present in the blood. Late in the disease, virus is also present in the blood. In between, virus is hidden away. So there are two 'windows' available for a vaccine to work—at the two times when the virus is present in blood.

Classically, vaccines have been used for the first purpose, to prevent infection. Most childhood vaccines do not prevent someone picking up the agent; they ensure that it can be destroyed quickly and efficiently by the body. So for a long time now we have been searching for vaccines against the HIV. Work continues and vaccine possibilities are becoming more and more practical and likely.

And there are two types of vaccines: those to prevent the illness by destroying virus when first it enters the blood and those to help treat people by destroying virus late in the disease when it ventures back into the blood.

But there is a great disadvantage of vaccines for this disease. The test for HIV is based on the presence of antibodies. Antibodies develop within (say) eight weeks of meeting the virus—22 days if you followed a recent Melbourne blood bank story. We say someone is HIV positive if they have antibodies to the virus in their blood.

And it is the presence of HIV positivity that is the basis of much discrimination. So anyone receiving a vaccine is likely to develop antibodies and to become HIV positive, even if they have never been exposed to the virus naturally. We expect that those people, who might not be infected, will then, sadly, be subject to all the discrimination that society levels at people with infection.

The question is: will the extra discrimination that we know follows people who are HIV positive make worthwhile the benefits that a vaccine might confer? Will a person's life be so awful from mindless discrimination in housing, in employment, in police services, in medical services, in dental services, in hospital services, in education, in funeral services, in ambulance services, in the military, and so on that the benefits from vaccination will just not be worthwhile? This is the question that continues to bug us.

Today, treatment has advanced and HIV/AIDS is rather like *Diabetes mellitus*—a chronic illness with bad effects but one lasting a long time for which much can be done. Complicating the picture is the fact that the rate of infection has dropped now in Australia to about 600 new infections a year. It is possible that denial will rule again and that people will pretend that AIDS does not exist. It is almost as if we never learn.

So today we have considered several matters: first, that the traditional clinical trial is no longer acceptable, and secondly, that discrimination against HIV infected people is widespread and not yet coped with.

AN APOLOGY TO ABORIGINAL AUSTRALIA FOR THE 'STOLEN GENERATION' (1997)

On 17 October 1997, I was invited to deliver a graduation address at the University of Tasmania in which I decided to give a public apology to Aboriginal people for the evils of the 'Stolen Generations'—10 years before the then Australian Prime Minister did the same thing in the Australian Parliament.

First, congratulations to the new graduates. You have good awards from this university and I congratulate you on your successful negotiation of difficult courses. To your families, to the significant others in your lives, go congratulations too. These special people have sacrificed for your success and today belongs to them as it does to you.

Your city and your state need your skills now. You have so much to contribute and your society will be richer when you are giving to it the benefits of the expertise and training you have on board. You are now members of the worldwide community of scholars and will be so from now on. It is a good community, often under attack in an anti-intellectual country like Australia, and one of your new obligations is to defend that community from mindless attacks, such as those that occur from time to time, not least in the outer states of Australia.

You now have the duty, a duty you will keep for the rest of your lives, to speak out, to say what you think, to express values you hold, to weigh difficult issues, to formulate views, and to lead your communities. You should be brave and fear nothing—your leadership will then be that more effective.

You are all voters. This is your society. Not only do you belong to it, but also you participate in it, and must help, for the rest of your lives, to shape the views that it expresses.

Pericles, standing over the bodies of those who had fallen in the defence of Athens, is supposed to have said, 'We do not think those who take no part in politics are minding their own business. We think they have no business here at all.'

One of your duties is to speak out on issues—for if you do not, it is possible that no-one will. And a healthy society is one in which many points of view are presented, so that citizens can listen to several arguments and make up their own minds on the basis of reasoned argument—can choose from among many points of view much as one does in a cafeteria.

It is usual for the speaker at graduations to choose some subject of current importance or interest. It is important that a speaker does raise a topical matter and sets out views and in view of what you have just had to listen to, it is important that this speaker puts his money where his mouth is, so to speak. So let us talk about Aboriginal reconciliation. It is topical, and it is important.

Let us start with Mabo and Wik. These were just two decisions of the High Court of Australia. That court exists to tell us what our laws mean, what our Constitution says. The judges of that court do not necessarily get every decision right but they work to interpret the law as they see it. They act as referees or umpires when people disagree about words, or the meaning of laws. To attack a decision of the court seems to me to be something we can accept, something contemplated, something proper. To attack the judges seems to me to be unfair, wrong and dangerous. Those politicians who have attacked the justices have done the society no good and have weakened the concept of the rule of law to which I hold, as you no doubt do too. Let us take care in appointing justices, but let us confine our criticism to judgments and avoid directing our comments to persons who are doing what they have been asked by society to do, and are doing it with diligence and care and to the best of their ability.

In any event, any fair reading of the judgments reveals that leasehold land in Australia continues to be safe enough, that Aboriginal claims are likely to fail unless claimants have the particular combination of characteristics exhibited by Eddie Mabo. Wik says only that pastoral leases do not extinguish all native rights except where there is conflict between rights.

Eddie Mabo lived on a Torres Strait Island with his family. They had unbroken occupation going back centuries. They had unbroken cultural traditions going back into antiquity. The court held that the older concept of Australia as an

AN APOLOGY TO ABORIGINAL AUSTRALIA FOR THE 'STOLEN GENERATION' (1997)

empty land, as *terra nullius*, was wrong, that Eddie Mabo's people had always been on Murray Island and that their continuous occupation and cultural links established their rights to that land.

Very few groups or communities can establish a case like that. So I think the 10-point plan, currently being debated in Parliament, is not necessary and is a move by pastoralists to gain more secure title to 42 per cent of Australia—to vast amounts of land. Nothing more. And passing it to the states and territories to determine is like asking the early Christians to pass matters to the lions to determine. About as much justice is likely to emerge from some state and territory governments.

Now let me tell you a story and develop another theme. Many years ago, a senate committee travelled from Adelaide to Oodnadatta by light aircraft. It was accompanied by the then acting director for South Australia of the Department of Aboriginal Affairs. Her name was Lois (now Lowitja) O'Donoghue. Just before the plane took off, fresh fruit and vegetables in a box were loaded into the plane and were delivered later to Lois's mother, an Aboriginal woman in Oodnadatta.

In September of this year, Lois O'Donoghue, former Australian of the Year, recently retired as chair of the Aboriginal and Torres Strait Islander Commission, addressed a crowded meeting in Mosman in Sydney. She told that audience how she, along with her siblings, had been taken from her mother and brought up in an orphanage outside Adelaide. Her dignity was impressive, her account was tragic. No-one should have to endure what she did. And it was not only her. Thousands—no, tens of thousands—of people were taken from their parents under misguided policies which held sway over decades, beliefs which arose from the view that Aboriginality is deficit, that Aboriginal culture and heritage are worthless.

If my children were taken in similar circumstances, I do not know what I would do. Grief, anger, hopelessness, bitterness, consternation, despair, alcoholism—who can guess, who can begin to understand. Just think of your children or your parents and ask how you would have coped had it been you.

Lois lost her mother for a quarter of a century or more. Her father was long dead; he never saw his children again nor did they see him. Lois became a nursing sister and had, in her own words, to be just that bit better, because she was black.

She later managed to re-establish contact with her mother and promised to return to visit. Her mother waited by the roadside to welcome the daughter taken from her as a child. She waited each day for three months at the edge of the highway and then, when her daughter arrived, they had to converse with non-verbal language because Lois had been forced to forget her native tongue when she learned English. Given that circumstance, given those realities, given that history, it is impossible not to be ashamed, not to want to apologise. That our national leaders will not do so is their judgment and their business. But Tasmania has apologised. And we are different. We have no constituencies to worry about. We have no opinion polls to dominate and guide us. We have only ourselves to live with and a future to leave to our children.

So may I say now, as a former minister for Aboriginal affairs, on behalf of all such of my generation as may wish to join me, that in respect of the Stolen Generations we are sorry for what was done, sorry for the hurt, sorry for the tragedies we caused, sorry for the unhappiness we inflicted, sorry for the lives we ruined, sorry for the families we parted. That it was done by people like us, for the best of reasons, using the theories of the times, is understood, but we, with our present understanding, are ashamed of what went on while we looked away. If we can do anything to make it better, please tell us.

So there you are. I have spoken out for what I believe. It may be all wrong, of course, and may be a message you do not want to hear anyway. For this is really your day, your celebration, the beginning of your journey as graduates of this university. Congratulations to each of you. Enjoy the day.

AUSTRALIAN RACISM TODAY AND ABORIGINAL DISADVANTAGE (1997)

In May 1997 I was invited to address a graduation at the University of Canberra and to give the occasional address there. I was troubled as the evidence of a new racism had been appearing and was shocked that prominent people were slow to condemn it. I believed that a national tone was set by what those in leadership roles were saying.

To the new graduates, and to your families, congratulations. The qualifications of the University of Canberra, the degrees, the diplomas, the certificates, are valued by scholars, by the community, and by employers alike. If we really want a clever country then it is to people like you that we look to achieve it. It is people like you who will deliver it. Your families are proud that you have seen the distance, that you have prevailed, that you have succeeded in the exams with their support, and their sacrifices, and their encouragement. Remember, it is their success too and that it has been with their help that you have succeeded.

You have added to this university as well. It is different because you are among its graduate alumni. You are now members of the worldwide community of scholars and will be so for the remainder of your lives. It is a good community, this community of scholars. It adds to every society in which it is found. It provides much of the intellectual 'oomph' that impels us on and improves our lives.

It is a community often under attack, not least in an anti-intellectual country like Australia. What scholars must do, always, repeatedly, whenever asked, is to find ways of examining what happens, to state what they see and believe without fear. The message will not always be correct. But it is the duty of scholars to offer their constructions, their theories, their views. It is the message that is more important than the messenger. Actually, the tradition in Australia is to kill the messenger if the message is inconvenient or if the message challenges established orthodoxies, or established forms or established relationships.

Scholars are not frightened of new things, or new information, or new evidence, or new theories, or new ways of seeing old things. So now you are part of the worldwide community of scholars. Protect and further this community. After all, you cannot now leave it, so it had better do well. But now let me speak out as I have been urging you to do. Let me 'put my money where my mouth is'. Let us talk about racism in Australia.

A little more than a year ago a hitherto unknown candidate for Federal Parliament resurrected the race debate in her election campaign. To its credit, the party she sought to represent dis-endorsed her quickly and decisively. To its shame, the electorate she appealed to with her ugly message elected her. She then, in her first speech in Parliament, reiterated her racist views and has reiterated them since. She is appealing to a darker side of the character of Australia. It is a side that held sway when awful things happened to inhabitants of this continent who were here long before we whites were. It is a side which was associated with bloodshed, and which has resulted today in poverty, disease, death, disadvantage and dispossession.

Today the descendants of earlier Australians live in squalor, have disease rates which are shamefully high, have high premature mortality rates—life for blacks is 20 years less than for whites—have awful infant mortality rates, and so on. How can any of us be happy with any of these figures? How can any of us escape feelings of shame at these figures? I have never heard that particular constituency politician say, for instance, anything about the extreme degree of Aboriginal disadvantage, have never heard her say she cares. She blames the victims, instead of addressing the problems.

The extent of disadvantage for anyone, black or white, has no place in a wealthy and affluent country. And I expect—no, I demand—that national leaders speak for us, that they make clear the values that we hold on this and on other moral matters. That they have been relatively silent when they could have spoken out, when they could have spoken for the nation, is an indictment on them, on the standards they set, on what they are prepared to tolerate, on the values they articulate for us that they wish to transmit to the world.

To stay relatively silent when one has the platform and the opportunity to speak out is to put populism before principle. You new graduates must be brave and ready always to speak out, whenever need exists, for you are the future leaders of this society and it will be what you make it. Let us all assert that we will not tolerate extreme disadvantage, whomever it affects. Let us assert that we demand that it be overcome. Let us assert that we are angry—especially at a minister who boasts proudly that he will, during his time as minister, not become emotionally involved in his task, and at leaders who will not, on our behalf, when they are able, make crystal clear that we reject anyone who wishes to reactivate a race debate that should have ended with the referendum of 1967.

I was minister for Aboriginal affairs. I failed to fix the situation. But I tried, and things were better at the end of my stewardship than they were at the beginning. My fear is that we, as a nation, are going backwards now, that communal commitment is less, that racism, in the absence of its unequivocal rejection at the highest levels, is getting stronger, and is becoming more acceptable.

We are talking about an Australia that you will inherit, that you will shape, in which you will be movers and shakers, and in which the dominant values will be what you assert. I want no part of any nation such as I fear ours is becoming. I want no part of pretending things are other than as they are. I want no part of political leaders who fail to state clearly that racism is wrong, that it has no part in modern Australia, and that Aboriginal disadvantage demands action now from all governments acting on our behalf. I doubt that you want it either.

Reconciliation was always a worthwhile and important process. That is why so many prominent people wanted to be part of it. I believe that reconciliation points the way. I want the process to be valued and nurtured—not to have it sidelined.

A word too about Mabo and Wik. A lot of dangerous nonsense has been talked about both, and some quite disgraceful attacks have been mounted on judges of the High Court who are doing no more than tell us, as they see it, what the law and Constitution mean. The Mabo decision asserted that the concept of *terra nullius* was wrong. Fancy asking us to believe that the continent was uninhabited before white settlement and then basing a system of land tenure on that fiction. The Wik decision merely formalises what has happened for generations where pastoralists and Aborigines have worked together for access to traditional sites. There is no question of civilisation as we know it ending with either decision unless rednecks carry the day and compliant governments follow.

With those sombre thoughts, I congratulate all of you again, wish you well, hope that you will continue to support this splendid university that cares so much and which has given each of you such a good start for the journey that lies ahead. I ask only that you speak out whenever it is needed and whenever you can. And congratulations to you all.

ABORIGINAL HEALTH (2000)

On 17 May 2000, I was invited to speak at the Warringah Shire Council north of Sydney. My topic was Aboriginal health. I argued against John Howard, who was in favour of the equal provision, person to person, of health for Indigenous Australians. I argued that Indigenous Australians needed more health provisions in order to be equal.

First, let us set some context. This is important, as things are not as simple as they may seem. Australia's health generally is that of an industrialised nation. Most children survive; there is not much infectious disease; people generally live until some part or other wears out.

Many emerging nations are worse. Certainly, they have some older people, but they have a lower percentage than we do and they have a higher mortality in infancy and childhood than we do, and they have a much higher incidence of infectious disease. That means that the average age is skewed downwards—many more children and young people.

Of course, one wonders how we can say even those things with confidence—well, we measure many things and can actually see some patterns. First, we should realise that there is no such thing really as the typical Australian experience. Health outcomes in Australia are viciously unequal. Our politicians may say that there is 'equality of access' (although that too can be contested—just ask anyone who has had a moment of need for themselves or their families), but there is certainly not 'equality of outcome' in spite of some egalitarian preferences which we seem to hold as a society.

To be better off financially means to have better health as well. So the richer and better educated are more healthy. The poorer and less educated are sicker and die earlier. This relationship is true for most things. It is even possible to draw maps of a city like Sydney and show that diseases occur unequally in different LGAs [local government areas] across the metropolitan area.

In the UK in 1911 the then registrar-general divided that society into five groups and that classification, although it is grossly imperfect, has lasted. For all its defects, it has allowed us to track events over time and to determine that social class and health outcomes are related. Health outcomes in Social Class I are better than those of Social Class V. What is more, the improvements of recent decades, while they have occurred for the richest and the poorest alike, have occurred more for the richest and less for the poorest—at least in the UK.

This relationship applies here too. The richer and better educated do better healthwise. It is only with these backgrounds that we can begin to look at health.

Australian Aboriginals make up about 1 per cent to 2 per cent of the population. It is actually hard to know exactly how many, as the current definition has three parts: being of Aboriginal descent; identifying as Aboriginal; being accepted by others as Aboriginal. The previous policy was assimilation and many people 'hid' any Aboriginality in their families. More people have identified themselves as Aboriginal with each census, but we are still probably under-reporting and underestimating the Aboriginal populations.

The second main thing we should understand is that Australian Aboriginals are economically depressed. They are poorer than whites, have worse housing, less education, more unemployment and vastly more imprisonment. On almost every socioeconomic indicator, they are way below the Australian average. These facts notwithstanding, the Aboriginal middle class is increasing fast. And people in that class behave like other people in that class, be they Aboriginal or non-Aboriginal.

Perhaps the proper comparator for Aboriginals is with Social Class V—but the comparison is made generally with the whole Australian community. This was the point in asking you to consider some context; you may wish now to compare Aboriginals with Social Class V; I have to tell you now that the only figures I have are for comparison with the whole Australian community.

A digression here. When I was minister for Aboriginal affairs, the then prime minister wanted to know what certain measures would have meant for poor white families. They certainly had need but we lacked resources to respond. These poorer whites with a sense of grievance and unfairness were the ones who are part of the constituency of Pauline Hanson.

Let us come back to Aboriginal Australia. Aboriginal mortality is worse: Aboriginals have about 15–20 less years of life than do Australians generally. This means that there is less benefit for Aboriginals from programs directed towards the old—yes, there are some elderly Aboriginals, but less than we would want and certainly less than in the whole population. So programs for the aged favour non-Aboriginal groups.

There is a higher age-specific mortality for that particular community. Let me explain. One can allow for different numbers at different ages by doing some simple mathematics and working out how a population might behave if it was composed of defined numbers at each age. But even when this is done, Aboriginals do worse and have an excess of mortality at every age.

Next, if we look at each disease group we find that the cause of death from almost every disease was higher. It would be wearisome for you to have to go through recitations of figures for heart disease, for respiratory disease, for accidents, and so on. But the figures are clear: for most diseases, the Aboriginal experience is worse.

Over recent decades there have been some improvements in mortality. It would be worthwhile seeing if Aboriginals had enjoyed more benefit—after all, that would narrow any gap. Figures show, however, that improvement was about equal in Aboriginal Australians and all Australians—so there was improvement in both, but the gap remained big in Australia.

But we should be aware of some findings.

- Aboriginal infant mortality is about two to four times the national average.
- Aboriginal still-births and perinatal mortality are about two to four times the national average.
- Low birth-weight babies are two to three times more likely to be born to Aboriginal women.
- The rate of hospitalisation of Aboriginals is about 50 per cent higher than for the whole population.
- There are risk factors for disease more apparent in Aboriginal Australians. They have more obesity, they smoke more, they have problems with alcohol, having more teetotallers but many more problem drinkers than the whole population.
- Their self-reported health status is worse for age comparable groups.

With that knowledge, let us think for a moment what should be expenditures. We might take a moment to consider that there is Commonwealth expenditure: Aboriginal medical services, pharmaceuticals and Medicare. There is state and territory expenditure—particularly on hospitals—and there is local government expenditure, things such as rubbish removal.

Lest anyone think that local government provides for all, let me take you back to the sight of Justice Marcus Einfeld weeping at Toomelah—weeping because the local government body there gave to Aboriginals an insufficiency of services—certainly less than they gave to others. So there was drainage water pooled on the ground there and there was uncollected rubbish around that community.

Expenditure for Aboriginals in 1995–96 was 44 per cent higher than for the national average, mainly because state and territory expenditures were higher. There was much less through Medicare and PBS [Pharmaceutical Benefits Scheme] and even if we add the costs of AMSs [Aboriginal Medical Services], the Commonwealth expenditure on Aboriginals does not approach what would be needed for a sick and depressed group. The problem seems real. Many of the problems are susceptible to public health measures—just as they are in many developing nations. And here there is a dilemma: many people like me see the need for more public health measures while many others see the need for more disease-specific measures.

Of course, both are right. During my time as minister for Aboriginal affairs, I introduced the Public Health Improvement Program for Indigenous Australians, but it has not produced the improvements that were hoped for it. It has not been 'owned' by Aboriginals, and this need to 'own' programs is one of the things that stands in the way of progress.

So there it is. We are a wealthy and industrialised country within which there lives an identifiable minority with abysmal health that is not improving quickly enough. It is a blot on us as a wealthy country.

RATIONING IN HEALTH (1998)

On 5 May 1998, I was invited to address the (then) South West Sydney Area Health Service and the Simpson Centre at Liverpool Hospital, south-west of Sydney. I chose to speak on rationing in the health services.

You are very brave to discuss rationing and to invite an outsider to discuss this awkward matter with you. Rationing there is, but the standard of breakfast out here is still excellent. We might start by asking why each of you does not have a Rolls Royce car. It is, after all, the best available car, has the best motor, the best body, the best fittings.

It is also the most expensive kind of car.

You might respond that you cannot afford to buy or maintain such a car. That is called budgeting. You do it every day at home. You make careful decisions about the use of your money. It is being done in the hospital and medical services too. They are not purchasing the Rolls Royce equivalents for hospitals. And it is being done by governments.

There is another thing about the choice of car. Each of you will have made a decision that involves trading off the cost of purchasing and maintaining a car with alternative uses of your money, with the cash flow you might have and with your judgment about what is most important to you. You probably could have afforded an expensive car but decided to put considerations of initial cost, of cost of spare parts, of insurance costs, of maintenance costs, of servicing costs, into a big equation and to make a judgment that takes all those factors into account.

What you did was to use opportunity-cost thinking. The use of a dollar for one purpose means that it is no longer available for another purpose. This is called an opportunity-cost decision by economists. You use opportunity-cost judgments every day. You are skilled at making them. So do clinicians and administrators make opportunity cost judgments. So do governments. Now we are ready to consider rationing.

There is a story about this area that gives some flavour of south-west Sydney. My friend and predecessor Ian Webster set up a drug and alcohol service soon after he came here. It quickly became apparent that there needed to be a methadone maintenance program for heroin users living in the area. But he had to get authority for such a program. When he went before the august body which deals with such matters, he was asked did he want 20 or 30 places on his methadone program. He responded that he wanted 250 places—for a start. So we all understand that there is a lot of unmet need here.

A famous health economist once articulated three simple theorems for me. The first is that resources are finite. The second is that resources have alternative uses. The third is that people disagree about the alternatives and about their relative importance. Let us consider all three propositions.

First, there is the proposition that resources are finite. We could look at this by asking how much different economies spend on hospital and medical services. It ranges, in industrialised countries, from about 6 per cent of national income to about 16 per cent. Now that is quite a spread. The spread itself should set alarm bells ringing in our heads. It happens that the wealthiest of all countries spends the largest amount and the highest percentage on hospital and medical services and the United Kingdom spends towards the lower end. If trends continue almost all increases in the national wealth of the United States will be used in the hospital and medical areas over the next few decades. What is interesting is that such measures as we do have suggest that outcomes such as survival, patient satisfaction, infant mortality are no better in the country with the highest expenditure than in the country with the lowish expenditure. It seems that expenditure and outcomes are only proximately related at best; some say that there is little relationship between outcomes and services as far as society as a whole is concerned.

Some react to the shortage of resources by saying only that the cake should be larger. They say that they should exercise no discipline, they should be allowed to do whatever they wish—to meet the needs that individuals present to them, and that others should give more to allow all this to happen. Perhaps they are right—and incidentally, you here in south-west Sydney are gaining some money now under a complicated arrangement within New South Wales. But someday the increases will cease. And then you will be like most of us.

Let us return to the person who says the cake should be larger. Suppose it was larger. Just suppose for a moment that I was again minister for health and that, because of my eloquence, the Cabinet increased the percentage of the Budget going to health. Do you imagine that I could gain more than about 2 per cent—which has to come, incidentally, from other areas—or do you imagine that I could do the same thing year after year? Or do you think that after one or two years I would be back with a fixed cake—even if it was larger than it had been initially?

The second theorem says that resources have alternative uses. At the level of government those uses might be defence related, or education related, or for building dams or roads. Within an area or within a hospital there are also alternative uses for any dollar—and the competition for resources is unremitting and bitter. And do not forget—if we use a dollar for one purpose, we cannot use it for another.

The third theorem says that values are important, that people disagree about the relative values of different uses. This is important. Some people actually own Rolls Royce cars. Just because I see the importance of spending in hospitals or for medical services does not mean that someone else will give these matters the same relative importance. Most of us give lip-service to different perceptions—until someone disagrees with our set of priorities. But beware—on matters of judgment, they are as likely to be correct as we are.

Rationing has always been with us. It is just that it has been implicit and hidden away, made easier by two features of hospitals as they used to be. The first was the idea of hospitals as self-contained and self-serving entities instead of hospitals as area resources. In the old system of belief, they were answerable only to themselves; when I worked at Royal North Shore, we did not know and did not care what the health of the lower North Shore of Sydney was like. That is no longer the case.

The second feature had to do with the more extreme paternalism of the professions that made decisions and controlled resources back in the bad old days. You will have to decide for yourselves if that has changed at all. I think it is still a problem.

So let us state some basic points. There is not enough to go around. There is not enough to do for everyone what we would wish to do. Such a proposition may offend your sense of social justice. You may feel that people in medical need should be able to access whatever is needed.

Well, they cannot. People miss out. People suffer and die when treatment for them exists, or they wait, when treatment is available for some, but not for them. By the way, a wait of nine months for someone aged 70 is a substantial percentage of their remaining average life span.

We had an unwritten rule when I was a young doctor. Haemodialysis was new and rationing was essential; there were more people with renal failure than there were places on the then new dialysis program. We determined that no-one over the age of 60 could receive dialysis. I am now 63—and believe that was a ridiculous restriction. But it was never discussed, never justified, never argued, never made explicit, never publicised. It just existed and it was implemented. People won and lived and people lost and died with treatable renal failure.

Sometimes rationing is by failure to provide service at all, sometimes by restricting new modalities so that MRI machines or lithotripters are restricted in number and location, sometimes by making people wait—rationing by queues, we call it—and people get around that by fudging the urgency of their condition or by paying or by calling in political support. People do all kinds of things to get around rationing. Let me tell you a story about that.

Some years ago a person developed a form of leukaemia for which an unrelated donor marrow transplant was considered. The person was eleventh on the list but pulled out political stops; the local paper and television publicised the case—shock, horror—and the minister eventually ordered the area to give the treatment, irrespective of the medical imperatives, thus bumping someone else down the list. Incidentally, the patient died rapidly.

It does not matter how many resources the government gets into this area or how well Ken Brown deploys what is available. There will never be enough, people will always have to wait, some will find that they cannot access services, some new modalities will not exist here, and so on. Rationing will be as real here as it is elsewhere—and as it has always been.

One US philosopher has put up for consideration that we might have to limit use of publicly provided resources to those below a certain age. Above that age they would have to demonstrate poverty or provide for themselves. You may find this offensive but it is really no more reasonable or unreasonable than almost any other system of rationing.

What they did in Oregon in the United States was instructive. There they made a threshold decision that choices about rationing should be made by the public and not by the providers of services. Having made that decision, they then set up a process and ended up with a list of procedures in priority order, which they funded until the money ran out. Now, there were faults in almost every part of the process—but the principle is what we need to look at. Oregon asserted that those who pay taxes and provide revenue should have some say in how that revenue is spent.

The United Kingdom took a different approach to what I will call explicit rationing. In one part of that country they established citizen juries, randomly selected, to hear submissions from experts, rather as barristers put submissions before a court. People argue for and against particular interventions and set out the opportunity costs of each. The juries then do as juries do elsewhere—and decisions are made. No providers can serve on juries. Neither can advocates for any particular group or disease.

The real questions for you include:

- do you believe that the public should make decisions about how their taxes should be used? If so, how might community input be obtained
- do you believe that 'best decisions' are being made now
- how might you design a process to make those decisions?

There are existing models elsewhere that you could use. There is a lot of interest in the subject of how we share what is available. There is a need for an important area like this one to get things correct.

Lest I be accused of cowardice, let me state my position. Those who pay taxes have the right to say how revenue should be spent. Providers have few rights to make decisions for competent people. And limited resources should serve citizens ahead of providers. It is over to you. This is the issue of the time. I hope you can provide some answers.

HEALTH: AN 'AWFUL' DEBATE (2011)

In February 2011, I was invited to deliver the Malcolm Schonell Memorial Lecture at St George Hospital in Sydney. I chose to speak about the poor nature of what passed for a debate on health issues in Australia. It repeated my concerns that people were being disadvantaged because the debate was so poor. I felt, as a philosophical liberal, that this was preventing informed discussion and entrenching inequality.

Malcolm Schonell is the special person after whom this presentation is named. Many of you would remember him well. But, strange to say, so do I from a previous life. He is remembered because he was such a fine clinician and teacher.

Malcolm Schonell was born in 1934 in London, England. He died suddenly, far too young, at Somerset on Cape York on 15 July 1999. During World War II, he was evacuated to Wales when his home was bombed in the Blitz. His father was a professor of education who became vice-chancellor of the University of Queensland. His mother was a distinguished educational psychologist.

In 1950, the Schonells migrated to Australia and Malcolm finished his secondary schooling at Geelong Grammar School before going to study medicine at the University of Queensland, from where he graduated in 1958. He gained a membership of the Royal College of Physicians of Edinburgh and a Doctorate in Medicine from the University of New South Wales. When my cohort went to England, just a year later, we all eschewed the London and Edinburgh memberships—a generational change. He was ahead of that change and the Edinburgh Membership was rightly valued, and demonstrated to the world that he was a trained physician.

Malcolm was senior lecturer and then associate professor in medicine at the University of New South Wales, working at this hospital establishing an absolutely first-class clinical school. He published a successful textbook of respiratory medicine in 1974. He met his beloved wife, Margaret, on a zoology expedition on Stradbroke Island near Brisbane. His sister regarded Margaret fondly as the sister she did not have until Margaret arrived.

One of my friends reported that the world was made up of healers and warriors. Malcolm Schonell was a healer, and an enabler. A college document records that he had a good 'listening ear' and he was revered here as a clinician, as a colleague, and as a teacher. He was called the 'ultimate encourager' by one student and his skill was legendary. It is a great privilege to be here, with his colleagues, to remember him and his fabled skill. To be allowed to give this address is an honour indeed.

It was made clear that the remarks today in this named lecture could be on any topic. Other grand rounds, of course, are different, and more like the grand rounds we all know, but this one is special and different. So, your permission was all that was needed for me to proceed. Let us consider the health debate first and then the so-called health reforms second.

The health debate in Australia is awful. For that matter, most public policy debates in Australia are awful.

The wrong language is used. Wrong choices are made. The real main problems are ignored. No courage is shown. There is too much spin and pandering to the popular press and to the shock jocks. Kerry O'Brien was the person from the media who asked really penetrating questions and caused all politicians to be very careful and very fearful. Should not that be standard practice?

It is not that we do not have dedicated practitioners. We do. They work against the odds to look after their patients. But there is no morality in advocating tax cuts when there are hunger, homelessness and unmet need in so many areas. Did you know that dementia is emerging as the top illness in Australia and services are already inadequate to deal with it? In such a situation we do not need, or want, tax cuts. We want decent services and we are willing to pay for them.

To hell with focus groups as a substitute for leadership. Their use is to give us a snapshot of 'what is', 'what people are thinking', and not to act as a replacement for leadership. Let us have leaders who tell us something new and who lead us, who show us possible futures—who inspire us just as Anna Bligh inspired us in the Queensland flood crisis. It is as if political leaders do not understand, or do not care, about the very real problems you face every day in your work in this fine hospital. You all know the phrase, 'Of course I must follow them, I am their

HEALTH: AN 'AWFUL' DEBATE (2011)

leader'. Our political leaders do not lead; they follow. Not only are the debates awful, but also the Federal Government is awful and the Federal Opposition is worse as regards vision and purpose.

But let us look at the health debate and at health specifically. People sometimes wait too long for admission to hospital, people are sometimes discharged from hospital prematurely, common conditions are often despised in teaching hospitals, there is not enough money, morale is low in the sector, there are not enough trained people, and the public system is not always the employer of choice. That is just for starters.

Now some doctors are better and some doctors are not so good, and some nurses are better than others and so, part of what happens to people might reflect personal factors, *but* the system is also no good. Doctors see problems naturally enough in terms of the needs of the patients they interact with every day. That is how doctors are trained. So there is nothing surprising about the viewpoint they bring to the table. But they are rather Ptolemaic, seeing *their* needs and those of their patients as the centre of the universe, with other things rotating around.

Medical practitioners often seem to have blinkers on. They show too little understanding of the resource implications of what they propose. Additionally, they often display what has been called 'the technological imperative', which can be stated as, 'if something can be done, it should be done'; or, 'if it is done elsewhere, it ought to be done here and done now'. One suspects that some medicos would want all of GDP spent on their area. And, if not all, one wonders what percentage of GDP would satisfy them. They generally will not say.

And what medicos propose usually ignores other realities, for example:

1. other legitimate needs such as housing, education, refugee policy, foreign affairs, road and bridge building, pension levels, social services, river health, flood relief and so many other things in different worthy, needy areas
2. levels of taxation
3. current politics.

And, because the representative medical associations sometimes behave like militant trade unions and nothing more—painters and dockers in white coats, waving shrouds—no-one acts entirely on what comes out of the profession (although no political leader wants every surgery across the country to be a centre of adverse comment).

The bureaucrats, on the other hand, are often obsessed with process and not with outcomes. They look at how things are done, at the details and the language used, instead of looking at the outcomes achieved. They do what political leaders tell them to do—and that is sometimes wrong from the politicians; that is not the fault of bureaucrats, of course. They are very aware of the power games that go on in Canberra and Macquarie Street and they play in those games. Sir Humphrey Appleby is alive and well in the public services here. For bureaucrats, one has to achieve a budget balance whatever the social effects of doing that. They would actually be comfortable with appalling social outcomes if their bureaucratic needs were met. So they do not have it right either.

But let me say something in their defence. If we want numbers (for example, the length of waiting times in emergency departments or the size of surgical waiting lists), we might need a bureaucrat to do some of that measurement and collation for us.

Neither do health funds get it right. Neither do other professional organisations. Neither do political leaders. Political leaders have not served us well for decades, making silly promises—particularly in the health area—mostly close to elections, and expecting people like us to deliver on those promises. But they were always silly promises. We were not party to them being made. In fact, one prime minister made a silly announcement in the health area when worse for liquor, just a few miles from here. We, who had no part in the announcements, were just expected to deliver what other people promised.

The promises often had nasty implications for our capacity to deliver something else we valued or wanted. For there *are* opportunity costs involved in any promise and the Minister for Health might be instructed by Cabinet colleagues to incorporate the silly promises into the existing departmental budget, with no increase to meet those promises. Luckily, most often the promises are considered as 'extras' to the budget. So if that happens something else has to go.

Some initiatives just skew the system in awful ways. An example is the spending on pharmaceuticals that was taking an increasing percentage of the cash and limiting what was possible in other areas. We only became really knowledgeable about the exact amounts in the months following any accounting period, but Treasury knew the approximate amounts and did not let us forget them.

Some of our outcomes—length of life, maternal mortality, child mortality, infant mortality—are very good by international standards and are achieved with only average expenditure. There are many good features—very good features—about what we do have, particularly our universal insurance arrangements, which were introduced only after a joint sitting of the Parliament, and over the angry protests of the AMA [Australian Medical Association], the then Federal Opposition and the medical profession.

But we in Australia do not have as perfect a system as we sometimes think. In a recent study conducted by the Commonwealth Fund and involving 11 nations, Australia did poorly. We were the fourth-worst ranked nation on the numbers of people who do not see a medico when they are sick. We were the third-worst ranked nation in the numbers who do not fill prescriptions or who skip doses; we ranked second worst in the numbers who skip tests or follow-up; we ranked third worst in the numbers who pay more than US$1,000 for their care in one year and a larger percentage (55 per cent) of Australian respondents reported difficulties in accessing after hours care—we were the fifth worst there. The most devastating statistic was that 75 per cent—the highest percentage of the nations surveyed—said that Australia's system needed fundamental changes.

A 2008 Commonwealth Fund study found that over a third (36 per cent) of Australians with chronic conditions reported problems with accessing health care, a higher percentage than any other of seven countries except the United States. So we should not be complacent about our system now.

Added to that we have in Australia a continuing scandal that has black Australians living 20 years less than white Australians and with worse levels of almost everything that can be measured. By the way, if we advocate equality of resources according to need then extra resources should go to black Australia today.

If we want a better system, we need to get this awful debate back on track. To do this, we need urgently, among other things, an honest debate about rationing in the health system. Such an honest debate is not sufficient to fix the whole problem, but it is a necessary element in any repair. Rationing exists and coherent rationing is essential if the system is to survive and if the system is to have the capacity to introduce anything new.

We do not have an honest debate about rationing now. No-one talks openly of what we can and cannot do, what we will and will not pay for, and essential rationing decisions are made 'off stage' by people the general public (the payers) might not select and away from the people who bear the effects of the decisions. For example, a decision that only so many hip joints will be made available to orthopods in any month rations the number of hip replacements any hospital can do, or the Victorian decision a few years ago that uncomplicated cataract removals could not be paid for in public hospitals was a rationing decision. Queues are a form of rationing. The non-availability of beds is a form of rationing. Waiting times in emergency departments or for tests are forms of rationing. Limitations on operating time are a form of rationing. And so on.

They tried to address rationing in Oregon but we can do better than they did. In Oregon they just got the vested interest groups pushing their own barrows. There are other approaches. In some other jurisdictions they empanelled citizen juries who then listened to learned counsel arguing for or against certain interventions, after which they voted like juries do between alternative initiatives. A much better idea.

One problem is that there are necessary, unpopular interventions—things like treatment of drug addicts, or the care of people afflicted with HIV/AIDS, or measures to prevent unnecessary hepatitis C infection, or much mental health expenditure, that people do not want to vote for, but which a compassionate society should provide. But until we address rationing people will expect a Rolls Royce system and will not be happy to receive a Holden instead.

At the end of the day, some publicly funded procedures will have to go or be limited in number, so that other procedures can be accommodated or introduced—rational rationing. And as our clientele becomes older we might have to consider withdrawing public funding for some procedures at certain ages. For example, we might decide to withdraw public funding for certain cardiac procedures at (say) the age of 75. There are many more examples. A friend was told that if he had been two years older, his cardiac valve replacement would not have been done. So age-related procedure withdrawal already exists. This approach might outrage some people, but it frees resources to treat others—to do hernias and cataracts and prostates and varicose veins and provide good quality palliative care for more people, for example. We cannot do everything possible for everyone. The sooner that unpleasant reality becomes part of the public discourse, the sooner we decide what we will do, and for whom we will do it, and what we will not do, and for whom we will not do it, the better off we will be. People might still want more than we will pay for—if so they can pay themselves or they can take an airplane to America.

We provide a public subsidy. We do not provide everything. There is no 'right' involved. There is another fallacy that might be discussed here. Some initiatives, for example, 'hospital in the home', or community-based palliative care, or more money for prevention, have benefits for the whole society but at an additional cost. They would keep some people from needing to go into expensive hospital beds at all. Then other people could occupy those beds. But while *beds* remain the same number and remain full, there are no cost savings from any new initiatives. People, sometimes medically trained people, say there are cost savings. They are wrong. Society would be better off but at extra total cost to the budget. It takes Treasury officers about 15 seconds to demolish that argument.

The way to save money is to close beds. Many sector workers do not understand this. They do not understand Treasury thinking. It is like a bridge with people on one side speaking French and people on the other side speaking Hungarian. Communication is poor. Almost non-existent. And our future survival depends on finding people who can understand both languages so that there can be some real communication across the bridge.

Now let us look at the so-called health reforms that are upon us. Let us look at famous hospitals like this one. They are staffed with good clinicians, doctors, nurses, allied health professionals (especially those who attend grand rounds), who are just trying to help sick and suffering people and who are staying up-to-date so that they can do it better.

And the money to run hospitals comes from several sources. It comes, as to the majority of the money, from the Commonwealth, and from the state—the dual government provision of hospital funding has been a problem recognised for at least 40 years. The money also comes, in lesser amounts, from other sources like the health funds and private pockets. What was said about rationing might mean that an extra amount might have to come from private pockets.

And there is not enough money overall. Actually you cannot promise a Rolls Royce and then provide a Holden and then say that you are surprised that expectations cannot be met. Those who have only enough resources to provide a Holden cannot satisfy those who have been promised a Rolls Royce by people who should know better.

The current system is characterised by:

1. Big deficits in most hospitals. Those at area levels responsible for budgets are tearing their hair out at the deficits and their size. You see, community expectations and available money do not match.
2. A 'blame game' in which each level of government blames the other for deficiencies and shortfalls.
3. Cost-shifting as each level of government tries to shift costs to the other level. It is sometimes obscene—and funny. Did you know, for example, that one state once tried to put all its ambulance service under hospital control and thus get the Commonwealth to pick up part of the tab for its ambulances?
4. A shortage of trained staff. You know all about this. You know how impossible it is when someone on annual leave or prolonged maternity leave is not replaced and yet you are expected to deliver just the same standards of service. Not only that, when you do get permission to advertise the job, often some months later, there are often too few applicants, particularly suitable applicants. Not only that, but sometimes new staff can be obtained only by poaching staff from someone else—the recruitment of overseas nurses and

other clinicians comes to mind as one form of poaching, as does the story of the new radiotherapy unit at Wagga Wagga that was staffed only by poaching staff from a unit in nearby Canberra.

That tells me that opening new facilities is not going to solve the problems. For a start, we do not have enough doctors or nurses or therapists or physicians to service new facilities. Cost-shifting games are played with deadly seriousness and are played hard. A premier once told me that his job was 'to take the socks off the Commonwealth' at every opportunity. Nothing about desirable social objectives. All about money.

Prime Minister Rudd talked a lot about health in 2009. Let us summarise what Kevin Rudd promised us when he was prime minister. You recall that he pushed for hospital reform, that he spoke of it, that he appointed a special commission to go into it, that he made an announcement in March 2010, that he called the states together in a Council of Australian Governments meeting, and that he bullied everyone until a package emerged in April 2010. And that package was taken to a subsequent election by Julia Gillard, who won the election.

Now Julia Gillard has changed it again. There will be no GST clawback. There will be only 50 per cent funding from the Commonwealth—eventually. A national pool will be established. There is some talk of an extra $16.5 billion—but details are sketchy. She has abandoned a Rudd promise to fund 100 per cent of primary care in hospitals. In fact all details are to be worked out mid-year. We are entitled to be confused and a little sceptical. There is already a 43 per cent Commonwealth contribution, so the new offer is not worth much.

The details are all-important. Only if the detailed promises are any good will health care be any better. The process started by Kevin Rudd would have had to involve reform of primary care eventually to include a greater emphasis on prevention; you know that a prevention focus offers big gains for little expenditure—just think of obesity and smoking and alcohol.

So now we are seeing:

1. Local health networks replacing the eight baronies that we were used to. There used to be 17 areas so it is 'back to the future' in some ways. By the way, Kevin Rudd and Julia Gillard spoke of local *hospital* networks, whereas this state has established local *health* networks—a subtle difference in terms—which inter alia keep real control with the state and away from local boards.
2. New funding arrangements where:
    a. all money will go into a proposed national pool
    b. the Commonwealth will be responsible for payment of 50 per cent of agreed costs of hospitals instead of 43 per cent at present.

HEALTH: AN 'AWFUL' DEBATE (2011)

Going back to the speeches that were made when the whole thing was announced and after the Council of Australian Governments meetings that led to the agreements, we learn that the first was touted as a 'landmark plan to seize control of the ailing hospital system', that the Commonwealth would become the majority funding agency of hospitals and that the Commonwealth would provide 100 per cent of the agreed costs of GP primary care in outpatient clinics.

There was a statement that it would end the blame game, and that it would eliminate waste, and that it would provide a basis for dealing with rapidly rising health costs. Macho words! Hair on the chest! But it is not so. The claims are wrong.

Rifts did appear—and quickly too. For example, the ACT Government considered that the agreement would be based on state and territory borders. Kevin Rudd, for his part, thought it logical (as would most people looking at a map) that the Canberra hospital, the Queanbeyan hospital and the Yass hospital should be one 'natural' administrative unit. So that was one disagreement; the ACT Government showed no inclination to take on the management of the neighbouring New South Wales hospitals, different Commonwealth subventions notwithstanding.

Before we look at the likely effects of the changes, just remember that real reform would come only if one level of government had, and took, total funding responsibility, and just remember that the promise is of 50 per cent Commonwealth funding rather than 100 per cent funding.

And let us relate my prognostications to the world you know and work in. We can predict that the move to local health networks will have mixed effects—few benefits and many problems. Yes—in theory administration will be closer to you, and more responsive to your local needs, but not much, there will still be an inadequacy of resources and real control will still be exercised from the Department of Health in North Sydney.

Then there are some functions that are greater than a small health area can provide for—medical research, for example—and it is likely that all players will want someone else to be responsible for that. Another matter that a local area board cannot handle well is the provision of super-specialised services like some transplant surgery. That could only happen at some hypothetical hospital, for instance, at the expense of something else or if extra money was provided, and then only in a limited number of selected places in the state.

So the so-called reforms will not likely mean any of you will be able to introduce anything new. Anyway the state has appointed three super-administrators—a new level of bureaucracy—so that the Health Department in

North Sydney will still be in charge in actuality. By the way, does it not smack of *1984* and Orwellian double-speak that anyone speaks of a *health* department when the business is largely related to sickness?

With all that said, let us look at some of the effects of the so-called reforms. First, there will be no end to cost-shifting. The state will still be responsible for up to 50 per cent of agreed costs and the imperatives to cost-shift will be almost as great as ever. Secondly, there will be no end to the blame game. The Commonwealth will say that state and territory systems are not good enough, not robust enough, not efficient enough; the states and territories will deny this and say that the Commonwealth is heartless, is bleeding them dry, and does not understand.

What should happen of course is that all funding and all control should be from one level of government.

You might know about Willie Sutton. The story is that he was on the FBI list of the 10 most wanted men. Anyway he was a noted bank robber who spent half of his adult life in prison. Someone asked him why he robbed banks and he is said (incorrectly) to have responded that he robbed them because they were where the money was.

Now you might also know that the states and territories gave up their taxing powers in 1942 in the darkest days of World War II and have never got them back. Before that we received a separate tax notice from the state—rather like the rate notices we receive from local government today. At the same time as they surrendered their taxing powers, the states and territories kept their constitutional responsibility for the health system—but without much money to run it. So the whole shebang, the constitutional responsibility added to the financial powers that the Commonwealth already has, should go across to the Commonwealth. (That was spoken like a 'Fed'.) That *would* end cost-shifting. It *would* end the 'blame game'.

But until that happens, ladies and gentlemen, do not expect the so-called health reforms to deliver anything much. Waiting times will be just as long in good emergency departments. Surgical waiting lists will be just as long. The 'blame game' will not end. Cost-shifting will not end. The new so-called reforms will not make your busy lives any different or any better. They will not make 2011 a better year for you.

And you do deserve better. The work you do is important and needed and appreciated. Not only do you treat the sick. Not only are you the flagship for an important geographical area that plays good rugby league too, but you prepare the next generation of doctors. The current arrangements are not good enough to support you now. The current debate is bad and ill-focused. And both will become increasingly inappropriate as time passes, especially if they are not changed substantially and quickly. And most Australians want a better system. You are exemplars on whom future generations of medicos will base their practice. Good luck in your important work. We are in your debt just as we all are in the debt of people like Malcolm Schonell, who we remember today.

BIBLIOGRAPHY

Ayres, Philip. 1987. *Malcolm Fraser: A biography*. Melbourne: William Heinemann.

Barwick, Garfield. 1983. *Sir John did His Duty*. Sydney: Serendip Publications.

Baume, Peter. 1991. *A Question of Balance: Report on the future of drug evaluation in Australia*. Canberra: AGPS.

Baume, Peter. 2000. Service in three careers. *Medical Journal of Australia* 173: 643–6.

Brown, Wallace. 2002. *Ten Prime Ministers: Life among the politicians*. Sydney: Longueville Books.

CCH Australia Limited. 1975. *The Asprey report: An analysis*. Sydney: CCH Australia Limited.

Chipp, Don and Larkin, John. 1978. *Don Chipp: The third man*. Adelaide: Rigby.

Chipp, Don and Larkin, John (eds). 1987. *Chipp*. Sydney: Methuen Haynes.

Cohen, Barry. 1996. *Life with Gough*. Sydney: Allen & Unwin.

Edgar, Don. 1975. La Trobe University survey of Diamond Valley voters 1975. Unpublished reports.

Encel, Sol, Horne, Donald and Thompson, Elaine (eds). 1977. *Change the Rules: Towards a democratic constitution*. Melbourne: Penguin Books.

Fraser, Bryce. 1983. *The Macquarie Book of Events*. Sydney: Macquarie Library.

Fraser, Malcolm and Simons, Margaret. 2010. *The Political Memoirs*. Melbourne: Melbourne University Publishing.

Freudenberg, Graham. 2009. *A Certain Grandeur: Whitlam in politics*. Revised edn. Melbourne: Macmillan.

Grattan, Michelle. 1998. *Australian Prime Ministers*. Revised edn. Sydney: New Holland Publishers.

Hall, Richard and Iremonger, John. 1976. *The Makers and the Breakers: The Governor-General and the Senate v the Constitution*. Sydney: Wellington Lane Press.

Herman, Anton. 1993. *Alan Missen: Liberal pilgrim*. Canberra: The Poplar Press.

Horne, Donald. 1976. *Death of the Lucky Country*. Melbourne: Penguin.

Institute of Public Affairs (IPA). 1976. *The FACTS and the Law: A summary of important documents including a copy of the Australian Constitution relating to the political crisis of 11 November 1975*. Sydney: Institute of Public Affairs (NSW).

Kelly, Paul. 1976. *The Unmaking of Gough*. Sydney: Angus & Robertson.

Kelly, Paul. 1983. *The Dismissal: Australia's most sensational power struggle— The dramatic fall of Gough Whitlam*. Sydney: Angus & Robertson.

Kelly, Paul. 1984. *The Hawke Ascendancy*. Sydney: Angus & Robertson.

Kelly, Paul. 1995. *November 1975: Inside story of Australia's greatest political crisis*. Sydney: Allen & Unwin.

Kerr, John. 1978. *Matters for Judgement: An autobiography*. Melbourne: Macmillan.

Kuhn, Thomas S. 1962. *The Structure of Scientific Revolutions*. Chicago: Chicago University Press.

Lunn, Arnold. 1933. *Now I See*. New York: Sheed & Ward Inc.

MacArthur, Douglas. 1964. *Reminiscences*. New York: McGraw-Hill.

MacCrae, John. 1919. *In Flanders Fields and Other Poems*. New York: G.P. Putnam's Sons.

McMinn, Winston. 1979. *A Constitutional History of Australia*. Melbourne: Oxford University Press.

Mayer, Henry (ed.). 1973. *Labor to Power: Australia's 1972 election*. Sydney: Angus & Robertson.

Menadue, John. 1999. *Things You Learn along the Way*. Melbourne: David Lovell Publishing. Available from: www.johnmenadue.com/book/Menadue.pdf.

Menzies, Robert. 1943. *The Forgotten People and Other Studies in Democracy*. Sydney: Angus & Robertson.

Nolan, Sybil and Hocking, Jenny. 2005. *The Dismissal: Where were you on November 11, 1975?* Melbourne: Melbourne University Press.

Oakes, Laurie. 1976. *Crash through or Crash: The unmaking of a prime minister*. Melbourne: Drummond.

Odgers, J.R. 1976. *Australian Senate Practice*. 5th edn. Canberra: Commonwealth of Australia.

Parliament of Australia. 1902. *Senate Hansard*. No. 15.

Parliament of Australia. 1941. *House of Representatives Hansard*. vol. 168.

Parliament of Australia. 1955. *House of Representatives Hansard*. vol. H of R 6, [NS], 4 Eliz II.

Parliament of Australia. 1974. *Senate Hansard*. vol. S60.

Parliament of Australia. 1975a. *Journals of the Senate—56th Session*.

Parliament of Australia. 1975b. *Senate Hansard*. vol. S64.

Parliament of Australia. 1975c. *Senate Hansard*. vol. S66.

Parliament of Australia. 1985. *Senate Hansard*. vol. S109.

Parliament of Australia. 1988. *Senate Hansard*. vol. S127.

Penniman, Howard R. (ed.). 1977. *Australia at the Polls: The national elections of 1975*. Canberra and Washington, DC: ANU Press and American Enterprise Institute for Public Policy.

Podger, Andrew S., Raymond, Judy E. and Jackson, Wayne S. 1980. *The relationship between the Australian social security and personal income taxation systems: A practical examination*. Canberra: Department of Social Security.

Puplick, Christopher and Southey, Robert. 1980. *Liberal Thinking*. Melbourne: Macmillan.

Reid, Alan. 1976. *The Whitlam Venture*. Melbourne: Hill of Content.

Russell, Bertrand. 1948. *History of Western Philosophy*. London: George Allen & Unwin.

Sawer, Marion. 2003. *The Ethical State? Social liberalism in Australia*. Melbourne: Melbourne University Press.

Schlesinger, Arthur M. 1999. *The Cycles of American History*. Boston: Houghton, Mifflin, Harcourt.

Schneider, Russell. 1980. *War without Blood*. Sydney: Angus & Robertson.

Schwoerer, L.G. 2004. *The Revolution of 1688–89: Changing perspectives*. Cambridge: Cambridge University Press.

Sexton, Michael. 1979. *Illusions of Power: The fate of a reform government*. Sydney: Allen & Unwin.

Shem, Samuel. 1978. *The House of God*. New York: Richard Marek.

Shilts, Randy. 1987. *And the Band Played On: Politics, people and the AIDS epidemic*. London: St Martin's Press.

Solomon, David. 1976. *Elect the Governor-General*. Melbourne: Nelson.

Tennison, Patrick. 1976. *The Lucky Country Reborn*. Melbourne: Hill of Content.

Tennyson, Alfred. 1849. *In Memoriam A.H.H.*

Thucydides. 1972. *The Peloponnesian War*. Rex Warner, trans. Harmondsworth: Penguin Classics.

Trevelyan, George Macaulay. 1942. *A Shortened History of England*. London: Longmans, Green.

Valder, John. 1983. *Facing the Facts: Report of the Liberal Party Committee of Review*. Canberra: Liberal Party of Australia.

Watson, Don. 1979. *Brian Fitzpatrick: A radical life*. Sydney: Hale & Iremonger.

Weller, Patrick. 1989. *Malcolm Fraser PM: A study in prime ministerial power*. Melbourne: Penguin Books.

White, D.M. and Kemp D.A. (eds). 1986. *Malcolm Fraser on Australia*. Melbourne: Hill of Content.

Whitlam, Gough. 1979. *The Truth of the Matter*. Melbourne: Penguin Books.

Whitlam, Gough. 1997. *Abiding Interests*. Brisbane: Queensland University Press.

www.ingramcontent.com/pod-product-compliance
Lightning Source LLC
Chambersburg PA
CBHW061127010526
44116CB00023B/2991